The W. C. Fields Films

The W.C. Fields Films

James L. Neibaur

McFarland & Company, Inc., Publishers
Jefferson, North Carolina

ALSO OF INTEREST AND FROM MCFARLAND
Chaplin at Essanay: A Film Artist in Transition, 1915–1916, by James L. Neibaur (2008), *Arbuckle and Keaton: Their 14 Film Collaborations,* by James L. Neibaur (2007), *The Bob Hope Films,* by James L. Neibaur (2005), *The Jerry Lewis Films: An Analytical Filmography of the Innovative Comic,* by James L. Neibaur and Ted Okuda (1994; softcover 2013), *The RKO Features: A Complete Filmography of the Feature Films Released or Produced by RKO Radio Pictures, 1929–1960,* by James L. Neibaur (1994; softcover 2005)

Frontispiece: Sketch of W.C. Fields by James L. Neibaur.

LIBRARY OF CONGRESS CATALOGUING-IN-PUBLICATION DATA

Names: Neibaur, James L., 1958– author.
Title: The W. C. Fields films / James L. Neibaur.
Description: Jefferson, North Carolina : McFarland & Company, Inc., Publishers, 2017. | Includes bibliographical references and index.
Identifiers: LCCN 2017011480 | ISBN 9781476665306 (softcover : acid free paper) ∞
Subjects: LCSH: Fields, W. C. (William Claude), 1880–1946— Criticism and interpretation.
Classification: LCC PN2287.F45 N45 2017 | DDC 791.4302/8092—dc23
LC record available at https://lccn.loc.gov/2017011480

BRITISH LIBRARY CATALOGUING DATA ARE AVAILABLE

ISBN (print) 978-1-4766-6530-6
ISBN (ebook) 978-1-4766-2748-9

© 2017 James L. Neibaur. All rights reserved

No part of this book may be reproduced or transmitted in any form or by any means, electronic or mechanical, including photocopying or recording, or by any information storage and retrieval system, without permission in writing from the publisher.

Front cover: W.C. Fields, 1880–1946 (film strip © 2017 Shutterstock)

Printed in the United States of America

McFarland & Company, Inc., Publishers
 Box 611, Jefferson, North Carolina 28640
 www.mcfarlandpub.com

For my old friend
Joseph Kane (1957–2016)

and

my new one,
Marshall Lynch (born 2015)

Acknowledgments

Thanks to the following who helped with this project:

Katie Carter and Terri Lynch, my small staff of two, who always work so hard on my projects, chapter by chapter, film by film.

Paul Gierucki, Ron Hutchinson, and Ted Okuda, for sharing invaluable materials from their own collections.

James Zeruk, Jerry Lewis, Joe Kane, Ronald Fields, Donald Deschner, William K. Everson, Ted Wioncek, David T. Rocks, Dave Stevenson, Buster Crabbe, Gloria Jean, and Scott MacGillivray.

Table of Contents

Preface 1

The Early Life of W. C. Fields: 1880-1915 5

♦ The Films ♦

Pool Sharks 9
His Lordship's Dilemma 11
Janice Meredith 13
Sally of the Sawdust 16
That Royle Girl 19
It's the Old Army Game 23
So's Your Old Man 29
The Potters 33
Running Wild 35
Two Flaming Youths 39
Tillie's Punctured Romance 42
Fools for Luck 47
The Golf Specialist 50
Her Majesty, Love 54
Million Dollar Legs 57
If I Had a Million 63
The Dentist 66
The Fatal Glass of Beer 70
The Pharmacist 74
The Barber Shop 76

International House 79
Tillie and Gus 85
Alice in Wonderland 90
Six of a Kind 93
You're Telling Me 97
The Old Fashioned Way 103
Mrs. Wiggs of the Cabbage Patch 109
It's a Gift 111
David Copperfield 118
Mississippi 121
Man on the Flying Trapeze 125
Poppy 134
The Big Broadcast of 1938 138
You Can't Cheat an Honest Man 144
My Little Chickadee 150
The Bank Dick 155
Never Give a Sucker an Even Break 164

Table of Contents

The Final Years: 1942–1946 173

The W. C. Fields Legacy 177

Notes 181

Bibliography 185

Index 189

Preface

W. C. Fields is one of the most brilliant comedians ever to appear in motion pictures. His work and manner have influenced many, and his courage in challenging established methods continue to make his movies relevant in the 21st century. At the height of his career, during the mid-to-late 1930s, W. C. Fields was a major motion picture star, and his likeness found its way into cartoons and advertisements. Films like *It's a Gift* (1934), *Man on the Flying Trapeze* (1935), and *The Bank Dick* (1940), remain essential classics of their era.

During the late 1960s and early 1970s, high school and college students discovered Fields' old films. Younger people responded to his put-upon Everyman character, while his ultimate ability to rebel, triumphing over his adversaries, provided a satisfying climax to his pictures. Even his catch phrases, like, "Any man who hates babies and dogs can't be all bad," were considered amusingly reactionary and bold rather than mean and cantankerous. (Nobody bothered to research the quote and discover that someone else said it *about* Fields: it was not said by Fields himself.) It was part of his persona, his mystique, his relevance to his own era and to the new one in which later generations embraced him. During this period, Fields' popularity soared, resulting in film festivals and Fields-lookalike contests on college campuses. He became an icon a quarter of a century after his 1946 passing, and his character became firmly established in the pop culture lexicon.

However, by the mid–1970s, American pop culture had changed. Television's *Saturday Night Live* focused on the here and now, and the cultural zeitgeist moved away from nostalgia and the embracing of past stars as pop culture heroes. By the end of the 1980s, movie magazines had occasional articles discussing how popular Fields had been only twenty years earlier, but whose notoriety had dwindled to where that current era's young people were not even aware of him.

This, thankfully, did not stop Fields from continuing to be marketed to movie buffs. His films were released to VHS and, later, DVD. In 2015, the 100th anniversary of his first film appearance, was celebrated at the Magic Castle in Hollywood. Various Fields family members, including Ronald Fields, who had years earlier compiled existing material from his grandfather's notes and released them in book form, were on hand to lend an air of respectability. In fact, there were a handful of books discussing Fields' films that came out while he was enjoying a nostalgic resurgence of popularity. Since that time, however, many of his silent movies, then considered lost, have been found, restored, and made available. Some of his silents remain lost, while others are represented only by existing fragments. Because of these developments over the decades, this author decided it was time for a fresh assessment of Fields' screen work.

This book is a film-by-film look at that work, from his debut in *Pool Sharks* (1915) through his final starring feature *Never Give a Sucker an Even Break* (1941). A concluding chapter will look at the cameos he did as his career—and his life— were coming to an end. Each chapter contains background information, some discussion of the creative process, an assessment of the film, and its continuing impact on viewers. Lost films will be examined through period reviews and the description of existing clips and scene stills. Along with his starring movies, there will be an exploration of the smaller roles he played in such films as *Alice in Wonderland* (1933) and *Mrs. Wiggs of the Cabbage Patch* (1934). Photos, ads, or one-sheets will illustrate each chapter.

According to the late critic and essayist Roger Ebert, the career of W. C. Fields

> resides not so much in individual films as in scenes and moments scattered here and there between his first short subject, in 1915, and his last films in the mid–1940s. He recycled material tirelessly. Bits from his vaudeville act were being dusted off forty years later, and he always played more or less the same character. Even as Mr. Micawber in *David Copperfield* (1935), his most disciplined and polished performance, he was recognizably himself in costume (or, it could be argued, Micawber was simply an earlier fictional version of Fields). It is the appeal of the man who cheerfully embraces a life of antisocial hedonism, basking in serene contentment with his own flaws. He is self-contained. As a comedian, he had unusual timing: His dialogue does not end in punch lines that invite laughter, but trails off into implications and insinuations of things better left unsaid. Audiences suspected he was sneaking double meanings past the censors, and they were right.[1]

Fields' films were often a meandering series of scenes, not all of which were organic to the narrative. That narrative might reflect his cynical look at the American family dynamic, the success of unscrupulous businessmen, the judgment of persnickety women's groups, the seamy underbelly of small-town life, and untrustworthy children. Regardless of the films' lack of a disciplined structure, they remain fascinating works, replete with a hilarious mixture of slapstick and satire.

Whether or not a book of this sort, along with the existing films that are readily available, can restore the legacy of W. C. Fields to the mainstream spotlight where it belongs, cannot be predicted. But we *are* prepared to provide the most thorough examination of his work, celebrating the classics while acknowledging the occasional misfire.

The Early Life of W. C. Fields: 1880–1915

William Claude Dukenfield was born on January 29, 1880 (not 1879, as has been reported elsewhere). Since he frequently embellished his biography in interviews, many studies take him at his word, and report that he ran away from home at the age of nine, and survived on the streets by his wits and his fists. He explains that he perfected his juggling during this time, picked up work in a few shows, developed his act in vaudeville, and ended up in the *Ziegfeld Follies*. This is only partly true.

Young William *did* run away from home frequently, starting at the age of nine, but sought refuge at the home of relatives. He would stay for long periods with his grandmother, and he did attend school as a child. Although he never advanced past grade school, young William learned to read and write, unlike other members of his family. Rather than continue with his studies, the restless youth chose instead to obtain employment, and worked a variety of different jobs.

Eventually, William began working with his father, who would deliver fruits and vegetables in a horse-drawn carriage, charging significantly more than he had paid for the items. While delivering fruit, William would try to juggle the apples as he waited for the patrons to come to the door. Having a knack for balance, the boy would practice juggling all manner of items, and even rigged a tightrope on which he practiced. Drawn to circus and stage performers, William had his sights set on show business.

In the meantime, however, he continued working closely with his father. It was not a harmonious relationship. At one point, William's father tripped on an errant shovel his son had left in the way, and threw the tool at the boy. William retaliated by throwing a bushel basket at his father's head. The irate father chased the boy down the street. William once again sought refuge with his grandmother. However, by the arrival of the 20th century, when he became established in show business, he gave his father enough money so that he no longer had to work, and encouraged his siblings to learn to read and write so they could communicate to him by way of letters.

William Claude Dukenfield began juggling in vaudeville in the late 1890s, and in the early 1900s he was already being billed as "W. C. Fields, The World's Greatest Juggler." He became popular throughout North America, Europe, and Australia. Along with juggling, Fields would mutter asides during his act, reprimanding the ball for not coming to his hand quickly enough, or the cigar for not landing in his mouth as planned. Audiences found him immensely entertaining and, by 1905, Fields was appearing on Broadway in a show called *The Ham Tree*, starring the comedy team of McIntyre and Heath.

On April 8, 1900, Fields married the former Harriet Hughes, who, as Hattie Fields, became a part of his act. Whenever he would flub one of his juggling routines, he would blame Hattie as part of the performance, which always amused audiences. Hattie was very intelligent and well read. She helped the barely literate Fields to expand his command of the English language, and he became a voracious reader, often traveling with a trunk of books. A son, William Claude, Jr., was born in 1904. Fields and Hattie separated in 1907, but they never divorced. Fields voluntarily sent Hattie a stipend each week for the rest of his life.

W. C. Fields as a young man.

Fields continued his successful vaudeville appearances until 1915, when he joined the *Ziegfeld Follies*. By this time, Fields had evolved from his juggling act and performed a pool routine with a specially rigged pool table. He was recruited by the French Gaumont Company, which had been producing films in

W. C. Fields vaudeville publicity.

the United States since 1913. It was Gaumont's intention to feature various Broadway stars in a series of short films, produced at their studio in Flushing, Queens, New York. Fields made two films for the company, neither of which he felt had merit.

In 1916, Fields met dancer Bessie Poole, and they entered a relationship that lasted ten years and produced a son, William Rexford Fields. Whereas Hattie left show business to care for their child, and insisted that her husband do likewise, Bessie made no such demands on the dedicated performer. Young William Rexford, in fact, was placed in foster care with a childless couple. Bessie died in 1928, and Fields helped support their son until the age of nineteen.

Continuing with the *Follies* until 1922, Fields was back on Broadway the following year in the musical-comedy *Poppy*, then returned to movies with a small role in a 1924 feature. In 1925, Fields starred in a feature film, based upon the play *Poppy*, and, from that point on, he continued a pretty steady movie career for the remainder of the silent era. W. C. Fields was a longtime show business veteran by the time he became established as a recognizable movie actor. Throughout his screen career he continued to explore his dry, wisecracking character, with occasional moments of tenderness. In his first films, we see just a faint glimmer of the screen persona he would eventually hone to perfection. But in his silent features, these elements of his character had been further developed onstage. He also adapted, both in his silent and sound features, sketches and gags he had performed for years in the *Follies* as well as vaudeville. Now that additional examples of his silent era work are available, we can more clearly understand his development onscreen.

By the mid–1920s, W. C. Fields was doing as much movie work as stage work, and when talkies came along, he was pretty much exclusively a motion picture comedian.

THE FILMS

Pool Sharks

Production: Gaumont Company
Distribution: Mutual Film Corporation of America
Director: Edwin Middleton
Release date: September 19, 1915
Running time: One reel (approximately twelve minutes)
Cast: W. C. Fields (a pool shark), Bud Ross (his chief adversary), Larry Westford (another adversary), Marian West (the object of the men's affections).

According to historian David Pierce, roughly 73 percent of American silent films made between 1912 and 1929 no longer exist.[2] It is heartening, therefore, that W. C. Fields' screen debut is among those still available and accessible. It allows us to see Fields, the performer, as a young man, the way he carried himself in his act, how he reacted and responded, and how these basic elements formed what would become important factors in an iconic presence.

Pool Sharks was made by the Gaumont Company and released through the Mutual Corporation of America, which, a year later, would acquire the services of Charlie Chaplin, promising him an enormous salary and full creative control over each production. Records were poorly kept during this period, especially from smaller companies, so little statistical information can be uncovered about a film's credits.

Fields had no interest in becoming a steady film actor at that time. He, like many stage personalities, saw movies as an amusing novelty that would permit him to have a sample of his work filmed for posterity—before some other comedian beat him to it.

Pool Sharks is pure knockabout slapstick, obviously inspired by the then-popular Keystone comedies produced by Mack Sennett. The Keystones were frantically funny slapstick farces involving cops, bathing beauties, and bug-eyed mustachioed comics running and tumbling about within the parameters of a basic plot structure. With a roster that, at one time or another, included such greats as Charlie Chaplin, Roscoe Arbuckle,

Trade ad for Fields' debut movie, *Pool Sharks* (Gaumont, 1915).

Mabel Normand, Al St. John, and Charley Chase, the Keystones were immensely popular portions of any movie theatre's program.

In *Pool Sharks*, the narrative structure is simple. Fields is attracted to a woman at an outdoor dinner party. A diminutive rival has designs on the same woman. They both vie for her attention, and the results are consistently unpromising. They sit together on a hammock and it collapses. The two men shove each other and bop each other on the head. The woman is both appalled at their antics, albeit flattered that she is receiving so much attention. They sit down to eat, and the two rivals are so overzealous in their attention that they spill a dessert on her new party dress, causing her to leave in a huff. Enter a group of men who have witnessed all. They decide to have the two rivals engage in a pool game on which the men can bet. After a series of trick shots, the men start throwing pool balls at each other. One of them flies out a window and shatters the woman's goldfish bowl. She comes to the poolroom to confront the men. The rival ends up head first in a rain barrel, but Fields, that scallywag, gets away.

The simplicity of *Pool Sharks* is part of its charm. And although it is very basic knockabout humor, as we examine Fields' performance we see some nuance emerging that would remain a part of his fully realized screen character. One such element in this embryonic effort is his reaction to children. When the adults sit down to eat, Fields sees there are no chairs for him, so he pulls a chair out from under a little kid.

Fields wears a black clip-on mustache in his silent movies, and keeps it in his first couple of talkies as well. What is striking about the mustache is that it is such a radically different color from his blond hair and is so obviously fake. It's funny, and lets you know from the start that this is a man you won't be able to take seriously. However, for those of us who are more familiar with his prime sound films, this prop is something of a distraction. It isn't needed, but apparently this sort of facial prop was quite common among silent movie comedians so it fits his earlier movie ventures.

Pool Sharks also features some very early stop-motion animation, which were state-of-the-art special effects at that time. It's a really impressive bit of animation that moves quite fluidly and has just the right comedic effect. One can only imagine how enthralling they would look to an audience of more than a century ago, when cinema itself was still something of a novelty. However, that leads to the real disappointment with this film. *Pool Sharks* never makes use of Fields' prowess at the pool table, nor does it feature any of his own routines that he had perfected on stage.

This film was part of the Gaumont Company's attempt to bring the top stars of Broadway to the screen. W. C. Fields was enjoying worldwide popularity on stage, and was enough of a draw to lend some level of name value to a one-reel comedy.

Reel Life stated:

> The filming Fields of the *Follies* for the first of the Gaumont single-reel comedies is a proof in action that the company was bringing Broadway star quality even in the single reelers.[3]

His Lordship's Dilemma

Production: Gaumont Company
Distribution: Mutual Film Corporation of America
Director: William F. Haddock
Release date: October 3, 1915
Running time: One reel (approximately twelve minutes)
Cast: W. C. Fields (His Lordship), Bud Ross (the valet), Walter Dukenfield (a bartender)

Although we have ready access to W. C. Fields' film debut, his second film for Gaumont remains lost. *His Lordship's Dilemma* appears to be quite similar in structure to *Pool Sharks*, and it features Fields' first movie appearance in a barroom, as well as the first screen version of his comic golf game. According to past publicity reports, the film goes something like this:

Fields is a phony lord who is down on his luck, and forced to leave his luxurious mansion. He is accompanied by his loyal valet. His Lordship must find regular employment, and decides to attempt whatever situation is available, having no real ability other than the leisurely activities of the wealthy, such as golf. He and his valet first work advertising a restaurant, with His Lordship carrying a sign promoting the diner, followed by his valet with a similar sign promoting antacid tablets.

W. C. Fields (left), Bud Ross (center), and Fields' brother Walter Dukenfield (far right) in *His Lordship's Dilemma* (Gaumount, 1915).

The two men take their one dollar in pay, and go to a nearby bar for a drink. And while, unfortunately, specific details are not available, the existing material on this movie indicate that His Lordship and the valet manage to swindle the bartender (played by Fields' real-life brother Walter) into giving them several drinks and a free lunch.

The two men go to the park to eat, where His Lordship reads in the newspaper about an actual member of the aristocracy who has won the hand of a pretty heiress due to his prowess in golf. Relaxing in the sun after drinks and a full meal, His Lordship dreams of playing a golf game that is so impressive, it attracts a wealthy heiress. He goes to her home to ask her father for her hand in marriage, and manages to rescue him from a bomb that has been tossed by his adversaries onto his front steps. His Lordship bats it away with his cane, using a golf swing. Emerging as a hero on the links, and a bigger hero in her father's home, His Lordship is given consent to marry the heiress, whom he embraces. This pleasant dream disappears when His Lordship awakens and finds he has his arms around his valet, who is laughing uproariously. Angered, he tosses his valet into a nearby lake and wanders off, alone.

There are a lot of factors here that serve as harbingers to what Fields would eventually do in his prime films. His predilection for chicanery is exhibited in the scene in which he and the valet manage to con the bartender.

Fields would perform variations of his golf game in his first talkie, *The Golf Specialist*, as well as in the later short *The Dentist*, and the features *You're Telling Me* and *The Big Broadcast of 1938*. Seeing how the routine was presented this early in his career, when it was more immediate to his doing it onstage, would have a considerable amount of cultural and historical interest. Finally, his tossing the valet in the water and leaving him to drown shows his character's irascibility, an element of his noted screen persona that would also be honed later on.

His Lordship's Dilemma was well received. A review in *Moving Picture World* called it "amusing" and stated that it was "a rather novel comedy that is scheduled for a good many laughs."[4] However, despite its popularity, Fields did not pursue a movie career at this time. He instead returned to the stage and would not appear in another film for nine years.

Janice Meredith

Production: Cosmopolitan Pictures Corporation
Distribution: Metro-Goldwyn
Director: E. Mason Hopper
Screenplay: Lillie Hayward, based upon the novel by Paul Leicester Ford
Camera: George Barnes, Ira H. Morgan
Editor: Walter Futter
Release date: December 8, 1924
Running time: 153 minutes
Cast: Marion Davies (Janice Meredith), Harrison Ford (Charles Fownes), Maclyn Arbuckle (Squire Meredith), Joseph Kilgour (General Washington), Mrs. Macklyn Arbuckle (Martha Washington), George Nash (Lord Howe), Tyrone Power (Lord Cornwallis), Mae Vokes (Susie), W. C. Fields (a British sergeant), Olin Howard (Phiemon), Hattie Delaro (Mrs. Meredith) Spencer Charters (Henion), Douglas Stevenson (Mowbray), Helen Lee Worthing (Mrs. Loring), George Cline (Bruner), Harlan Knight (Larkin), Marie De Bourbon (Marie Antoinette), Lionel Adams (Thomas Jefferson), Lee Beggs (Benjamin Franklin), Edwin Argus (Louis XVI), Walter Law (General Lee), Ken Maynard (Paul Revere), Burton McEvilly (Alexander Hamilton), Wilfred Noy (Dr. Joseph Warren), Robert Thorne (Patrick Henry), George Siegmann (Rahl).

After his two one-reel comedies were released in 1915, W. C. Fields returned to the *Ziegfeld Follies*. He did 112 performances at the New Amsterdam Theatre in New York during June of 1916, 111 performances in June of 1917, 151 performances in June of 1918, but did not participate in the regular *Follies* in 1919. That year he appeared in Florenz Ziegfeld's Sunday offerings, in another show called *Midnight Frolic*, and appeared in a Christmas show at Keith's Hippodrome in December. Fields returned to the regular *Follies* in 1920, and continued with them through 1922. In 1923, his play *Poppy* played at the New Apollo Theatre in New York for 346 performances. He took a small role in the movie version of *Janice Meredith* in October of 1924.

Based on a novel and a Broadway play, *Janice Meredith* was an epic movie release, with an astronomical (for its time) million-dollar budget. A historical drama, *Janice Meredith* was a huge hit and received critical acclaim. It has little to do with W. C. Fields, however, as his is a very small part, but he makes the most of his screen time, performing many bits of comic business.

Marion Davies stars in the title role. She loves an American soldier and is sent from her home in New Jersey to live with an aunt in Boston. When the solider is captured by British troops, Janice helps him escape. It is this scene in which Fields appears. He plays a British sergeant who is guarding the American soldier. He is something of a ladies' man, flirting with a maid in the room where the soldier is tied to a chair. When his superiors enter the room the sergeant quickly grabs a broom instead of his gun and stands at attention, as he places his hat on the tip of the broom handle instead of his head (a staple in virtually all of his later films). While the sergeant is distracted, Janice cuts the rope that is tied around the hands of the solider. She distracts the sergeant with a drink (another aspect of Fields' noted screen persona) and the soldier gets away.

Janice Meredith ran over two hours and thirty minutes, and maintained a solid narrative trajectory throughout. It has both action and drama and holds up fairly well as a historical piece. Some interesting marketing was utilized to promote the film, including having a series of scene stills on display in libraries, emphasizing its historical context.

Critics of the time were impressed. In the August 7, 1924, issue of *Film Daily*, a column called "Newspaper Opinions" offered comments from film reviewers throughout the country, including:

- *Janice Meredith* will be loved by every American who feel it is a pleasant homage to this great historical photoplay.

Janice Meredith

W. C. Fields had a small role as a British sergeant in the Marion Davies vehicle *Janice Meredith* (Cosmopolitan Pictures/Metro-Goldwyn, 1924).

- *Janice Meredith* should go on this list of things to see if one wishes to have a thrilling time.
- It is a picture that breathes the spirit of American independence in every sense.[5]

Fields' cameo did not seem to register with critics, as his name does not turn up in reviews. The concentration, naturally, was on the film's star, Marion Davies. However, since the film was produced by Cosmopolitan Pictures—William Randolph Hearst's film company, founded primarily to feature his mistress, Davies—there is some speculation as to the validity of the reviews. Davies was not a bad actress, and had a flair for comedy (as later demonstrated in two brilliantly funny King Vidor-directed films, *Show People* [1927] and *The Patsy* [1928]), but Hearst insisted she play in epic dramas and melodramas, which, he believed, held greater artistic merit than comedies.

Looking at it today, *Janice Meredith* holds up fairly well, although its long running time results in some slow-moving scenes. The cast is strong, the historical backdrop is interesting, and the addition of Fields adds a lighter touch to the otherwise heavy proceedings. In fact, the only thing for which the film is remotely known is that it marked W. C. Fields' first appearance in a feature-length film.

Sally of the Sawdust

Production: D. W. Griffith, Inc./Famous Players Lasky
Distribution: United Artists
Director: D. W. Griffith
Screenplay: Forrest Halsey, based upon the play *Poppy* by Dorothy Donnelly.
Camera: Harry Fishbeck, Harold S. Sintzenich
Editor: James Smith
Release date: August 2, 1925
Running time: 118 minutes
Cast: Carol Dempster (Sally), W. C. Fields (Prof. Eustace McGargle), Alfred Lunt (Peyton Lennox), Erville Alderson (Judge Foster), Effie Shannon (Mrs. Foster), Charles Hammond (Peyton Lennox, Sr.), Roy Applegate (detective), Florence Fair (Mrs. Vinton), Marie Shotwell (society lady), Glenn Andres (Leon), William "Shorty" Blanche (McGargle's sidekick), Steve Murphy (bandit).

Between the years 1908 and 1912, D. W. Griffith defined the grammar of filmmaking, directing some four hundred short films for the Biograph Company in New York. His epic films, *Birth of a Nation* (1915) and *Intolerance* (1916), both produced in Los Angeles, expanded the scope of the motion picture. By the mid-1920s he had been responsible for a number of features, some good, some not. An artist but not a businessman, Griffith lost his studio in Mamaroneck, New York, and was now a contract director for Famous Players-Lasky (later, Paramount). His new employers allowed Griffith to make his last independent film at their facilities in Astoria, as they wanted to expedite production so he could begin making movies for their studio. They were also interested in capitalizing on W. C. Fields' stage popularity. Fields had received a tremendous response appearing in *Poppy* for 346 performances at the New Apollo Theatre in New York during the 1923–1924 season. Although Griffith had little experience with

Trade ad for Fields' first starring feature film, *Sally of the Sawdust* (D. W. Griffith, Inc./Famous Players–Lasky, 1925).

comedy, he responded well to the underlying melodrama of the play's narrative. Fields had little experience with film, but was comfortable with the role he had essayed onstage. The title was changed to *Sally of the Sawdust*, because Norma Talmadge's film company had produced a film by the name of *Poppy* in 1917 (coincidentally, as it had nothing to do with Dorothy Donnelly's play).

Sally of the Sawdust opens with a woman on her deathbed in a circus tent, as her only child plays nearby. She is the daughter of wealthy Judge Foster, who disowned her when she married a circus performer. Before she dies, she entrusts her daughter Sally's care to her trusted friend Eustice McGargle (Fields). Sally grows up in the circus, referring to McGargle as "Pop," and never knowing her true heritage. When the two are performing in a carnival near the home of Judge Foster, Sally goes for a walk and meets the son of a judge, who becomes smitten with her. Their disparate stations in society will not allow their romance, so McGargle proves her true parentage. Sally marries the man, and McGargle is hired to use his carnival savvy in the world of real estate, where he becomes a great success.

Sally of the Sawdust has both good and bad elements. It is important as being the first feature film in which W. C. Fields has a leading role. It has further significance for having been directed by D. W. Griffith. But it is very uneven. Griffith was romantically involved with actress Carol Dempster at the time, so it is her dramatic exploits as Sally that are focused upon, while Fields seems more like a supporting player. While he professed to be a fan of low comedy, Griffith is obviously more comfortable with drama. Fields was able to convince Griffith to film lengthy scenes of his juggling act, but the director edited them down to only seconds and used them as transitional filler, while allowing Carol Dempster to perform an entire dance routine.

Despite having garnered a reputation for being of meager talents during her short film career, appearing mostly in Griffith's least successful movies, Carol Dempster comes off well as Sally. She is cute and disarming, effectively bringing forth her character's understanding of her place in the world, as well as her longing for something better. There are a number of rather harrowing dramatic scenes, including one early in the film when a leering acrobat tries to rape Sally; fortunately for her, Pop comes to her rescue. There are also draggy sequences, such as the one in which Sally leaves the carnival and takes a walk in an upscale neighborhood, seeing children playing and a mother and daughter communicating, responding to a world very different from the one she understands.

Dempster and Fields also share a positive onscreen chemistry, playing some nice father-daughter moments together. One shows McGargle and Sally as penniless, having spent their last twenty-five cents on a street vendor's meal. They hop a train in order to get to their next carnival engagement, clinging tightly to each other and trying to avoid being discovered as the train bumps along over the tracks. The sequence displays the emotional depth of their relationship, and is the sort of visual storytelling that defines Griffith as one of cinema's most important directors.

With the limited footage he is allotted, W. C. Fields still manages to add interesting elements to his screen character. He is a classic carnival fakir: a con man who knows all the angles. At the same time, he is a good-natured and understanding man, and his devotion to Sally is unwavering. Fields has moments of broad comedy and genuine pathos, and seems comfortable performing both. Still, making the film was an exhausting experience for him, as he was acting in the movie during the day and appearing in the *Follies* at night. When hired for the role, he was offered $250 per day, but held out for $300, with a four-day guarantee. This situation was lucrative, and helped Fields learn more about acting in a role for the camera, but it was a real challenge regarding time and effort.

Critics were pleased with the film, *Photoplay* calling it "the gayest, most delightful Griffith picture; and one of his most popular."[6] The film *was* popular, and it was W. C. Fields' performance that everyone was talking about. A climactic scene where McGargle steals a flivver and races to prove Sally's true heritage in court is a near harbinger to the massive chase sequences that would conclude much later movies like *The Bank Dick* and *Never Give a Sucker an Even Break*. McGargle is funny, skilled, and concludes this movie as its hero. Audiences responded in kind. In the magazine *Picture Play*, their critic wrote:

> For years I wanted to see W. C. Fields in a picture. Mr. Fields has been a star in the *Ziegfeld Follies* for a number of seasons. For no reason I can see he has been overlooked by motion pictures and now Mr. Griffith has chosen him to play the part of Eustace McGargle in *Sally of the Sawdust*. I can think of nothing more pleasant than Mr. Fields' constant company.[7]

This positive response from critics was helpful to Fields in his attempts to make an impact in movies. While he enjoyed his success onstage, he understood how important motion pictures had become by the mid–'20s and was interested in exploring this opportunity further.

That Royle Girl

Production: Famous Players–Lasky
Distribution: Paramount

Director: D. W. Griffith
Screenplay: Paul Schofield, based upon the novel by Edwin Balmer
Camera: Harry Fishbeck, Harold S. Sintzenich
Editor: James Smith
Release date: December 7, 1925
Running time: 114 minutes
Cast: Carol Dempster (Joan Daisy Royle), W. C. Fields (Mr. Royle, Joan's father), James Kirkwood (Calvin), Harrison Ford (Fred), Paul Everton (George), Kathleen Chambers (Adele), Ida Waterman (Mrs. Clarke), Dorothy Love (Lola), Dorothy Davidson (Elman), Frank Allworth (Oliver), George Regas (Henchman), Florence Auer (George's girl), Alice Laidley (Calvin's fiancée), William "Shorty" Blanche (bit).

After *Sally of the Sawdust* was completed and enjoying success, Griffith decided *That Royle Girl* would be his next screen venture, with Carol Dempster once again in the title role. And, not surprisingly, Griffith wanted Fields to again play her father. *That Royle Girl* was already in production, as it originally was not intended to include Fields. But Griffith wisely realized that the inclusion of the comedian would bolster the film's eventual box-office success.

For his part, Fields was interested in doing another movie, if only to capitalize on his success in *Sally*. Fields, who claimed he had willingly accepted half his usual stage salary to work with Griffith, investigated what movie actors in the bigger studios were being paid. He also calculated how his contribution to the movie might bolster its success. So, while *That Royle Girl* was in production, he was ready to negotiate. Insisting on receiving $2,500 per week, Fields believed his success on the stage, coupled with a starring role in a hit feature, warranted a much larger payment for his services. It was a gamble his career could afford. If he was turned down, he still had all of the activities he was enjoying onstage.

Griffith—and the studio—balked at Fields' demand. Plans were instead made to cast another actor in the role, but Fields' continued popularity with critics and moviegoers caused Griffith and the producers at Paramount to realize that in order to build from the success of *Sally of the Sawdust*, it was important to have both Dempster *and* Fields. Consequently, they gave in to the comedian's salary demands.

Fields was pleased with his opportunity in that film and was happy to again work with D. W. Griffith. In an interview for *Motion Picture Magazine*, he said:

> Although I had been in *Janice Meredith* doing exactly one day's work, it didn't in any way count as a start. Griffith liked the performance I gave on stage in *Poppy*, and hired me to take the same part in the picture. He gave me my first opportunity.[8]

In *That Royle Girl*, Carol Dempster plays Joan Daisy Royle, a peasant girl who becomes friendly with the leader of a jazz band. When the bandleader's estranged wife is murdered and he is accused, Joan helps to clear his name, believing the real killer is a gangster with whom his wife had been keeping company.

Critics at the time seemed impressed with the movie, but unhappy with so little contribution from Fields, not realizing his inclusion was an afterthought. The film concludes with a massive cyclone sequence that is said to have been truly epic in scope. Reaction shots of Fields were edited in later.

While literature on Fields indicates *That Royle Girl* received bad reviews, a critic in *Photoplay* praised both Griffith and Dempster:

> D. W. Griffith can't, apparently, make a poor picture. Even when he steps out of character for a moment to depict swift melodrama with jazz and the younger generation, he does it pleasingly. Carol Dempster gives a performance that skyrockets her into any ten best list of players named from now on. *That Royle Girl* presents a fresh idea on the screen—that is, that a girl can mean different things to different men. Daisy Royle doesn't love the jazz orchestra leader, and she certainly is not a bad girl; but she makes the very feminine error of leading a man on and then trying to close the door in his face. What follows is highly dramatic and interesting with the keen surprise that characterizes all Griffith's pictures.[9]

However, the reviewer for *Motion Picture Magazine* stated, "W. C. Fields will make you laugh but his opportunities are few."[10] This is understandable, given that the film was advertised as a drama, not a comedy.

That Royle Girl was released amid several very big movies, including Charlie Chaplin's *The Gold Rush* and King Vidor's *The Big Parade*, starring John Gilbert. *That Royle Girl* did not perform as well at the box office, doing nicely in some areas but not in others. It broke box-office records in Chicago and Baltimore, for example, but in New York, where it was scheduled for a two-week run, it was shelved after a few days of poor attendance.

Fields would continue to credit Griffith for using his services in a couple of high-profile studio movies, as it resulted in his getting a contract with Paramount Pictures. The studio heads noticed how he had been embraced by moviegoers and singled out by critics as a highlight in two of their feature releases, even to the point where a flop film would have been considered to be more interesting if Fields had been allotted more footage. In that it figures with some prominence in the filmography of both W. C. Fields and D. W. Griffith, it is unnerving to think *That Royle Girl* is a lost film.

Paramount Pictures offered W. C. Fields a contract to continue making

Trade ad for *That Royle Girl* (Famous Players-Lasky, 1925), a melodrama Fields was added to at the last minute to ensure its box-office success.

movies. The timing couldn't have been any more fortuitous. His contract with the *Follies* would end on January 16, 1926. Fields was deemed by the studio to be worth his salary demands, as the comedian pointed out how signing with movies would have to be as lucrative as his stage success. Of course, Fields was allowed to continue to work onstage while making movies, but he realized that being the star of a film would likely allow him little time for much else.

A contract was drawn up and signed, and W. C. Fields made plans to uproot and head to California after his current *Follies* contract ended. Paramount scheduled his first day of shooting to be January 25, 1926. A publicity story in *Motion Picture News* called Fields "Paramount's newest star," adding, "Fields has been an outstanding comedian for several years. On the screen he is funnier than on stage. When he entered pictures he made this comment: 'My idea is to bring back slapstick two-dollar up.'"[11] This meant that Fields planned to approach his screen vehicles with a subtler approach to physical comedy.

It's the Old Army Game

Production: Famous Players–Lasky
Distribution: Paramount
Associate Producer: William Le Baron
Director: A. Edward Sutherland
Screenplay: Tom J. Geraghty, based upon the play by J. P. (Joseph Patrick) McEvoy, with special material by W. C. Fields; titles by Ralph Spence
Camera: Alvin Wyckoff
Editor: Tom J. Geraghty
Release date: May 24, 1926
Running time: 70 minutes
Cast: W. C. Fields (Elmer Prettywillie), Louise Brooks (Marilyn Sheridan), Blanche Ring (Tessie), William Gaxton (George Parker), Mary Foy (Sarah), Mickey Bennett (Mickey), Josephine Dunn, Jack Luden (society bathers), George Currie (artist), Elise Cavanna (early morning stamp customer / dowager customer asking for change), John Merton (fireman).

For his first starring film under his new Paramount contract, W. C. Fields had the opportunity to display his stage-honed routines more effectively than in any movie thus far. Surprisingly, for those who are most familiar with his later, more noted, sound films, his screen character is already quite well defined. The character he plays in this film is clever, unscrupulous, at odds with society's conventions and its citizens. He has a young woman friend who looks up to him and with whom he is smitten, an overbearing sister who does not appreciate him, and her bratty youngster who frustrates him. These elements, the way Fields presents the dysfunctional family dynamic, and his reactive comedy, would all be ingredients in later, classic films.

Motion Picture News announced in its January 1926 issue:

> When W. C. Fields makes his first starring vehicle for Paramount, he will have as his leading lady Louise Brooks. Clara Bow was originally slated for the leading feminine role but will be unable to assume it because of a previous engagement in a West Coast Paramount production.[12]

Filmed on location in Ocala, Florida, *It's the Old Army Game* is enhanced by several ideas Fields had used onstage, including scenes from *Poppy* as well as sketches he had performed in the *Follies*, and, most notably, a 1925 show called *The Comic Supplement (of American Life)* by noted satirist J. P. McEvoy. Fields plays Elmer Prettywillie, a small-town druggist, who lives above his shop. He and his pretty young clerk, Marilyn Sheridan (Brooks),[13] do their best with marginal business. Into this slow-paced business comes a snappy fellow named George Delevan, a man with a lot of sharp ideas about real estate. He stops in Elmer's drug store and is immediately smitten with Marilyn. He makes a deal with Elmer to lease part of his store for his real estate business, arranging to share his profits with the shop owner. Soon business is booming, and the store is filled with people looking for real estate investment deals. After several deals have been made, George then leaves for New York on business. While he is gone, a detective enters the store looking for him, telling Elmer that George is a crook and the real estate deals are no good. Elmer decides to drive to New York and confront George, but after several mishaps on the road, he returns home. When, upon returning home, Elmer sees a large mob of townspeople heading toward him, he believes they are upset about being swindled and have formed a lynch mob. He starts to run away, and the people run after him. When they finally catch up to Elmer, he discovers that the deals are indeed good and the townsfolk were running up to *thank* him, not hang him. It turns out that while George was indeed swindling the others at first, his relationship with Marilyn changed his mind, and he therefore altered his tactics. Everyone in town made money, especially Elmer.

The basic premise here, with Fields playing a well-meaning character who is struggling, put-upon, only to triumph in the end, would be a standard narrative basis for all of his best films. *It's the Old Army Game* falls into that category, at least as far as his surviving early films are concerned.

The viewer cannot help but notice how deftly Fields handles the silent medium. Pantomime was hardly new to him as, for years with his juggling

One-sheet for *It's the Old Army Game* (Famous Players–Lasky, 1926), a silent feature containing many scenes Fields had performed in the *Ziegfeld Follies*.

act, he did not speak on the stage—he merely muttered unintelligible asides when a trick seemingly went wrong. Overcoming a stutter, Fields became known for his skill with dialogue and frequently brought the house down with his hilarious ad-libs. Now, as a star of the silent screen, he was back to relying solely on his ability to communicate his comic ideas visually. The artful double-takes he displays here, his body language and facial nuances serve him well. With little cinematic background, Fields demonstrates that he is able to respond to the intimacy of the movie camera without using the broad gestures necessary for stage work.

The story opens when Elmer is awakened early by a customer who needs a stamp to mail an important letter. He gets out of bed, goes down to his shop and obliges her. She foolishly sets off the fire alarm off by opening its door, wherein she places the letter and goes cheerfully on her way. Fire engines then come roaring to the shop. When the firemen arrive at the scene and realize it is a false alarm, they expect free sodas as compensation. Elmer sets off yet another alarm to fool them into leaving. After they are gone, a genuine fire starts in the store. Naturally, he tries to put it out, with less than successful results. His fire extinguisher can't be removed from the wall. His attempts to bring water to the fire cause him to spill the contents before he gets there. It is a nice example of mounting frustration and a great gag sequence for silent comedy. Clearly, W. C. Fields does not need dialogue to be funny.

Next up is the first film version of the "Back Porch" routine that Fields had performed so successfully onstage. The concept is remarkably simple: Elmer attempts to sleep outside on a porch swing and is constantly being interrupted. First, he tries to quiet a crying baby. When he does, the baby shatters a full milk bottle over his head. By the time a vegetable man comes walking by, hollering for business, Elmer brandishes a shotgun. While this sketch would work much more effectively in his 1934 sound feature *It's a Gift*, it is fascinating to see what Fields does with the sketch in a silent movie, especially as the conflict in the scene deals specifically with noise. It comes off as one of the highlights of this feature.

Another of the most noted elements of the Fields screen character is his reaction to children as adversaries. Planning to leave the store for a while, bratty nephew Mickey throws a tantrum, insisting that he be allowed to come along. He grabs Elmer's leg tightly and won't let go, as hard as Elmer tries to extricate himself from the child's grasp. A woman says to Elmer, "Be careful, you'll break his leg!" Fields' reaction is far better seen than described, but he has Elmer open his eyes wide and point to himself in a "Who, *me*?" manner, completely aghast that the woman would accuse him of being violent when it is *he* who is the victim. As Elmer breaks free, he falls into a line of soda fountain stools, which topple over like dominoes.

In *Motion Picture Junior*, a movie magazine aimed at the younger set, child actor Mickey Bennett is credited with writing the following:

> The other day we shot fifty scenes for *It's the Old Army Game* and we were finished by three-thirty. Now fifty scenes in a day is a very great deal and we were proud of our record. We wanted to celebrate in some way, and do you know what we did? Why, Mr. Sutherland, our director, and Mr. Fields, the star, organized a ball team and we played until six o'clock. That was real fun.[14]

Since Bennett was only around ten years old at the time, it is all but certain a studio publicist actually wrote this article. But it is interesting to imagine an impromptu ball game on the set of the movie, however apocryphal such a thing might be.

Another of Fields' stage routines, again based upon J. P. McEvoy's sketches, is a picnic scene involving a rambunctious family. Elmer and his brood stop at what they believe is a park, when it is, in fact, the grounds of a private estate. As they picnic, they systematically make a mess of the grounds. With no concern for their surroundings, they litter the place with paper and other debris and trample the carefully manicured lawn. Louise Brooks recalled this scene in *Lulu in Hollywood*:

> The picnic scene was shot on the most lavish estate in Palm Beach, the winter home of a J. P. Morgan partner, Edward Stotesbury. What the producing unit did to the lawn was frightful. During the five days of shooting the littler converted it to a garbage dump, and when the trucks and forty pairs of feet finished their work, it looked like the abandoned site of a soldier's reunion. But Mr. and Mrs. Stotesbury were thrilled. "Everybody," said Mrs. Stotesbury, "in Palm Beach is driving by to see what is going on here!"[15]

Whereas several scenes (the drug store, the back porch, the picnic, etc.) were recycled stage routines that would be used to greater effect in Fields' sound films, at least some of the material in *It's the Old Army Game* is exclusive to this movie. Fields does a lot of business with the car when he attempts to drive to New York. Elmer is first shown driving the wrong way on a one-way street, carefully dodging the oncoming traffic. After more mishaps, Elmer lifts the hood of the car and the engine explodes in his face.

Finally, the scene with Elmer running from the townspeople is brilliantly shot. Fields is shown in the foreground, running toward the camera with the mob well in the background, chasing him. Elmer is pretty far ahead, but in order to run faster, he starts emptying his pockets. He throws out weightless items like a handkerchief, but when he pulls out a bottle he puts it back in his pocket. The way director Sutherland frames this scene, showing the furious action in both the background and foreground, and how he has the shot concentrate on Fields closely enough so that we can see him taking items from his pockets, is impressive.

It's the Old Army Game is a solid comedy feature. The critics, including Lillian Brennan of *Film Daily*, agreed:

> *It's the Old Army Game* offered the big laughs of the past week. W. C. Fields, with his trick mustache stuck out on the edge of his nose, makes merry in a right jolly fashion. It isn't the easiest thing in the world to make a picture consistently amusing without some definite plot basis but director Edward Sutherland handled this one very well. The funniest sequence is the back porch business where Fields tries to sleep in a couch hammock. Louise Brooks is a real eyeful when it comes to looks.[16]

Brennan is correct in stating that the film has no real narrative structure. It has a basic story, one that is sustained primarily with gags and sketches. These are not only funny, they are historically important. We get a glimpse of what Fields had been doing in the *Follies*, during a period just after he had been touring with them (in fact, he had met co-star Louise Brooks in the *Follies* the year before and they became good friends). We also see early cinematic presentations of these routines that were often revamped and embellished when reused in his later sound films. New York audiences, familiar with these routines from the stage, were chagrined that Fields was merely recycling material. However, the rest of the country was seeing these sketches for the first time and were delighted with them. The July 1926 issue of *Motion Picture Classic* stated:

> No comedian since Chaplin has appeared above the screen horizon with so much original humor as W. C. Fields. Recruited from the stage by D. W. Griffith for *Sally of the Sawdust*, he has brought to the films a distinct personality and a talent for creating spontaneous laughter.[17]

The review in *Moving Picture World* also raved about Fields' originality and the amount of comedy contained in *It's the Old Army Game*:

> As the result of the hit he made in two Griffith productions, W. C. Fields is being starred in the Paramount production *It's the Old Army Game*, a rollicking farce comedy plentifully punctuated with chuckles and laughter. There is an exceedingly rapid fire collection of gags. We don't believe we have ever seen more in one picture. Many of them are new and even the more familiar ones are more effective by Fields' inimitable acting. There is hardly a minute when he is not engaged in some gag or bit of amusing clowning. *It's the Old Army Game* provides genuine amusement for any kind of theatre where patrons enjoy laughter.[18]

Despite these accolades, *It's the Old Army Game* was not the box-office hit Paramount hoped it might be. The studio heads tempered their disappointment with the understanding that Fields might need a film or two in order to become more established to moviegoers in the Midwestern states who had never seen him onstage. Despite disappointing returns, Paramount remained pleased with having a stage star with Fields' reputation under contract.

The importance of *It's the Old Army Game* to the W. C. Fields filmography is rather significant. It is quite a turnaround from his previous features, in which he played supporting roles and was primarily relied upon for comic relief. It is deeper and infinitely more satisfying than the short comedies in which he had appeared a decade earlier. As the principal lead in a feature film, W. C. Fields gets to do so much more here; it is starting with this film that the viewer can plainly see how talented a comedian Fields is.

So's Your Old Man

Production: Famous Players–Lasky
Distribution: Paramount
Associate Producer: William Le Baron
Director: Gregory La Cava
Screenplay: J. Clarkson Miller, Howard Emmett Rogers, based upon the story "Mr. Bisbee's Princess" by Julian Street; titles by Julian Johnson
Camera: George Webber
Editor: George Block, Julian Johnson
Release date: October 25, 1926
Running time: 67 minutes
Cast: W. C. Fields (Sam Bisbee), Alice Joyce (Princess Lescaboura), Charles "Buddy" Rogers (Kenneth Murchison), Kittens Reichert (Alice Bisbee), Marcia Harris (Mrs. Bisbee), Julia Ralph (Mrs. Murchison), Frank Montgomery (Jeff), Jerry Sinclair (Al), Charles Byer (Prince Lescaboura), Walter Walker (mayor), William "Shorty" Blanche (stooge).

Paramount obviously had faith in the sustainability of W. C. Fields as a starring comedian in feature films, judging by the fact that they were announcing a second vehicle just as he was going into production with his first. *Motion Picture News* announced in their March 1926 issue:

> A second starring vehicle has been selected by Paramount for W. C. Fields to follow *It's the Old Army Game*, which goes into production at the Long Island studios next week. The newest story is titled *So's Your Old Man*.[19]

As discussed in the previous chapter, there are several elements in *It's the Old Army Game* that would find their way into later talkies, including *It's a Gift*, *The Pharmacist*, and *The Bank Dick*. But *So's Your Old Man*

Lobby card for *So's Your Old Man* (Famous Players–Lasky, 1926), a rather disappointing follow-up to *It's the Old Army Game*.

was to be completely remade eight years later as *You're Telling Me*, which is not only the better film, but also much more accessible and notable. Because it was remade much more successfully, *So's Your Old Man* is just a disappointing curio today—particularly so in that it is a rather lackluster follow-up to the very funny *It's the Old Army Game*.

Fields plays Sam Bisbee, a low-income dreamer in the small town of Waukesha, New Jersey, who fancies himself an inventor. His daughter is smitten with a boy from a high society family, who lives in a palatial estate that is as much a tourist attraction of the town as the shoe factory. There is a social conflict brought about by Sam, who is a crude, earthy, rather ordinary sort.

Bisbee believes he has invented a shatterproof windshield and brings it to be tested in front of several potential backers. It gets switched before the experiment takes place, and the windshield promptly shatters during testing. On the train home, a despondent Sam contemplates suicide. At that moment, he sees an attractive woman he incorrectly believes is about to do the same. He stops her, and she is moved by his attention and kindness. They talk so long he misses his stop and must double back. Some town gossips see him talking to the woman, and by the time he arrives home he finds himself the subject of a scandal. Little does Sam realize that the woman he spoke to on the train is a visiting princess whom a small-town society family is expecting. When she comes to town and asks for Sam, calling him a dear friend, his status changes for the better.

While it is vastly inferior to its sound remake, *So's Your Old Man* is not completely without merit. For the first time, Fields offers a sardonic look at small-town life, class systems, gossip, and judgmental people. And there are some good gags. Fields does some fine pantomime in the attempted suicide scene: he holds the poison near his mouth, but cannot summon the courage to drink it. When he buys his wife a pony as a makeup gift (believing a larger pet is necessary for a large problem), there is a great visual of him being led down the street by the energetic animal.

The highlight of *So's Your Old Man* is the earliest surviving filmed record of W. C. Fields' golf routine, which he performed often in the *Follies* (an earlier filmed record is reportedly in the lost film *His Lordship's Dilemma*). The setup has Sam, now well regarded due to his association with the princess, breaking in the new course at a newly built exclusive country club. It is the sort of place at which Sam Bisbee would otherwise be unwelcome.

The golf game is performed similarly to how Fields played it onstage. He even has his *Follies* sidekick, William "Shorty" Blanche, appearing in his role as the caddy. While it shows how the sketch can be funny without the necessary dialogue, it would be far better showcased in his first sound short, *The Golf Specialist*.

Along with exploring what would become common themes in subsequent Fields features, *So's Your Old Man* features a pretty well-defined presentation of his Everyman character. Sam Bisbee is unfazed by the society people who shun him, and goes about his business with enthusiasm and confidence. When he finally meets failure, he is unable to fully comprehend its impact and believes suicide is the only answer. However, when he assumes that the woman on the train is about to do the same thing, he interrupts her and displays the sort of qualities that make him likeable. We feel sorry for Sam; he is misunderstood and lacks encouragement. Fields would utilize these qualities often in subsequent films, albeit more effectively.

Mrs. Bisbee, as portrayed in this film, is not as haughty and overbearing as future wives in Fields' films. When this movie was remade, that same dynamic remained. Mrs. Bisbee is more of the long-suffering type who functions within the parameters of her social existence, but longs for a better situation. Sam enthusiastically believes his inventions can provide that. This film also features Sam as more boisterous than in the later talkie. When the refined mother of the boy who likes Sam's daughter agrees to visit, Mrs. Bisbee does the best she can to host her. And, despite the Bisbees' much lower income level, the society woman tries to be understanding that good, cultured people can come from challenging surroundings. However, when Sam enters, pleasantly sloshed and walking around without a shirt, smoking a cigar, wearing his hat, and basically destroying every social convention, that good impression is destroyed.

It is notable that Gregory La Cava directed this film. Eddie Sutherland, who had helmed *It's the Old Army Game*, reportedly did not care for W. C. Fields and wasn't interested in working with him again. Conversely, La Cava liked Fields, and Fields liked him. They became good friends, enjoying golfing, gambling, and drinking together. However, La Cava would direct Fields in only one more film. Both men agreed that they preferred their friendship to working together.

So's Your Old Man was well liked upon its release. The critic for *Film Daily* stated: "With W. C. Fields the principal laugh perpetrator, its entertainment value is assured. There is some great hilarity in the complications that follow."[20] In *Exhibitors World*, a Missouri theatre owner stated: "Showed this on a family night and it went over with a bang. They all have a good time when you show a comedy like this. Let's keep them laughing."[21]

Again, despite generally positive reviews, Fields' second effort for Paramount was a letdown at the box office. The studio heads, of course, were approaching the Fields films as a business, expecting returns similar to their other, more successful features. Paramount had recently begun distributing the films of comedy star Harold Lloyd and his latest offering, *For Heaven's Sake*, was huge commercial hit. What Fields might have been searching for was an effective way to blend his comic sketches within the structure of a feature film, where they would appear to be an organic part of the movie rather than merely isolated scenes. His first starring features appeared to be arriving at this by creating a distinctive screen character who could play within these established sketches. Paramount executives continued to search for the property they thought would best showcase Fields' unique talents. What they failed to realize is that this had already occurred. It just needed to find its audience.

The Potters

Production: Famous Players-Lasky
Associate Producer: William Le Baron
Distribution: Paramount
Director: Fred C. Newmeyer
Screenplay: J. Clarkson Miller, Ray Harris, Sam Mintz, based on the play by J. P. McEvoy
Camera: Paul Vogel
Editor: Julian Johnson
Release date: January 29, 1927
Running time: 71 minutes
Cast: W. C. Fields (Pa Potter), Mary Alden (Ma Potter), Ivy Harris (Mamie), Richard "Skeets" Gallagher (Red), Jack Egan (Bill), Joseph W. Smiley (Rankin), Bradley Barker (Eagle).

The Potters was based upon a play by J. P. McEvoy that ran on Broadway during the 1923–1924 season, while Fields was appearing in *Poppy*. It was an attempt by Paramount to place W. C. in a narrative context for which he could play a solid role, and not merely rehash his stage routines. They even hired frequent Harold Lloyd director Fred Newmeyer to helm it.

The film deals with Pa Potter (Fields) gullibly investing $4,000 in oil stock. He figures that he will soon net $20,000 per day due to his investments. He tries to contain his enthusiasm around his family and not tell them anything, preferring to surprise them when the money starts rolling in. Unfortunately, he soon discovers that the stocks are worthless and that he has been swindled. He admits everything to his family, who are furious with him. A few days go by and Pa Potter hits rock bottom, but then he learns that the oil wells turned out to be gushers. The men who sold him the stock come to see him and attempt to buy their shares back, but Potter is on to them, holds out for a huge amount, and gets it. He comes home with a brand new radio and expensive gifts for each member of his family. They are confused as to what has happened, so he turns on their new radio for them to hear the news. He wins back their respect.

The Potters has a rather small cast, and appears to be an intimate production with Fields as the star and the others in clear support. Based upon the available information, it does not seem to have been an ensemble piece. In order to assess the film properly, it would be necessary to see it. Alas, this is not possible: *The Potters* joins the ranks of other "lost" Fields films.

Using *So's Your Old Man* as a comparison, we can imagine Fields' character suffering from depression. The description offered in the trades,

Lobby card for *The Potters* (Famous Players–Lasky, 1927), based on the play by J. P. McEvoy, featuring Richard "Skeets" Gallagher (left) and W. C. Fields.

however, states that he does not play this emotion for dark comedy as he had in the previous movie. He actually plays it straight, and evokes sympathy, in that he had invested in the wells in good faith and did so altruistically, wanting the best for his family. Indeed, from what we can deduce about *The Potters*, the Fields character appears to be more accepting and understanding of the people in his immediate world. Despite how his family turns on him when he earnestly invests in what he thought was a good idea, he still shares his ultimate wealth with them. Compared to the grotesque portrayals of future family members (particularly in *The Bank Dick*), the family's reaction may have been played for subtlety by the actors. It would even be understandable if they had been upset, given that it was *their* money Pa Potter was thought to have lost in a scheme. But, again, none of this can be accurately determined without seeing the movie.

Someone who *did* see the movie was Mordaunt Hall, critic for the *New York Times*. And judging by his reaction, *The Potters* was quite good.

W. C. Fields, the veteran stage comedian, has struck his stride as a screen actor in the picturization of J. P. McEvoy's play, "The Potters." Yesterday afternoon this film aroused many a round of hearty laughter from the large audience in the Paramount Theatre. The role of "Pa" Potter fits Mr. Fields like the proverbial glove. His performance is a real achievement, for he has resisted the temptation to be extravagant or to duplicate his mirthful actions. The moods of "Pa" Potter are reflected admirably by Mr. Fields, and whether it is a lowering of an eyelid, a gesture of his right hand, a frown or look of exuberance, one feels delighted with this Mr. Potter. The tale contains a nice quota of suspense, and the adapters, Sam Mintz and Ray Harris, have been far more restrained in translating this stage effort into a scenario than is usually the case. Fred Newmeyer, who directed several of the most successful of Harold Lloyd's comedies, is to be congratulated on his work in directing this picture.[22]

Laurence Reid, in the *Motion Picture News*, was slightly less enthusiastic about the film:

> When J. P. McEvoy wrote *The Potters* he just about dashed off the best piece of family hokum as it concerns middle class life that has come along in many a day. It was natural that the play would become a picture, even though much of its pointed incident would miss the mark with the dialogue silenced. W. C. Fields is splendid in those moments where he begins to dream of success.[23]

The box-office take for *The Potters* was still not at the level of Paramount's expectations for a stage star of Fields' magnitude, but it was an improvement over his previous features. The studio felt that perhaps the Fields films were gaining momentum with moviegoers who were not familiar with his work in the *Follies*. The following announcement appeared in the *Motion Picture News*:

> Associate Producer William Le Baron at the Long Island studio has signed W. C. Fields to a new Paramount starring contract. Responsible for the new arrangement were the pictures *So's Your Old Man* and *The Potters*, which were shown a few days ago at the studio theatre. Under the terms of the new contract, Fields will begin his next effort in March, a search for a suitable story being made in the meantime.[24]

With the relative success of *The Potters*, Paramount believed they had finally landed on a screen persona that worked for Fields. The comedian seized the moment, and made a proposal to the studio that would build upon this success. Paramount accepted Fields' proposal to hire Gregory La Cava to produce and direct his next film. The studio executives were also considering closing their Long Island studio and concentrating on their facilities in Los Angeles. If they decided to do so, it would mean Fields would have to move west as well.

Running Wild

Production and Distribution: Paramount
Associate Producer: William Le Baron

Director: Gregory La Cava
Screenplay: Gregory La Cava, based upon the story "Fearless Finch" by Roy Briant, who co-wrote the screenplay and furnished the titles
Camera: Paul Vogel
Editor: Ralph Black
Release date: August 20, 1927
Running time: 68 minutes
Cast: W. C. Fields (Elmer Finch), Marie Shotwell (Mrs. Finch), Mary Brian (Elizabeth Finch), Claude Buchanan (Dave Harvey), Frederick Burton (Mr. Harvey), Barnet Raskin (Junior), Frank Evans (Amos Barker), Edward Roseman (a hypnotist), J. Moy Bennett (Johnson), Tom Madden (a truck driver), John Merton (a cop).

Running Wild is the best of W. C. Fields' surviving silent vehicles. Here's why: Fields is allowed, for the first time onscreen, to exhibit the full gamut of his skills as an actor, exploring a wildly diverse set of emotions. While he has effectively conveyed elements of his stage character in all of his screen appearances thus far, he has clearly embellished those traits and acquired a host of subtle gestures and mannerisms for the intimacy of the movie camera. And, with *Running Wild*'s Elmer Finch, he has a complex and layered character to play.

Finch is a very timid man who is bossed around by his harridan of a second wife, and her fat, lazy son. Even his stepson's dog attacks him. The only love he gets is from his young daughter from his first marriage. (There is a tangential subplot regarding Elmer's daughter and the son of Elmer's boss having a romance, but that is something of a distraction to the central part of the narrative.) Finch is equally timid at the workplace, where he cowers at every minor confrontation. This is unlike previous characters Fields played. While he had already parodied the dysfunctional family dynamic and played a put-upon Everyman within that structure, he never played a character as defined as Elmer Finch. Finch isn't a hardworking man who simply wants to quietly avoid confrontation. He is a patsy who is bullied by nearly everyone in his immediate world. Fields, as Finch, evokes both humor and sympathy.

The firm for which Elmer works is intent upon securing an important contract from a Mr. Johnson. Elmer wants to buy his daughter a new dress; in order to do so he decides to approach Mr. Johnson himself, arrange for the contract, and obtain the commission. This attempt fails when a nervous Elmer places his lit cigar too close to a string of firecrackers, disrupting the meeting and destroying the deal. The firm is displeased, but decides to instead use Elmer to collect an important debt from a Mr. Barker. Everyone who has tried to get the money from Barker has come

Fields and Mary Brian made a sympathetic father and daughter in his best silent film, *Running Wild* (Paramount, 1927).

back beaten up, with torn clothing and bruises. Elmer is the veritable sacrificial lamb.

Elmer enters the lobby of Mr. Barker's office and hears him pummeling somebody behind closed doors. Barker bursts into the lobby and throws the man out. He then confronts Elmer, flattening his derby over his head. Elmer runs away.

The development of the film, although still played for comedy, has given further depth to the Elmer Finch character. His timidity extends beyond being generally bullied, and manifests itself when he, for once, has an opportunity to make good. The bit with the firecrackers is funny, but the underlying situation is that Finch just simply cannot win. Failing at his assignment with Barker, Finch is now desperate.

And that leads to the next plot development.

Elmer finds a horseshoe and, in his desperation, tosses it over his shoulder, making a wish. The horseshoe shatters a storefront's window. To avoid a confrontation with the store's proprietor, Elmer runs into a vaudeville theatre, where a hypnotist is performing his act. Elmer unwittingly ends up onstage as one of the hypnotist's subjects. During the course of the show, Elmer is hypnotized into having the courage of a lion. Elmer, responding to the spell, uncharacteristically yells, "I'm a lion!" and leaves the stage.

The newly lionized Elmer returns to Barker's office, and punches him until he agrees to pay his debt. After this violent display, Elmer bursts out of Barker's office, back into the lobby, and finds Mr. Johnson waiting to see Barker. Elmer says to Johnson, "I'm a lion!" and Johnson misunderstands, believing him to be a member of the Lion's Club. Recognizing him as a fellow club member, Johnson signs the contract with Elmer's firm.

It is interesting, in the early scenes, to see Fields play a character who is so completely timid, who responds to everyone with such cowardice. Indeed, Finch is the very antithesis of Fields' cunning con man roles in earlier movies. While Fields employs all of his established comic gestures, he adds some new mannerisms as well, including wincing, cringing, keeping his head down, shrugging his shoulders, and speaking to people without looking them in the eye. Then, when he is hypnotized, all of these elements are reversed. He jumps, he flails, he yells, and he completely dominates every situation.

After succeeding with both Barker and Johnson, Elmer returns to his own firm, bursts into his supervisor's meeting room, violently insists the executives at the meeting all sit down. Once they do, he reveals the signed contract from Johnson. He bellows a series of demands to his shocked superiors. This portion of Elmer Finch's world has been reversed in his favor.

Upon returning home, Elmer enters the house with a beautiful, expensive new dress for his daughter. He then disrupts his wife's tea party, frightening the other women away. His wife eventually succumbs to his overbearing manner, but not until *after* he takes down a prominently displayed framed photo of her late husband and dances on it. The stepson comes home. Elmer chases him up the stairs, removes his trousers, and spanks him with a razor strap.

Fields' bravura performance is the axis of the film, and it is he who dictates its rhythm. He takes us as far as he can with Elmer's timidity, then, just as we become frustrated with the character, he makes the complete turn with the hypnosis scene and changes direction. This structure is most effective, making the later scenes that much more amusing than the earlier ones.

The hypnotist is called to take the spell off Elmer and he returns to his settled, mannered self. He doesn't remember what happened, but his daughter, who proudly witnessed everything, clues him in. Elmer is amazed, and has a large commission check in his pocket for securing the Johnson account. When the stepson arrives at the door and asks his mother if he can come in, she says (by way of a title card), "Ask your father, he knows what's best." Elmer is now fully in charge. Not remembering the spanking he had given his stepson, he chases him down the street to do so again.

Critics deemed this movie Fields' best when it was released in early 1927. Laurence Reid, in *Motion Picture News*, stated:

> The comedian has discarded his *Follies* tricks—tricks, you might say, which were keeping him back. In this offering he demonstrates he has some different aces up his sleeve. The antics are mostly original, well-fortified with chuckles, many of which come deep from the diaphragm.[25]

Norbert Lusk, in *Picture Play*, was equally pleased:

> The best picture of W. C. Fields is found in his latest, *Running Wild*. The picture has a human quality that raises it above the ordinary screen farce of the worm who turns, and Fields is unique in the portrayal of this sort of character.[26]

Despite its aesthetic brilliance and its critical reception, *Running Wild* was still not the moneymaker Paramount hoped it would be. Fields continued to work hard and was appearing in vehicles that were tailored to his abilities, but he still had not established himself in films.

Two Flaming Youths

Production and Distribution: Paramount
Associate Producer: Louis D. Lighton
Director: John Waters
Screenplay: Percy Heath, Donald Davis (uncredited: Grover Jones, Julian Josephson, Norman Z. McLeod, Eddie Moran, Gilbert Pratt), based upon "The Side Show," a story by Percy Heath; the film's titles were supplied by Jack Conway
Camera: H. Kinley Martin
Editor: Rose Loewinger
Release date: December 17, 1927
Running time: 55 minutes
Cast: W. C. Fields (Gabby Gilfoil), Chester Conklin (Sheriff Holden), Mary Brian (Mary Gilfoil), Jack Luden (Tony), George Irving (Simeon), Cissy Fitzgerald (Madge), Jimmy Quinn (Slipper Sawtelle), John Seresheff (The Strong Man), John Aasen (the giant), Clark and McCullough, Moran and Mack, Pearl and Bard, Weber and Fields, Beery and Hatton, The Duncan Sisters, Baker and Silvers, Savoy and Brennan (themselves).

Paramount had another, and final, idea as to what they could do to bolster Fields' box-office standing: They chose to try him in a comedy team. Stan Laurel and Oliver Hardy had just been teamed by Leo McCarey in a series of two-reel comedies for the Hal Roach studios, and their onscreen antics caught on with the public immediately. Paramount had erstwhile Keystone comedian Chester Conklin under contract, so the decision was to put Conklin and Fields in a few movies together. They would not always function as a bona fide team like Laurel and Hardy, but the studio thought these two talented veteran comedians would function quite effectively as co-stars. If they did we will never know for certain; all three films they made together are lost.

Two Flaming Youths features Conklin as small-town sheriff Ben Holden, who is smitten with hotel manager Madge Malarkey. Fields is Gabby Gilfoil, a carnival man, whose traveling show rolls into town on a wagon, which promptly breaks down. A mechanic needs a few days to fix it, so Gabby sets up his carnival in the town. While trying to generate business, Gabby runs into Madge. Each believes the other has money (neither does) so they become attracted to each other on that level. This causes the sheriff to become jealous, and a rivalry ensues. Meanwhile, Gabby's daughter falls for the mechanic working on the wagon.

The sheriff believes Gabby is a notorious criminal, Slippery Sawtelle, not realizing that Slippery was recently captured and jailed. At one point, Gabby lures the sheriff into the kangaroo cage at the carnival. The kangaroo starts boxing the sheriff, and Gabby starts barking to the crowd, "See the sheriff battle the boxing kangaroo!" Tickets sell quickly and enough money is made for Gabby to pay off all of his debts. Once the sheriff is out of the cage, he rushes back to Madge, who is now smitten with the wealthy Simeon Trott. Both losing Madge, Gabby and the sheriff join forces to dupe Simeon in a shell game, and win away his money. They succeed, splitting the spoils between them. Meanwhile, Gabby's daughter ends up with the mechanic.

What research tells us about the film is intriguing, and the use of Fields and Conklin as adversaries has solid comic potential. The con man aspect of the Fields character is once again explored, and the idea with the sheriff and the boxing kangaroo is an example of his screen persona's cleverness in manipulating the situation for his own benefit. Finally, the fact that the two comic adversaries team up against a common enemy at the end of the movie (and each enjoys his own triumph), tells us that the film features the two actors' onscreen relationship on several levels.

Another intriguing aspect of *Two Flaming Youths* is that it appears to have been fleshed out to (barely) feature length by presenting carnival acts and allowing them some screen time to perform at least part of their act. Since most of the vaudeville performers appearing in the film usually rely on dialogue, it is curious as to how they conveyed their comedy in the context of a silent movie.

Certainly the most shocking fact about *Two Flaming Youths* is that W. C. Fields was nearly killed while making it. In a scene in which Conklin is chasing Fields while both are on bicycles, Fields was supposed to look over his shoulder to see if Conklin was gaining on him, just as a truck was backing out into the street. He was then supposed to hit the truck with his bike, roll under the axle, and escape as the truck blocked Conklin from pursuing him. However, when Fields fell, he broke bones in his spine and was unable to move. The truck kept moving, and Fields could not roll under the axle. The vehicle's huge tire was heading straight for Fields' skull. Crew members yelled out, but the driver could not hear them. Stuntman John Sinclair ran out, pulled Fields by the legs,

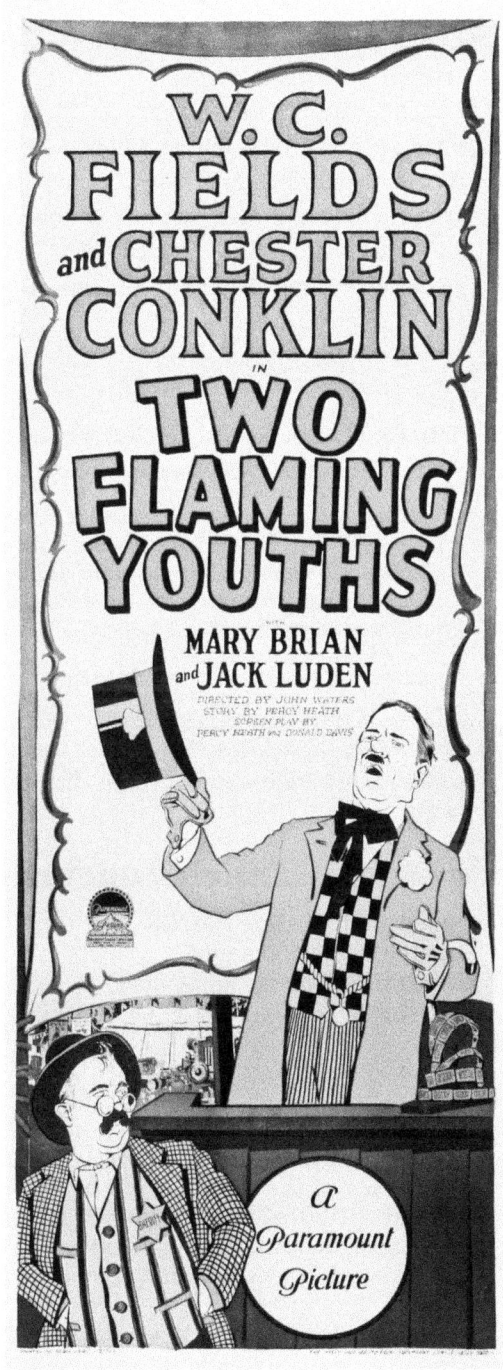

In an attempt to make a new "Laurel and Hardy," Fields was teamed with former Keystone comedian Chester Conklin in three features, the first being *Two Flaming Youths* (Paramount, 1927).

and dragged him to safety in the nick of time. It was the last scene being filmed, so *Two Flaming Youths* was released on time. But it took several weeks for Fields to recover.

In gratitude for his heroism, Fields offered Sinclair money, but Sinclair only wanted a job on Fields' next movie. From that point on, John Sinclair worked on every W. C. Fields film project, often as the comedian's stuntman, but he also, at least on occasion, contributed gags.

Past studies have stated that *Two Flaming Youths* received poor reviews, but one theatre owner reporting in *Exhibitors Herald* stated:

> A surefire comedy that will please. Some great jugging by Fields, and the race for the widow's hand by Fields and Conklin with a surprise ending are the highlights. Very good comedy. Fields is extra good.[27]

That same theatre owner added the warning to his fellow exhibitors: "Not for the older folks." As he explained:

> I may be a bit isolated in my tastes, but I am in total agreement with the idea that the proper target for the comic picture is the middle-aged citizenry. This is that sort of a comedy, not the best in the world, and not the worst, a comedy out of which a self-respecting man or woman of more than thirty years of age can get a giggle. I'm for more of them.[28]

Apparently, not enough middle-aged people went to see *Two Flaming Youths*; it was another in what was becoming a long line of box-office disappointments starring W. C. Fields. Recovering from his injuries, Fields—a chronic worrier—probably felt that his movie career might not recover at all.

Tillie's Punctured Romance

Production: Christie Film Co.
Distribution: Paramount
Director: A. Edward Sutherland
Screenplay: Monte Brice, Keene Thompson
Camera: Charles Boyle, William Wheeler
Editor: Arthur Huffsmith
Release date: March 3, 1928
Running time: 70 minutes
Cast: W. C. Fields (the ringmaster), Louise Fazenda (Tillie) Chester Conklin (owner of the circus), Mack Swain (Tillie's father), Grant Withers (the hero), Doris Hills (the heroine), Tom Kennedy (prop man), Babe London (strong woman), Billy Platt (midget), Mickey Bennett (brat), Mike Rafetto (lion tamer), Kalla Pasha (axe thrower).

Producer Al Christie, who made short comedies for Educational Pictures, was interested in producing a remake of the 1914 Keystone production *Tillie's Punctured Romance*. Amazing in its cinematic approach, a real triumph within the parameter of director Mack Sennett's vision, *Tillie's Punctured Romance* is a landmark film, being the first feature-length comedy in movie history. It was based upon a play, *Tillie's Nightmare* by A. Baldwin Stone and Edgar Smith, and starred stage actress Marie Dressler (recreating her role as Tillie in her film debut), as well as Charlie Chaplin, Mabel Normand, and the Keystone Cops. Al Christie and company wanted to revamp the story and feature W. C. Fields and Chester Conklin. Paramount—by now desperate for a hit—agreed to their terms.

Producer Al Christie had been producing comedies since 1910, joining the old Nestor Company, which became part of Universal, in 1911. In 1916, Al Christie and his brother Charles formed Christie Film Company, which was best known for producing short comedies that were much gentler in tone than the anarchic Keystones. By 1922, the Christie corporation had become quite successful and began expanding their scope. According to James Curtis's excellent 2003 biography of Fields:

> [Christie] held the rights to such staples as *Charley's Aunt* and *Up in Mabel's Room* and made creditable screen versions of both. He also owned the rights to *Tillie's Punctured Romance*, the landmark slapstick feature directed by Mack Sennett. Christie proposed a remake for Paramount release and [the studio] agreed to fund the project, contributing Fields, Conklin, and director Eddie Sutherland to the package.[29]

However, Christie did not plan to use the same story as Sennett's production. That one was about a farm girl (Dressler) who is lured away to the big city by a slicker (Chaplin) who dupes her and goes off with his girl (Mabel Normand), leaving the ignorant Tillie broke and alone in the big city, where she has to wait on tables at a seedy diner in order to survive. When she comes into an inheritance, the slicker wants Tillie back, but only to bilk her of that money as well.

Christie's story is different. In this one Tillie is again a farm girl (with Mack Swain repeating his role as her father from the Sennett movie), but she runs away to join the circus. Tillie becomes a performer in the circus where Fields plays the ringmaster and Conklin the owner. In the middle of the story, war is declared and the narrative shifts to overseas, with General Pershing and the American Expeditionary Forces. Conklin and Fields try to enlist first, but they are both too old, so they decide to help out by entertaining the troops on the battlefield. They get lost, end up in enemy territory, the former circus lions escape and cause the enemy soldiers to scatter out of the foxholes, helping the Allies win the war.

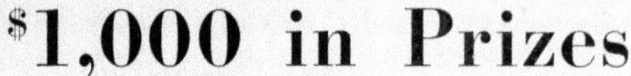

The studio tried contests and prizes to entice customers to see the all-new version of the classic *Tillie's Punctured Romance* (Christy Film Co./Paramount, 1928). They might have had more success with a better film.

There are tangential subplots involving the ringmaster planning to kill the circus's owner by feeding him to the lions, but getting himself in danger instead. There is also a budding romance between Tillie and the Strong Man, and the Ringmaster and the Strong Woman. As the film ends, all the leads are happily coupled with whom they desire.

Tillie's Punctured Romance began shooting in December of 1927. Fields was a bit careful on the set, still recovering from his injury on the previous movie, while Conklin spent a lot of time between takes telling amusing stories about working in the previous Sennett version. A blurb in *Film Daily* appeared in January:

> Six thousand feet is the limit set by Al Christie for the releasing footage of *Tillie's Punctured Romance*, a Christie special that Eddie Sutherland is cutting. "The reason for this radical departure," says Christie, "is that a contributing factor in the success of feature comedies in the past was the short running time." It is expected that the cutting and previewing of *Tillie* will require several more weeks, with the release date set for February 18th.[30]

There continued to be updates in the trades, right up to the time *Tillie's Punctured Romance* was ready to be released. In one advertisement, Paramount listed this movie among their ten upcoming features for 1928, including Harold Lloyd's *Speedy*, *The Last Command* with Emil Jannings, and other highly anticipated films. About *Tillie's Punctured Romance*, the publicity read:

> Millions roared at the old *Tillie's Punctured Romance* and called it the comedy classic of all time. The same millions—and millions more—hail with delight at Al Christie's new 1928 *Tillie's Punctured Romance* (everything bigger and better but the title).[31]

If Paramount had been displeased with the level of box-office returns from previous W. C. Fields movies, they must have been downright angry about this one. *Tillie's Punctured Romance* was an enormous flop, bombing with critics, exhibitors, and moviegoers alike. Movie theatre owners stated in the October issue of *Exhibitors Herald*:

- This is the kind of picture that causes vacant seats in a theatre. Got plenty of razzing from my patrons.
- Absolutely the dumbest thing ever shown in our theatre.
- Fewer laughs than an ordinary two-reel comedy. It was an awful flop at the box office.
- Paramount should be ashamed to put out such a picture as this.
- It might be a puncture for *Tillie* but it was a blowout for me. I made $8.60 and I wanted to give that back.[32]

The film was also savaged by the critics, who found the story laughable (not in a good way) and incomprehensible. But it did have its defenders. The resident critic for the *Motion Picture News* stated:

> The old dame still has a lot of life left in her. With the capable staff of Christie comedy constructors, a new cast of frolic adapts, and general goofiness everywhere, this new Tillie is an attractor for laughs. The story doesn't obey any of the rules of logic. It is merrily crazy and has an ending which can be met with any time in the one-reel quickie comedies turned out by various studios. But, it is obvious, that everything is in good fun and seriousness would seem out of place in the burlesque of events. So don't look for logic. Some will undoubtedly regard it as silly, but it is funny, nevertheless.[33]

It is interesting that what most critics called "incomprehensible," the *Motion Picture News* review identified as "merrily crazy" in its not obeying "any of the rules of logic." But Paramount was much more interested in the bottom line. *Tillie's Punctured Romance* was a fairly expensive production, with sets, animals, and special effects during the battle scenes. It did not make back its costs.

Despite its lack of success, it is unfortunate that we cannot see for ourselves just how bad *Tillie's Punctured Romance* is, or whether it, in fact, seems funnier than it did in 1928. Would we agree with the critics and moviegoers who found it incomprehensible, or would we side with the *Motion Picture News*, believing that its silliness is part of its charm? With the ability to actually screen *Tillie's Punctured Romance*, we could also determine whether it merits any significance in the overall film career of W. C. Fields.

Usually, in the case of lost films, there isn't much evidence to determine just why they are lost. Sometimes prints turn up decades later, often in the most unlikely places. Other times all existing prints seem to have disappeared. But there does seem to be a trail back to this version of *Tillie's Punctured Romance*. In 1932, producer Charles R. Rogers bought the rights to the original 1914 Mack Sennett version, with the camera negative for the 1928 version tossed in as part of the deal. Rogers had no interest in the more recent version, then only four years old, and obviously did not have the foresight that this box-office flop would have any future historical interest. It is unknown as to what Rogers did with the negative. Did he destroy it? Did he disregard it and allow it to decompose?

We can only assess a lost film like *Tillie's Punctured Romance* based upon what research can provide. It's failure certainly didn't bode well for Fields' continued employment with Paramount.

Fools for Luck

Production and Distribution: Paramount
Director: Charles F. Reisner
Screenplay: Sam Mintz, Jr., J. Walter Rubin (uncredited Grover Jones, Hank Mann), based upon "Men About Town," a story by Harry Fried
Producer: B. P. Schulberg
Camera: William Marshall
Editor: George Nichols, Jr.
Release date: June 11, 1928
Running time: 60 minutes
Cast: W. C. Fields (Richard Whitehead), Chester Conklin (Samuel Hunter), Sally Blane (Louise Hunter), Jack Luden (Ray Caldwell), Mary Alden (Mrs. Hunter), Arthur Houseman (Grogan), Robert Dudley (Jim Simpson), Martha Mattox (Mrs. Simpson).

Fools for Luck is the last of Paramount's attempts to team W. C. Fields and Chester Conklin, and also has the distinction of the most recent of the lost Fields films. Every movie hereafter is available and accessible. *Fools for Luck* seems to rely on past ideas that had been somewhat effective, both in plot development as well as the character dynamic between Fields and Conklin.

Fields is Richard Whitehead, a crooked oil man who descends upon the small town of Hunstville, where Sam Hunter (Conklin) is known as the city's richest citizen and its greatest pool player. Whitehead manages to convince Hunter to help him sell stock in oil wells to most of the township, and the trusted Hunter vouches for Whitehead and the oil wells' authenticity. When the wells turn out to be dry, there is a series of skirmishes between the two of them. However, in the end, the wells turn out to be gushers and everyone ends up happy.

This plot is similar to that of *It's the Old Army Game*, and that is not the only familiar element in *Fools for Luck*. There is also a scene where Hunter needs to dress up for an evening gathering, but when his butler brings out his suit, it is almost completely moth-eaten. Hunter hastily runs into a clothing store and buys a suit off the rack, but when he puts it on he discovers it is much too large for him. It is quickly taken in with basting, but when he appears on the dance floor, the basting starts to give away. This had already been done by Harold Lloyd in his feature *The Freshman* the year before, a fact not lost on critics of the time.

One scene that shows good comic potential is a pool game between the two leads. Hunter readily accepts a challenge from Whitehead, as he is the town's pool champion. Whitehead at first plays poorly, improperly holding the cue and making other amateurish mistakes. Hunter sees him

Fields (left) and Chester Conklin shoot pool in a scene from *Fools for Luck* (Paramount, 1928).

as an easy mark, so he agrees to play with one hand behind his back. Whitehead then proceeds to sink five balls, one after the other, with solid, professional shots.

The conflict between the principal characters seems to provide the gist of the comedy in *Fools for Luck*, including Hunter being unable to convince his wife and daughter just how unscrupulous the oil man is. They invite Whitehead into their home and give him the master bedroom. A funny scene occurs when Hunter comes home to find Whitehead sleeping in his bed. There is also a tangential romance between Sally Blane, who plays Hunter's daughter, and Jack Luden. Blane, who had a brief career in pictures, was Loretta Young's sister. Luden was a popular actor for a short time, but ended up getting hooked on heroin; he later died in prison. He had previously appeared in a bit role in *It's the Old Army Game*.

Fools for Luck was yet another commercial failure at the box office. Critics, like those few who saw the film, were also unimpressed. Mordaunt Hall, in the *New York Times*, complained:

Periodically Messrs. Conklin and Fields succeed in giving a second or so of fun, but when the inevitable silver flask is introduced the story is one in which originality is successfully avoided. Both Mr. Conklin and Mr. Fields are far better in more intelligent stories than this specimen. They are either very funny in their films or very silly. In this one the silly ideas predominate.[34]

A theatre owner wrote in *Exhibitors Herald* that "*Fools for Luck* might be a hit in a blind asylum, but it's not much for people who can see. This pair has no drawing power whatsoever."[35]

Fields did nothing to promote the film, at least not in Topeka, Kansas. A week before the film opened in that city, he was scheduled to appear at an auditorium for a live show, but held the curtain up for forty-five minutes until he received an extra $1,000 as a penalty against the theatre manager, because Fields' name was printed smaller than the opening act, Moran and Mack ("The Two Black Crows") in newspaper advertisements. As a result, angry Topekans stayed away from *Fools for Luck* when it opened a week later at the Jayhawk Theatre, resulting in the worst three days in the theatre's history.[36]

After this latest poor showing for their once promising star, Paramount chose not to renew his contract. At the same time, stage producer Earl Carroll was finishing a prison sentence after serving two years for embezzlement. He wanted to bring his *Earl Carroll's Vanities* back to Broadway, and hired Louise Brooks, among other performers. Carroll wanted Fields as his headliner, but realized he was now in movies and would be expensive to hire. He was correct. Fields indicated he wanted to be paid $6,000 per week and receive star billing. Carroll accepted the star billing, but didn't want to go any higher than $5,200 per week. Fields agreed to those terms, but only if his name was largest in all advertising, even larger than *Earl Carroll's Vanities*. Carroll accepted, and Fields remained in this Broadway show from late August of 1928 until March of 1930.

There is a story that one of the other comedians on the bill, Ben Blue, stole some bits from Fields' routines without obtaining permission. Fields hired some thugs to give Blue a beating near the stage door of the Palace Theatre, where they were then performing. The incident was reported in the New York papers. Ben Blue would later appear in various films and TV shows, including the Taxi Boys series at the Hal Roach Studios. He would even appear with Fields, nearly a decade later, in *The Big Broadcast of 1938*.

By the time W. C. Fields concluded his successful run with *Earl Carroll's Vanities*, a new decade had dawned. And by 1930, motion pictures were virtually all talkies. Ever since Warner Bros. had a hit with Al Jolson in the part-talkie *The Jazz Singer* back in 1927, theatres in the bigger cities began to be wired for sound. Fields' friend and chief supporter, William Le Baron, who had been helpful in getting him hired at Paramount, was now vice president in charge of production at RKO studios. He brought up Fields' name to short subjects producer Lou Brock, who realized that the comedian's silent films had been given a generally lukewarm reception. However, Brock, who was familiar with Fields' distinctive delivery, knew that he had yet to use that delivery onscreen.

Lou Brock told Le Baron that he was interested in hiring Fields to recreate his surefire golf act in a sound two-reeler. Fields was contacted and eager to return to movies, hoping that the addition of sound would give him the opportunity to add another dimension to his comedy, and better translate his stage routines to the movies, preserving them for all time.

When Fields' hiring by RKO was announced in the trades, theatre owners who recalled the lack of success they had with his past movies balked, stating that he was popular onstage, but was box-office poison at the movies. Le Baron and Brock disagreed, firmly believing that W. C. Fields would be a natural for talkies.

They were correct.

The Golf Specialist

Production: Radio Pictures
Producer: Louis Brock
Distribution: RKO
Director: Monte Brice
Screenplay: W. C. Fields
Camera: Frank Zucker
Editor: Russell G. Shields
Release date: July 24, 1930; re-released: 1975 (Janus)
Running time: 21 minutes
Cast: W. C. Fields (J. Effingham Bellweather), Shirley Grey (house detective's wife), John Dunsmuir, (house detective), Johnny Kane (Walter, the desk clerk), Howard Hull Gibson ("Deep Sea" McGurk, alias "The Slaughterhouse Kid"), Naomi Casey (bratty little girl), Allen Wood (caddy), Allan Bennett (double-jointed man), William Black (sheriff).

Despite its reputation, *The Golf Specialist* is actually not W. C. Fields' first appearance in a sound film. Fields appeared in a March 1929 Fox Movietone newsreel, shot in Florida. He is giving golf instructions to an unidentified female, and there is dialogue. In the existing footage, Fields does several takes instructing the woman on how to hit a ball, while she asks questions about his game.

> WOMAN: Have you ever played before?
> FIELDS: I haven't played since playing in the Canary Islands many years ago.
> WOMAN: The Canary Islands?
> FIELDS: Yes, we used to tee off on one island and drive to the other.
> WOMAN: Well, how far is it from one island to the other?
> FIELDS: Oh, about a half a mile. Of course, we had to have the wind behind us.

This raw footage also shows Fields do a bit where he steps on a club and it pops up and hits him in his rear. He blames the caddy, slapping off the man's hat. The caddy is a black actor, not Fields' regular player "Shorty" Blanche. In the background, we can hear the Movietone cameraman and crew laughing, and they applaud, much to Fields' delight. The raw footage then shows him doing the same bit again, with the camera positioned at a closer angle. In this next bit of footage, Fields is not wearing his clip-on mustache. He and the woman go through the Canary Islands dialogue again. Portions of each of these takes were used in the eventual Movietone release.

The idea of *The Golf Specialist* was simple: to capture W. C. Fields' golf act, "An Episode on the Links," in its entirety on film—with sound, in this case the RKO Photophone process. In order to make it appear that this was not simply one more filmed vaudeville sketch (a practice that had been overused at the time), a thin backstory was given, and more than one set was employed. Fields was eager to commit this sketch to film. One of his older stage routines, "The Family Ford," featuring another actor, had already been filmed by Vitaphone (a division of Warner Bros.) and was awaiting release (it came out in July of 1930, just a month before the release of *The Golf Specialist*). Fields was incensed that another comedian performed his material in a movie, so he wanted to commit his own routines to film before more of these situations happened.

The Golf Specialist opens on the lavish grounds of an upscale hotel in Palm Beach, Florida. (The film itself was shot at the Astoria Studios on Long Island.) In the hotel's lobby, a flirtatious woman, the house detective's wife, is attempting to seduce any man who comes through the door. Meanwhile, the burly "Deep Sea" McGurk comes in looking for a Mr. Bellweather, who has been "giving me the runaround" about getting paid "for taking him out in me fishing boat." He dictates a threatening note to be given to the miscreant once he arrives.

J. Effingham Bellweather (Fields) arrives immediately thereafter, reads the note, then rips it up. The house detective enters the lobby again, and

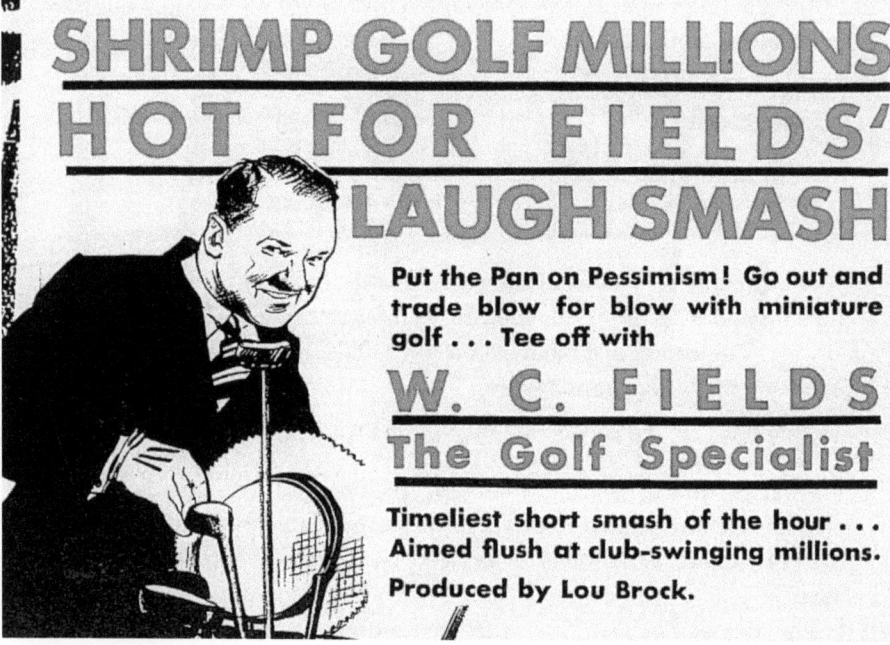

Trade ad for *The Golf Specialist* (RKO, 1930). In his first official talkie, Fields proved he was at least twice as funny with sound.

once again warns his pretty wife not to talk to *any* man. Actress Shirley Grey, making her third of nearly fifty film appearances, is quite amusing as the airheaded blond who is still clever enough to manipulate virtually anything in pants. When her husband accosts one of her admirers, she mechanically yells, "Help! Murder!" while casually applying lipstick and paying no attention to the punishment being meted out to her latest conquest. Bellweather mistakes the rough-speaking man for the young lady's father, an assumption she denies. She does not, however, reveal that he is her husband.

> BELLWEATHER: He's *not* your father and he was going to strike you?
> WOMAN: Perhaps he would have if you hadn't come along!
> BELLWEATHER: You know, I never struck a woman in my life!
> WOMAN (IMPRESSED): No?
> BELLWEATHER: Not even my own mother!

As Bellweather tries to make time with the promiscuous young lady, a strident little five-year-old girl tugs at his jacket and demands a dollar for her piggy bank. "I'll give you a dollar," he says, "if you'll sing me a song."

The little girl agrees, but wants the dollar *first*. Bellweather grumbles, "You're more than five—get out of here." The child is unfazed; she claims to have "fifty dollars in my bank already." Bellweather immediately tries to wrest the bank from her, while the child screams annoyingly. She gets even later by placing a stuffed dog behind Bellweather and sprinkling water on the back of his pants. Blaming the dog, Bellweather kicks the stuffed animal.

J. Effingham Bellweather is given all of the familiar traits—from dishonesty to cleverness, from unscrupulousness to friendliness. And some conflicts are set up, showing that Bellweather is a man wanted by the law for various petty offenses ("possessing a skunk" and "telling the facts of life to an Indian" are among the crimes indicated on a "Wanted" poster).

Bellweather, his caddy, and the hotel detective's wife make their way onto the links (a stagey-looking set with painted scenery) for a round of golf. The caddy is a sorry-looking little man with an oversized cap and ill-fitting clothes. He is played by vaudevillian Allen Wood, who had recently appeared with Fields at the RKO Palace Theatre in New York. (Fields' usual sidekick, William "Shorty" Blanche, was, apparently, unavailable.) From this point on, Bellweather attempts to tee off, and never manages to do so. Faulty clubs, the caddy's squeaky shoes, blowing papers, and even a pie disrupt his attempts. Bellweather offers a running commentary the entire time, from grumbling sarcasm to mixing metaphors. At one point he says to the caddy: "I'd like to wring your neck. I'd like to wash it first and give it a good ring. A ring you can hear from miles and miles." The hotel detective's wife stands earnestly alongside Bellweather, appearing interested, without really comprehending what is going on. Bellweather carefully explains what he is doing, endlessly repeating the phrase "Stand clear and keep your eye on the ball!"

The Golf Specialist received wide distribution and positive reviews. According to a writer for *Motion Picture News*:

> W. C. Fields clicks a lot of laughs in this amplification of the golf act he's used [for] so many years on the stage. The action has been elaborated to a considerable extent but it holds the attention throughout and keeps up a steady round of laughter. Fields' voice is ideal for talkers [later called talkies] and his camera presence excellent. All types of audiences will enjoy it.[37]

A critic for *Variety* stated:

> Fields used this sketch on and off in vaudeville and in the Follies. To anyone having seen this sketch in the show or vaudeville, the picture version will not seem as

comical; but to those who haven't, "The Golf Specialist" ought to be a laugh getter while those who have seen it before should laugh again at much of the action. Monte Brice directed and got most of the golfing pantomime and slapstick in the camera's eye effectively enough.[38]

As Fields spent only a day filming *The Golf Specialist*, he was soon on to other assignments. He took the role of Cap'n Andy in a revival of *Show Boat* for a two-week run at the Municipal Opera House in Forest Park, near the Mississippi River, in St. Louis. The role had originally been written with Fields in mind, but he was under contract to Paramount at the time and was unable appear in the Kern-Hammerstein show during its initial 1927–1928 Broadway run.

After *Show Boat*, Fields returned to New York and appeared in *Ballyhoo*. Producer Arthur Hammerstein lost money on the show and planned to close it in early January 1931, after a three-week run. Fields and the rest of the cast financed its further production and it lasted until the end of February. Having the performers take over the production of a show was revolutionary at that time.

Fields continued to feel that movies were to be his future. So he packed up his things and headed to California, where he planned to relocate and get into the movie business once and for all.

Her Majesty, Love

Production and Distribution: First National
Executive Producer: Hal B. Wallis
Associate Producer: Henry Blanke
Director: William Dieterle
Screenplay: Robert Lord, Arthur Caesar, based on a story by Rudolph Bernauer and Rudolf Österreicher.
Camera: Robert Kurrie
Editor: Ralph Dawson
Songs:
"You're Baby-Minded Now"
Music by Walter Jurmann, Lyrics by Al Dubin
Sung by Leon Errol, William Irving, Harry Stubbs, and Marilyn Miller
"Don't Ever Be Blue"
Music by Walter Jurmann, Lyrics by Al Dubin
Sung by Donald Novis and patrons of the cabaret
"Because of You"
Music by Walter Jurmann, Lyrics by Al Dubin
Sung by Ben Lyon and Donald Novis
Reprised by Marilyn Miller
"Though You're Not the First One"

Music by Walter Jurmann, Lyrics by Al Dubin
Sung by Donald Novis
Released December 31, 1931
Running time: 75 minutes
Cast: Marilyn Miller (Lia), Ben Lyon (Fred), W. C. Fields (Lia's father), Leon Errol (Baron), Ford Sterling (Otmar), Chester Conklin (Emil), Harry Stubbs (Hanneman), Clarence Wilson (Cornelius), Harry Holman (Reisenfeld), Ruth Hall (secretary), Mae Madison (Elli), Maude Eburne (Aunt Harriet), Virginia Sale (Laura), Irving Bacon (valet), Gino Corrado (clerk), Florence Roberts (Grandma), Lynn Reynolds (Trixie), Eddie Kane (cabaret patron), Gus Arnheim (himself).

Upon his arrival in California, Fields happened to run into actress Marilyn Miller, a friendly acquaintance from the *Ziegfeld Follies*. She had since become a hit on Broadway and had a contract with First National (a division of Warner Bros.). Miller needed someone to play her father in her next film, *Her Majesty, Love*, and Fields, she knew, would be perfect in the part. Of course, Fields was interested in being cast in a supporting role in a major film.

The story is one of a young man named Fred, from a wealthy industrialist family, who falls hard for Lia, an ordinary barmaid. He proposes to her, and she accepts. Fred's highbrow family objects to the engagement because the girl's father was once a lowly juggler in vaudeville. Fred is talked into giving Lia up when promised advancement in the family business, but soon realizes he prefers life with her. However, too much time has gone by and Lia is now engaged to someone else.

Pleased to have a part in this movie, happy to be reunited with former co-star Chester Conklin, Fields hoped his appearance in *Her Majesty, Love* would be the gateway to a career in talking pictures. However, despite reviewers taking note of the contributions of the veteran comics (who also included Ford Sterling and Leon Errol), *Her Majesty, Love* was a flop.

Miller, although only thirty-three years old at the time, was not aging well, due to an alcohol problem she developed after the sudden death of her first husband in a 1920 auto accident. This was her third movie, and her last. She would only live another five years, dying in 1936 from an infection following sinus surgery. Her co-star (and former lover) Ben Lyon comes off well enough in a decidedly bland part as the romantic lead.

Fields has some funny dialogue, such as: "After you're married I can just hear you saying those wonderful words: 'Dad, how much do you need?'" And when Leon Errol, as a wealthy baron, has designs on Lia, who

The manager of this theater chose to give W. C. Fields star billing in *Her Majesty, Love* (First National, 1931), even though his was only a supporting role. The actual star was Marilyn Miller, a former *Follies* girl, who had suggested Fields play her father in the story.

has no interest in him, Fields once again has only dollar signs in his eyes: "He's rich and he's old, what more do you want? You can look forward to a happy widowhood!"

Fields was also very cooperative during filming, getting along well with the cast and director, and even agreeing to wear an authentic-looking mustache as part of the character, rather than his clip-on prop. This would be the last film in which he wore a mustache (unless he happens to need a quick disguise, as in *The Old Fashioned Way* and *You Can't Cheat an Honest Man*, or to play a character part, such as T. Frothingill Bellows, in *The Broadcast of 1938*).

Fields was not above throwing in a few bits of his own, and director William Dieterle accommodated him. For instance, he recalled, for the director, a time when he once juggled the dinner plates at Will Rogers's home during a party. Fields does this in *Her Majesty, Love* in front of Fred's haughty parents. First, he flings some bakery goods across the length of the table to a waiting Chester Conklin. Then he juggles the plates with delightful dexterity. When interrupted by his daughter, he drops the expensive plates and they shatter on the floor.

Director Dieterle, making his second American film after getting his start in his native Germany, tries to offer some interesting establishing shots, and despite this being an early talkie, the camera does not remain stationary. There are sweeps and tracking shots that allow a better flow to the narrative structure. But, hard as he may have tried, there was little even a gifted director like Dieterle could do with such weak material.

Clarence Wilson, with whom Fields would work with again in *Tillie and Gus*, has a fun bit where he cracks nuts with his fists during a meeting, disrupting the proceedings. Ford Sterling is delightful as he exhibits the sort of fidgety mannerisms that had defined his silent screen roles. Chester Conklin and Leon Errol offer strong performances as well. Errol even does his drunk bit, offering lines like, "I once proposed to a gal because she smelled good!" The cast is comfortably rounded out with familiar veterans like Maude Eburne, Oscar Apfel, Gino Corrado, Eddie Kane, and Florence Roberts.

Despite all of this, *Her Majesty, Love* is not a good movie. Still, even in a poor film, Fields can charm the critics. According to a review in the *Motion Picture Herald*:

> Bill Fields tops the performances. As an ex-vaudevillian and father of the girl, Bill gets a swell opportunity to do his stuff, including just enough of his famous plate-juggling number.[39]

However, turning in a critically acclaimed performance in a flop movie didn't help Fields get more work in features. In fact, as we look at his movies historically, *Her Majesty, Love* is, arguably, one of the least important films of his career. Perhaps the most interesting aspect of *Her Majesty, Love* is that Fields would later use the clash of classes much more effectively in later films.

Fortunately for the comedian, over at his old studio Paramount a fan of his stage work had become one of the top producers. Herman Mankiewicz had once even written a screenplay with Fields in mind. When he heard that W. C. was looking for work, he met with him and asked if he would consider accepting a role in a new production he was putting together. Even though he would not receive star billing, Fields agreed, hoping it would lead to better things.

Million Dollar Legs

Production and Distribution: Paramount Publix
Executive Producer: B. P. Schulberg

Associate Producer: Herman J. Mankiewicz
Director: Edward F. Cline
Screenplay: Joseph L. Mankiewicz (story), Henry Myers (uncredited: Nick Barrows, Herman J. Mankiewicz, Sam Mintz)
Camera: Arthur L. Todd
Editor: LeRoy Stone
Songs:
"It's Terrific (When I Get Hot)"
Music by Ralph Rainger, Lyrics by Leo Robin
Sung by Lyda Roberti
"The Klopstakian Love Song"
Music based upon "One Hour with You" by Richard A. Whiting, Lyrics by Henry Myers
Performed by Jack Oakie
Release date: July 8, 1932
Running time: 64 minutes
Cast: Jack Oakie (Migg Tweeny), W. C. Fields (The President of Klopstokia), Andy Clyde (The Major-Domo), Lyda Roberti (Mata Machree), Susan Fleming (Angela), Ben Turpin (The Mysterious Man), Hugh Herbert (Secretary of the Treasury), Dickie Moore (Willie), Samuel Adams (Secretary of State), Tyler Booke (announcers), Billy Gilbert (Secretary of the Interior), Vernon Dent (Secretary of Agriculture), Ted Stanhope, Heinie Conklin, Al Bridge (emissaries), Bruce Bennett, Billy Engle, Bobby Dunn, Charlie Hall (athletes).
(Note: Hank Mann is listed in the credits but cannot be identified in the movie.)

Million Dollar Legs joins the Marx Brothers' *Duck Soup* (1933) and Wheeler and Woolsey's *Diplomaniacs* (1934) as one of the most wonderfully absurd political satires of the pre–Code era. This film is about the country of Klopstokia, where every citizen is gifted with athletic prowess and the presidency is decided by Indian wrestling. Enthusiastic brush salesman Migg Tweeny falls for Angela, the daughter of the President (Fields). Tweeny's boss has an interest in getting involved with the Olympic games, so Tweeny recruits the athletes of Klopstokia, including the President.

Because his starring silents had been box-office disappointments, Paramount felt Fields was better suited for an ensemble cast. *Million Dollar Legs* boasts many top-level comedians, several of whom worked for Sennett, and each is given a role appropriate for their talents (cross-eyed Ben Turpin is perfectly cast as a Mysterious Man who turns up throughout the entire film; Billy Gilbert is a sneezing cabinet member, etc.). Fields, as the President of Klopstokia, is central to the narrative.

This film's absurdity is immediate and relentless. First, every girl in

Trade ad for the wacky political satire *Million Dollar Legs* (Paramount Publix, 1932).

the country is named Angela (and the men are all named George), making it difficult for Tweeny to track down the one with whom he is smitten. When he does, he wants to marry her immediately. She suggests they ask her father's permission. When they arrive, he is auditioning future bodyguards by singlehandedly beating them up.

> TWEENY: If I go one round with you, can I marry your daughter?
> PRESIDENT: The Constitution says I can't hit a man under two hundred pounds.

The President then sets off a siren and several of his guards take Tweeny away. Angela confronts her father.

> ANGELA: They won't hurt him, will they?
> PRESIDENT: Only for about two hours. Then they'll shoot him.

Angela convinces her father that he can make use of Tweeny's prowess as a salesman, so he spares his life and promises that if Tweeny helps him raise the $8 million his country owes, he may marry his daughter. It is then that Tweeny decides to form an Olympic team out of the Klopstokian citizens.

Political rivals try to thwart Tweeny's plans by hiring the irresistible Mata Machree to distract the potential athletes. The scene where Lyda Roberti, as Machree, sings a seductive song as the rivals stare, slackjawed at her sensuality, weaving left to right as she sings, is one of the film's highlights.

Angela helps Tweeny recruit athletes, while also trying to teach him the Klopstokian love song (a bunch of gibberish to the tune of "One Hour with You," a hit song at the time). Tweeny is impressed with the athletic prowess of the townspeople, as he tells Angela.

> TWEENY: You know, I'll bet if they laid all the athletes end to end here they'd stretch—
> ANGELA: Four hundred and eighty-four miles!
> TWEENY: How do you know?
> ANGELA: We did it once.

The success of the Olympics hinges on the President lifting a series of heavy weights, but in order to do so he must lose his temper. Tweeny tries to rile him by calling him names, which is ineffective. But when he accidentally steps on the President's toe, he gets angry enough to hurl the heaviest weight (1,000 pounds) at Tweeny.

There really isn't much of a plot to *Million Dollar Legs*; its comedy is built on sharp dialogue and absurd situations. Director Eddie Cline, a veteran of the Sennett lot, was able to work quite comfortably with former Sennett players like Turpin, Andy Clyde, Vernon Dent, and Heinie Conklin. But Fields' penchant for ad-libbing initially confused the director. Wisely, he recognized the comedian's impeccable sense of comic timing, so he stood back and allowed Fields room to improvise. This ability to tap into Fields' way of doing things resulted in the two becoming good friends as well as collaborators.

Million Dollar Legs features one crazy scene after another. Andy Clyde, a sprinter, runs alongside the train carrying the Klopstokian athletes to the Olympic games, often passing the vehicle. Hugh Herbert plays Fields' chief rival, continually losing to him in Indian wrestling, despite working out. When he lifts weights against the President in the Olympics, it is Mata Machree's dancing that inspires him. When the President gets angry and throws the weight at Tweeny, he not only wins the weightlifting competition but also the shotput.

While his later popularity has caused *Million Dollar Legs* to be considered a W. C. Fields movie, it really belongs to Jack Oakie and Susan

Fleming, who play Tweeny and Angela. Fields has second billing to Oakie, but anchors the production with his presence, and the scenes in which he appears are the funniest. Oakie had great charisma and appeared in several winning comedies throughout his long career, his most noted being his hilarious turn as the Mussolini-like Napaloni in Charlie Chaplin's first talkie *The Great Dictator* (1940), for which he earned an Academy Award nomination for Best Supporting Actor. Fleming made a few films, retiring from the screen upon her marriage to Harpo Marx. Harpo is the one Marx Brother who enjoyed a long, happy, monogamous marriage. They had a large family and remained together until Harpo's death in 1964.

Sadly, Lyda Roberti, the young actress who was so outrageously funny as Mata Machree, also made few films. She died in 1938 at the age of thirty-one, a victim of heart disease. Before her passing, she replaced Thelma Todd as Patsy Kelly's comedy partner in a couple of short films for Hal Roach.

While the absurdity of *Million Dollar Legs* confused some audiences, others got the joke. The critic for *Hollywood Filmograph* stated:

> It may be said without any restraint or feeling of exaggeration that this is quite the maddest picture that ever galloped across a screen. *Million Dollar Legs* is an insane satire that is, pre-eminently, a funny picture to end all funny pictures. It contains slapstick musical-comedy scenes, a mythical kingdom, and even the Olympic games. *Million Dollar Legs* is a travesty on any comedy that every got mixed up with a serious idea.[40]

In the *New York Times*, a critic, identified only by the initials L. N., was also impressed:

> A hopefully mad sort of picture went on yesterday at the Paramount, where a series of comedians conducted themselves with a total lack of dignity. They made bad puns, took part in the Olympic games and casually parodied the drama of a more serious day than this. "What the country needs," said W. C. Fields, the president of Klopstokia, "is money." The winning of it provided the basis for the occasion, and that, in turn, gave entertainment good enough for any one. *Million Dollar Legs*—the name has nothing to do with it, of course—has won its laurels by its nonsense. In spirit it is something like *Of Thee I Sing* [the then-recent political musical with a score by George and Ira Gershwin, and a book by George S. Kaufman and Morey Ryskind], although without the satire and more definitely insane. It means nothing and proves nothing beyond the fact that everyone seems to be having a good time while getting on with it. It even, on occasion, goes so far as to parody the movies in their more sententious moments. The actors, of course, are clowns for the time being rather than somber comedians. Jack Oakie heads the cast, although it is Mr. Fields who does the greatest amount of damage. Lyda Roberti has the part of Mata Machree, Spy, and Ben Turpin pops up everywhere as the Mysterious Man. There are also secretaries of this and that, cabinet officers and all the rest. Joseph L. Mankiewicz, who was responsible for the story, apparently got it by writing down the most fantastic things that came into his head.[41]

And as time went one, the film continued to attract critics, including Pauline Kael, as recalled by Michael Wilmington in the *Chicago Tribune*:

> Late in her life, legendary critic Pauline Kael was asked to name her favorite movie. Somewhat perversely, she picked ... the crazy Depression-era W. C. Fields comedy *Million Dollar Legs*. Though *Legs* is rarely ranked by anyone else on a level with *Citizen Kane* and *Vertigo*, it is, by sheer yuks-per-minute power, a champion laugh-getter—or, as Kael wrote in *The New Yorker*, "one of the silliest and funniest pictures ever made, a lunatic musical satire on the Olympics with W. C. Fields, Jack Oakie, Andy Clyde, Ben Turpin and Lyda Roberti singing "It's Terrific."[42]

Fields was prepared to begin working on a series of two-reel comedies he had agreed to do for Mack Sennett. However, the executives of Paramount were so pleased with the success of *Million Dollar Legs* that they wanted to use him in another ensemble feature. At the time, Sennett's comedies were being distributed by Paramount Publix,[43] so it was relatively easy to arrange for Fields to do both.

A lot of changes had happened since Fields was starring in silent films at Paramount. First, the talking picture revolution had allowed the comedian to offer the one main ingredient missing in his work—his voice. Second, Fields had altered his character for sound movies. He was no longer wearing his clip-on mustache that he had been using since his earliest vaudeville days (when, as a young performer, he wanted to look older). Given that the silent era is filled with outrageously made-up characters with intentionally phony facial hair, Fields' clip-on did not serve as a distraction. But with sound, films became more realistic, and such props now seemed antiquated. Even though Groucho Marx continued to simply smear greasepaint across his face for mustache and eyebrows, Fields believed the clean shaven look best suited his new character in sound movies.

With this movie, it is already easy to see why Fields' sound films were more popular than his silents. His understated delivery is an essential element of his new image. The character he portrays in *Million Dollar Legs*, while containing many of the elements he had utilized since his vaudeville days, was more explosive, more dryly sarcastic, more uncompromising, more unscrupulous. And while his super strength in this movie is just an absurd plot device, Fields always found ways for his characters to triumph, be they wily con men or put-upon husbands. This would become especially evident in his next film.

If I Had a Million

Production and Distribution: Paramount Publix
Executive Producer: Emanuel L. Cohen
Associate Producer: Louis D. Lighton
Directors: James Cruze, H. Bruce Humberstone, Ernst Lubitsch, Norman Z. McLeod, Stephen Roberts, William A. Seiter, Norman Taurog
Screenplay: Robert Sparks (uncredited: Robert Hardy Andrews, Grover Jones, William Slavens McNutt, Lawton Mackall, Joseph L. Mankiewicz, Oliver H. P. Garrett, Harvey Gates, Claude Binyon, Malcolm Stuart Boylan, Whitney Bolton, John Bright, Sidney Buchman, Lester Cole, Isabel Dawn, Boyce De Gaw, Ernst Lubitsch, Walter De Leon)
Camera: Harry Fischbeck, Charles Edgar Schoenbaum, Gilbert Warrenton, Alvin Wyckoff
Editor: LeRoy Stone
Release date: December 2, 1932
Running time: 88 minutes
Cast: Gary Cooper (Steve Gallagher), Charles Laughton (Phineas V. Lambert), George Raft (Eddie Jackson), Jack Oakie (Private Mulligan), Richard Bennett (John Glidden), Charles Ruggles (Henry Peabody), Allison Skipworth (Emily La Rue), W. C. Fields (Rollo La Rue), Mary Boland (Mrs. Peabody), Roscoe Karns (Private O'Brien), May Robson (Mrs. Mary Walker), Roscoe Karns (Private O'Brien), Wynne Gibson (Violet Smith), Gene Raymond (John Wallace), Frances Dee (Mary Wallace), Reginald Barlow (Otto Bullwinkle), James Bush (Bowen), Wallis Clark (Monroe), Joyce Compton (Marie), Lucien Littlefield (Zeb), Blanche Friderici (Mrs. Garvey), Tom Kennedy (Joe), Edward Le Saint (Mr. Brown), Charles McMurphy (Mike), William V. Mong (Harry), Fred Santley (Marvin), Edwin Stanley (Galloway), Morgan Wallace (Mike), Irving Bacon (china shop salesman), Fred Holmes (china shop clerk), Bess Flowers (china shop customer), Harry Bradley (Guard), Bob Burns (Marine sergeant), James P. Burtis (jailer), Pop Byron (Murphy Beds proprietor), Cecil Cunningham (Agnes), Fred Kelsey (jailer), Marc Lawrence (henchman), Jerry Tucker (boy with balloon), Clarence Muse (prisoner), Dewey Robinson (cook), Ada Beecher, Vangie Beilby, Clara Bracy, Louise Emmons, Margaret Fealy, Harlene Hill, Margaret Mann, Gertrude Norman, Barbara Norton, Tempe Pigott, Mildred Pitts, Cora Shannon, Alice Smith, Emma Tansley, Mai Wells, Joy Winthrop (Idylwood residents).

The premise features a wealthy steel magnate who is dying, but cannot trust any of his relatives or employees. So he decides to give away his fortune to strangers. He randomly picks several names out of the phone book and personally delivers a million-dollar check to that individual. Each recipient is shown in his or her own separate episode, each having a different need for the money. While the episodes vary in quality and interest, fluctuating from farcical comedy to heavy melodrama, each is quite fascinating in its own right.

Henry Peabody (Charlie Ruggles) is a henpecked husband who works in a china shop. He uses his million to gleefully destroy all of the fragile vases in the store where he works, enjoying total catharsis in doing so. Eddie Jackson (George Raft) is a check forger who is so infamous, he can't find a way to cash a legitimate check. Violet Smith (Wynne Gibson) is a prostitute whose sudden fortune allows her to sleep in a bed, alone. Phineas Lambert (Charles Laughton) is a quiet, staid office worker whose sudden fortune results in his quietly walking into his employer's office and blowing a raspberry at him.

Not all of the vignettes are as effective. The scene with three army buddies interested in the same gal, only losing her to an old man after he gets the million-dollar check, is not quite as interesting or amusing, despite the presence of Gary Cooper, Roscoe Karns, and Jack Oakie. Gene Raymond's melodramatic turn as a man headed to the electric chair falls flat as well. It had been shot while Raymond had a day off from an MGM feature he was doing. He learned twenty-six pages of dialogue and shot the sequence all in that one day. He then could not talk for the next two, holding up the MGM production. The concluding sequence, with May Robson as a rebellious woman in a strictly structured old folks home, while ultimately rewarding, goes on too long.

The best of all the vignettes features W. C. Fields and Alison Skipworth as an old vaudeville couple who now own a tea room. They are comfortably prosperous, but have one dream: They want a new automobile. After having saved for years, one is being delivered. As they carefully venture out onto the road, a car comes by and slams into theirs, destroying it. When they are given the million dollars, they decide to buy an entire fleet of automobiles, hire drivers, and set out to eliminate all road hogs. They proceed down the road, and whenever they see a road hog cutting off another car, they chase the man down and destroy his vehicle. It is a wild slapstick sequence, and during screenings of the film in theatres, audiences related to the situation so well that it drew loud laughter and applause.

In his preparation for the role of Rollo, an ex-juggler, Fields looked over the dialogue provided him and worked out ways to augment it. The script had him often referring to Skipworth as "My little bird," but Fields decided to use a different bird for each time the script had him address her in that way. He addresses her as wren, turtle dove, and, most significantly, "my little chickadee," a phrase that would hereafter stay with Fields for the remainder of his career. Although, upon being hired for this film, Fields balked at being teamed with Skipworth. He knew her from the stage, and was fond of her personally, but the last time he was used in a team dynamic had been his unsuccessful pairing with Chester Conklin, which had also been generated by Paramount. However, he and Skipworth worked so well together that Fields fully enjoyed the experience. He realized their portion of the film was successful. Critics and moviegoers agreed it was the film's highlight.

W. C. Fields was teamed with Alison Skipworth for a segment in *If I Had a Million* (Paramount Publix, 1932), an episodic, all-star movie. To no one's surprise, Fields and Skipworth came off the best of the many stars in the cast.

The attraction of this movie was its being filled with some of the studio's top stars. However, *If I Had a Million* has a cultural and historical significance in that it was produced and released during the throes of the Great Depression. Its attempt to examine the varied effects a lot of money might have on various people from different walks of life evokes a level of interest that extends beyond its entertainment value. At a time when most Americans were struggling, the idea of falling into a million dollars was a real fantasy. As movies were affordable entertainment (the cost of a movie ticket in 1932 was 35¢),[44] the public used them as a means of escaping the doldrums of everyday life. Seeing everyone from elderly women to a lonely prostitute to put-upon shop clerk bettering their lives with this sudden windfall was attractive and gratifying.

The advertising campaign for *If I Had a Million* in the trades suggested that theatres exploit as many of the names in the cast as possible in their newspaper ads. Among the available ad materials were five hundred window cards, special twenty-four sheet stands, bumper strips for taxis, ten thousand heralds, and both lobby and street displays. Back-page ads on opening day and radio announcements were also suggested. The ideas were obviously effective since the film ended up being a box-office hit.

Taking several screenwriters and directors, each with a specific cinematic vision, and somehow tying everything together cohesively must have been a challenge, to say the least. That the film remains consistently enjoyable despite so many different approaches and perspectives is certainly impressive. It is uneven in that not every sequence maintains the high quality offered by the Fields-Skipworth piece, but it is consistent in that every episode offers a unique reaction to the obtaining a million dollars with no strings attached.

The critics seemed to like *If I Had a Million*. Lou Jacobs, in *Hollywood Filmograph*, called it one of the ten best pictures of the year, adding:

> It shows what the combination of a multi-star cast, multi-star directorial staff, and the brains of about a score of ace writers can do when properly blended. The result is perhaps one of the finest examples of flawless direction ever accomplished. One lone complaint is that it was a trifle too long, but we would hardly venture a guess as to what to eliminate. Perhaps the solider bit with Gary Cooper and Jack Oakie is the least important. That doesn't mean that it isn't enjoyable. *If I Had a Million* is a history-making talkie.[45]

The powers-that-be at Paramount set out to find another ensemble piece for Fields, and discussed another pairing with Skipworth. Meanwhile, Fields was now able to begin filming those two-reel comedies for Mack Sennett.

The Dentist

Production: Sennett Pictures Corporation
Distribution: Paramount Publix
Director: Leslie Pearce
Screenplay: W. C. Fields
Camera: John W. Boyle
Released December 9, 1932; rereleased: 1975 (Janus)
Running time: 21 minutes
Cast: W. C. Fields (a dentist), Babe Kane (Mary), Arnold Gray (Arthur), Dorothy Granger (Miss Peppitone), Elise Cavanna (Miss Mason), Zedna Farley (dental assistant), Billy Bletcher (bearded patient), Bud Jamison (Charley), Bobby Dunn (caddy), Harry Bowen (Joe), Barney Hellum (waiting room patient), Joseph Belmont (Mr. Bedford), Pete Rasch (Bedford's son), Joe Bordeaux (Bedford's caddy), George Gray (Bedford's golf partner), Emma Tansey (old lady on bench).

Mack Sennett and W. C. Fields had met years earlier when the producer was in the audience, laughing uproariously, for one of the comedian's performances in the *Follies*. Afterward, Sennett spoke to Fields backstage, telling him he would like, someday, to make a movie with him. At that time, Fields was riding high onstage and Sennett was one of the leading comedy producers in movies. Now, Sennett was struggling in the sound era and Fields was trying to retain some level of movie success. Each believed he could help the other achieve greater movie success. First, of course, they had to deal with the ever-pressing issue of money.

Since he made $5,000 per week working on *If I Had a Million*, Fields expected the same pay from Sennett. At the time, one of the stars of Sennett's short comedies was the up-and-coming crooner Bing Crosby, who was only getting $500 per week. Sennett balked at Fields' price, but didn't want to default on his deal with Paramount Publix. So he arranged that Fields receive $5,000 per short for five productions, and an option to do five more. According to Brent Walker's definitive 2010 book, *Mack Sennett's Fun Factory*:

> As things turned out, Fields would star in a total of four shorts for Sennett. Based upon Sennett's payroll records of those years, for his production arm Sennett Pictures Corp., it appears Fields' salary was amended so that he received $5,000 per picture. That made Fields Sennett's highest wage earner for those years, while Sennett paid himself a salary of only $8,500 for each of those years.[46]

Sennett knew Fields had a wealth of material from the stage that he could bring to the screen. He also knew that he was capable of structuring the films himself as a director. So, he arranged for company man Leslie Pearce to oversee the production and get director credit while Fields blocked the actors and helped choose camera angles. The result was exceptional. *The Dentist* pleased Sennett, pleased moviegoers, pleased critics, and pleased Paramount.

Fields often said that he preferred to play the put-upon henpecked husband who elicited audience sympathy; he felt there was more depth to such characters. And while he was quite good whenever playing such a role, Fields was also wonderful when playing the angry, irascible cynic whose cranky sarcasm helps him cope with the trials of everyday life. That is the role he plays in *The Dentist*, which is based upon a skit he did for the *Earl Carroll Vanities* in 1928.

The Dentist opens with Fields, as the title character, having breakfast at home. His daughter walks through the room, and the two snipe at each other. It seems that the dentist has discovered that his daughter is engaged to the ice man. He is against this arrangement, and lets her know it. He also abruptly throws the ice man out of the house as he makes a delivery. This means he must place the large block of ice into the ice box himself. He finally lifts it, but sets in on the stove while he takes a call. It melts to

Fields with patient Elsie Cavanna (center) and assistant Zedna Farley in *The Dentist* (Paramount Publix, 1933), the first of four short W. C. films produced by Mack Sennett.

the size of an ice cube, which he picks up easily with one hand and plops it into the ice box. The daughter inspects.

> DAUGHTER: There's just a little piece left. I'll have to order more.
> DENTIST: Keep that ice man out of here. I'm going to order a Frigidaire!

Fields augmented his stage material to expand it to two reels by finding a way to get the dentist character on the golf course. However, unlike his usual golf routine, this bit does not feature Fields trying to start his game and never succeeding. Instead, we follow the dentist as he plays a few holes, becoming annoyed at every possible inconvenience, including having to wait for other golfers to finish at each hole. Thus, he smacks the ball near a hole where another foursome is active, resulting in an elderly man being conked on the head. The scene culminates with the dentist throwing his clubs—and caddy—into a pond.

This opening footage introduces the dentist as someone who is continually frustrated by petty annoyances. He is also unable to control his surroundings at home or at play. When he shows up at the office, a friend is waiting.

> FRIEND: Want to play a bit of golf?
> DENTIST: No, I just threw my clubs away.
> FRIEND: What, *again*?

This lets us know that the dentist frequently reaches this level of anger and impulsiveness. It all perfectly sets up the dental-chair sequences that follow.

First, there is a female patient who is so intimidated, she squeals in fear as the dentist approaches her with a tiny mirror. She leaves before the examination even begins. She is followed by a haughty woman whose tooth extraction is so difficult, the dentist has to pull her along the floor as her legs are wrapped around his waist. Finally, a man with an enormously bushy beard offers another challenge: "I can't find his mouth." When the dentist explores further, a flock of birds come flying out.

These scenes are augmented by the unruly daughter, whom the dentist has locked in her room to keep her away from the ice man. Her room, it just so happens, is right above his office. She jumps up and down, causing the plaster to loosen and drop into a patient's open mouth. When the dentist scoops it out, the patient mistakes it for her tooth. "It came out easily, didn't it?" she says with a smile.

The dentist is informed by his assistant that his daughter is sneaking out of her room via a ladder to rendezvous with the ice man. The dentist hurries outside, only to be met by the bullying son of the man who was earlier hit on the head with the golf ball. The son punches the dentist. The ice man punches the bully. The dentist barks an order for more ice and walks away as his daughter and the ice man embrace.

The *Hollywood Filmograph* raved about *The Dentist*, opining that "it was a regular laugh fest for the audience ... it brought out spasms of laughter."[47] The *Motion Picture Herald* was equally enthusiastic, calling the short a "grand comedy,"[48] and stating that it reached its best when the dentist was tending to the female patients.

However, there was another element to the film—that of controversy—associated with this pre–Code short. At one point an angry Fields says, "Aw, the hell with her," in reference to a patient moaning in the waiting room while he's talking to a visiting friend. Shortly afterward, Fields tells his patient, "I knew a doctor who treated a man for yellow jaundice for nine years, then found out he was a Jap." But the scene that inspired the most attention (for better or worse) is the one involving the female patient getting a challenging tooth pulled, her legs tightly wrapped around the dentist's waist and being carried about the office. It is quite funny, but also, especially for the times, rather vulgar. In fact, when the film was reissued due to Fields' increasing popularity a few years later, that scene was removed entirely.[49] One exhibitor, running a theatre in a small rural town in Nebraska, wrote to the *Motion Picture Herald* that *The Dentist* was "Inexplicable! Rank! Uncalled for!"[50] Mack Sennett was delighted. He was no stranger to edgy, knockabout comedy, having pretty much invented the process back when he oversaw the Keystone studios nearly twenty years earlier. His films were often accused of being vulgar. *The Dentist* represented just the type of comedy he wanted from Fields.

For his part, Fields was basking in the creative freedom these shorts afforded him, and planned to tap into many of his old stage ideas. He was inspired by the creative challenge of putting them on film, augmenting them in a manner that made them more cinematic, even using the technology of film to create gags that would not have been possible onstage.

Sennett gave Fields the freedom to explore, to take chances, even risks. *The Dentist* contained a fair amount of controversial material, and that was fine. Even Paramount was comfortable. They had hired stage star Mae West, whose work was also the subject of controversy (and, later, censorship), while Fields' old vaudeville competitors the Marx Brothers were bringing another level of comic anarchy to the screen. However, *nobody* was quite prepared for the film idea Fields had next.

The Fatal Glass of Beer

Production: Sennett Pictures Corp.
Distribution: Paramount Publix
Director: Clyde Bruckman
Screenplay: W. C. Fields
Camera: Uncredited
Editor: Mack Sennett (uncredited)
Release date: March 3, 1933
Running time: 18 minutes
Cast: W. C. Fields (Mr. Snavely), Rosemary Theby (Mrs. Snavely), George Chandler (Chester, the wastrel son), Rychard Cramer (Officer Posthlewhistle), Ernie Alexander, Gordon Douglas, Junior Fuller, Ted Strobach (junior drinkers), Jack Cooper (officer), Marvin Loback (a bartender), George Moran, Artie Ortego (Indian chiefs).

There are two schools of thought regarding *The Fatal Glass of Beer*. One accepts its satire and finds the film hilariously funny and brilliantly absurd. The other responds to it as a confusing, laugh-less mess. This writer is of the former opinion.

The Fatal Glass of Beer (Paramount Publix, 1933), a satire on old-fashioned melodramas, was misunderstood in its time. Fields (left) is pictured with George Moran and Artie Ortego.

The story has Fields as Mr. Snavely, who lives with his plain wife in a barren cabin in the frozen wilderness. Surrounded by heavy blizzard conditions, every time Snavley opens the cabin door, he loudly proclaims, "It ain't a fit night out for man or beast!" and is met with a handful of fake snow thrown in his face.

There are several wonderfully ridiculous exchanges, including this reference to their heartless landlord:

> MRS. SNAVELY: He wants more money and if he don't get it, he'll take our malamutes.
> MR. SNAVELY: He won't take old Balto, my lead dog.
> MRS. SNAVELY: Why not, Pa?
> MR. SNAVELY: 'Cause I et him.
> MRS. SNAVELY: You *et* him?
> MR. SNAVELY: He was mighty good with mustard.

At one point Snavely states, "My uncle Ichabod said, speakin' of the city, 'It ain't no place for a woman, gal, but pretty men go there.'" Snavely sings a monotone song called "The Fatal Glass of Beer," which tells the sad story of his son, Chester, who went to the big city, where he took his first drink, which led him to stealing from his employer and, ultimately, prison. In his absent son's defense, Snavely says, "Our Chester never stole nothin' from nobody—hardly ever!"

Just then, Chester returns home, having completed his prison sentence. The tearfully happy reunion with his parents is presented in a deadly serious manner, with the florid gestures and exaggerated inflections inherent to melodramas.

> CHESTER: I feel so tired; I think I'll go to bed.
> MR. SNAVELY: Why don't you lie down and take a little rest first, Chester?
> MRS. SNAVELY: Be sure to open your window a little bit before you go to bed.
> CHESTER: I will, Ma, and, Ma, remember to open *your* window a little bit before *you* go to bed.
> MRS. SNAVELY: Good night, Chester.
> CHESTER: Good night, Ma.

This only ends after a final "good *night*, Chester!" from an exasperated Mr. Snavely.

One of the funniest scenes in *The Fatal Glass of Beer* includes some intentionally cheap back-projection effects. Snavely is shown operating a dog sled with several dogs, including a smaller one whose paws don't touch the ground. The movement of the rear projection offers the idea of the sled moving in a ridiculously poor manner. Later, Snavely announces he is going to "go milk the elk." He wanders about with stock footage of caribou on the back projection, their size dynamic not even matching Fields in the foreground. Fields responds to the creatures as if they are both performing together live in the same scene.

Chester finally admits to having stolen a large sum from his employer, but—he adds piously—he "threw the tainted money away." This is simply too much for the impoverished Mr. and Mrs. Snavely. They break assorted crockery over his head and toss him out into the darkness. One last time Snavley states: "And it ain't a fit night out for man or beast!" but this time no snow hits him. He winces in anticipation as the film ends.

When Fields had performed this sketch onstage, its New York audiences were quite familiar with the melodramatic clichés being parodied. Audiences in smaller cities, however, had no idea what they were watching.

In previous studies of Fields' work, the sorry reviews quoted are from the same period exhibitors, such as the theatre owner in North Carolina who reported to the *Motion Picture Herald*: "This is the worst comedy we have played from any company this season. No story, no acting, and as a whole has nothing."[51] In that same issue, an exhibitor from Michigan complained, "Two reels of film and twenty minutes wasted."[52] But in another issue of the *Herald*, a South Dakota theatre owner indicated that the film was "very funny" and a "good comedy," stating that "the scenes of the north were very interesting."[53] But this gentleman was definitely in the minority. *Variety* sniffed:

> In old-style manner of exaggerated melodramatics, it becomes a boresome, repetitious build-up until the obvious finale when both kick the prodigal youth out when learning he has none of the booty cached. Although it's not a fit night out for man or beast—after a painfully long buildup—he's kicked out in his pajamas. No real laughs and hardly a snicker.[54]

Even Mack Sennett hated *The Fatal Glass of Beer* and was sorry he had allowed Fields as much creative freedom. He tried to fix it in the editing room (by adding expositional scenes of Chester in the big city), but realized there was little that could change what Fields had created. It caused a rift between the producer and the comedian that hampered their working relationship thereafter. Fields was very proud of the finished product, and truly believed there was an audience for his satire. Unfortunately, the mainstream moviegoer did not respond favorably to *The Fatal Glass of Beer*, and for years it was dismissed as a misfire. It wasn't until the Fields renaissance in the late sixties that the film earned acclaim and was understood and appreciated.

Brent Walker stated in *Mack Sennett's Fun Factory*:

> On the face of it, Sennett's judgment seems wholly understandable and even astute. It is hard to picture 1933 audiences needing a laugh to lift them from the doldrums and despair of the Depression, laughing heartily at the very subtle and even subversive humor of *The Fatal Glass of Beer*.[55]

The rift between Fields and Sennett was such that the comedian lost his freedom on his proposed next project. Fields, along with Clyde Bruckman, wrote a script in which he played a put-upon Everyman who is tired of his sponging brother-in-law living with him. He wants to take a day off to see the fights, so he tells his boss he needs to attend his brother-in-law's funeral. When Sennett kept tampering with the concept and reworking Fields' ideas, this lack of freedom further widened the rift between the two men, and Fields abandoned the project. It was instead filmed with comedian Lloyd Hamilton under the title *Too Many Highballs*. Fields and Bruckman, who directed the short, would use this basic idea for a later feature, *The Man on the Flying Trapeze*.

Despite the tense work environment, Fields still owed Sennett more two-reelers, so he once again sought material from his stage work and came up with a more acceptable sketch that met with the producer's approval.

The Pharmacist

Production: Sennett Pictures Corp.
Distribution: Paramount Publix
Director: Arthur Ripley
Screenplay: W. C. Fields
Camera: George Unholz, Frank Good
Release date: April 21, 1933; rereleased: 1975 (Janus)
Running time: 21 minutes
Cast: W. C. Fields (Mr. Dilweg), Marjorie "Babe" Kane (Priscilla), Elise Cavanna (Mrs. Dilweg), Grady Sutton (Cuthbert), Lorena Carr (Ooleota), Si Jenks, Barney Hellum (men playing checkers), Arthur Thalasso (stamp customer), Joe Bordeaux (gunman), Emma Tansey (elderly lady customer), Julia Griffith (woman who faints), William McCall, Junior Fuller (men attending to fainting woman), James Donnelly (street sweeper), Efe Jackson, Jack Cooper (bits).

Fields plays Dilweg, another delightfully cranky character, although in this short he runs a small-town drug store, gritting his teeth with phony pleasantries while attending to customers, and also putting up with his dysfunctional family who reside upstairs from the store. Director Arthur Ripley, who had worked with Sennett in the previous decade writing some of Harry Langdon's best films, stood back and let Fields control the proceedings, which is the wisest way to direct him.

There is no story structure to *The Pharmacist*; it is just a series of occurrences in the Dilwegs' life. Dinner with the family is thwarted by a bratty younger daughter's disruptions until she is removed from the table. Complaining that she's hungry, she reaches in the birdcage and eats the pet canary (she later starts coughing up feathers). The older daughter spends most of the time on the phone with her boyfriend, Cuthbert, whom Dilweg insists is a sissy, despite never having met him. He mutters sarcastic comments in response to her phone call.

The scenes in the store are brilliant presentations of the troublesome customers with whom the beleaguered Dilweg must deal. In one case, he takes an order from someone who wants a box of cough drops delivered. He smiles and says that a truck will be coming to deliver them soon. He waits on a difficult man who wants one stamp, from the middle of a sheet, no less, and wants to pay for the three-cent purchase with a $100 bill. An older female customer insists on having a lady attendant. Dilweg runs upstairs and asks his wife to wait on her, but she insists on dressing up and putting on makeup first. When she finally makes her way down to the store, the woman quietly asks her where the Ladies Room is. This is all very well done, with Fields showing a contemptible view of the mainstream public. The druggist is giving away large vases free with each purchase. The man with the stamp not only gets one, but the woman who uses the restroom expects one as well.

Each customer is presented with some depth as to his or her sense of entitlement. The stamp customer wants a purple stamp. All the pharmacist has is green.

> CUSTOMER: A person hasn't got any rights in this country anymore! The government even tells you what color stamps you gotta buy!
> DILWEG: Yes, it's pretty tough. That's the Democratic Party for you. I've written to Washington about it.

When a man comes in and whispers if Dilweg has some liquor for sale (prohibition did not end until December of the year *The Pharmacist* was filmed), the druggist turns on a fan, which blows the man's jacket open and reveals his badge. Dilweg then proclaims, self-righteously, that he would never even *think* of carrying liquor just to satisfy the public's "depraved tastes."

It appears Fields wasn't quite sure how to conclude *The Pharmacist*, as it stumbles rather clumsily with a gunman coming into the drug store and shooting it out with police who are stationed in the street. A man comes out of the phone booth and knocks out the gunman. Dilweg is pleased that this courageous man saved his life. It turns out to be Cuthbert. While this concluding gag brings closure to that situation, the final scene remains a rather tepid conclusion to an otherwise inspired two-reeler.

It is interesting to see how *The Pharmacist* offers the two distinct personality types that Fields used in films. Outside of the store, including with his family, he is aggressively sarcastic and irascible. However, in the store, he is docile and striving desperately to please. When the stamp customer wants a purple stamp, Dilweg offers to paint one. When the man demands a stamp from the center of the sheet, Dilweg cuts around the other stamps, ruining several, in order to accommodate him. When the customer asks if Dilweg can break a $100 bill, the druggist replies, "No, but thanks for the compliment." In later films it will often be the meek, flustered character that is presented in the household scenes, while the character is more aggressive outside of the home.

Fields had performed the basis of this sketch in the 1925 *Ziegfeld Follies*, and again in his silent feature *It's the Old Army Game*. It is far more effective with dialogue and works nicely as a two-reeler. While they reportedly quibbled over the title (the star wanted to call it "W. C. Fields in the Drugstore"), the comedian and Sennett were on reasonably good terms and filming went smoothly. Fields had his friend Elise Cavanna in the role of his wife, and Grady Sutton as Cuthbert; he would use the pudgy, pasty-faced actor frequently over the next several years.

The critics were far more pleased with *The Pharmacist* than they had been with *The Fatal Glass of Beer*. The reviewer for *Film Daily* called it a "good comedy," stating, "Enough of the typical Fields gags make it generally enjoyable."[56]

The Barber Shop

Production: Sennett Pictures Corp.
Distribution: Paramount Publix
Director: Arthur Ripley
Screenplay: W. C. Fields
Camera: Johnny Boyle
Release date: July 28, 1933; rereleased: 1975 (Janus)
Running time: 20 minutes
Cast: W. C. Fields (Cornelius O'Hare), Elise Cavanna (Mrs. O'Hare), Harry Watson (Ronald), Dagmar Oakland (Hortense), John St. Clair (Mr. Flood), Cyril Ring (bank robber), Julia Griffith (Mrs. Scroggins), Fay Holderness (mother), Gloria Velarde (daughter), Dick Rush, Harry Bowen (cops), Frank Alexander (steam room customer), Billy Bletcher (steam room customer after the steam), George Humbert (violin salesman), William McCall (farmer), Joe Calder (bit).

W. C. Fields had one more Mack Sennett short to film: *The Barber Shop*, which was from a treatment he had written back in 1917 as a possible silent comedy for Gaumont, the producers of *Pool Sharks* and *His Lordship's Dilemma*. Fields wrote its basic outline on the back of a letter, but the idea was never fully fleshed out. He finally extended it to a screenplay for this production, which was his first two-reeler not based upon anything he had done onstage or in earlier movies.

What is most interesting about *The Barber Shop* is how Fields' character is presented. The irascible character found in *The Dentist* or *The Pharmacist* is still sarcastic, but mellower and more settled in his work and domestic life. It was something of a portent to what Fields would do in more ambitious features.

Fields plays Cornelius O'Hare, a barber, who sits in front of his shop in the morning and sardonically makes comments about the passersby, in this case to a man reading the newspaper.

> O'HARE: Hello, Mrs. Scroggins. How is Mr. Scroggins?
> MRS. SCROGGINS: Not every well; I'm worried about him.
> O'HARE: Yeah, me too.
> (after she passes, he turns to the man reading the paper)

Cornelius O'Hare (Fields) attends to Gloria Velarde's hair as her mother, Fay Holderness, looks on. *The Barber* (Paramount Publix, 1933).

> O'HARE: He was out on one of his benders again. How he can drink that raw alcohol and live I don't know. Fine mayor, he is.

The scene switches to the barber's domestic situation. He lives upstairs from his shop, not unlike the arrangement in *The Pharmacist*. Unlike the previous film, however, his current family is not dysfunctional. The wife is a bit haughty, however, and unnerved by the corny jokes told by their young son Ronald. Mr. O'Hare is delighted by his son's riddles.

> RONALD: How is a cat's tail like a long journey?
> O'HARE: I don't know. How is a cat like a long journey?
> RONALD: Because it's fur to the end!

O'Hare, like many husbands, believes himself to be misunderstood by his wife. She is a vegetarian, and does not allow meat in the house. He taps a bass fiddle with his bow like a drum, with no discernible rhythm, and balks at her low opinion of his musical abilities. In contrast to his relationship with his wife, O'Hare's relationship with his pretty manicurist has him bragging about past accomplishments, like being a firefighter and a detective. The young lady is impressed, believing every word the barber says.

> MANICURIST: It seems like you've been *everything*, Mr. O'Hare!
> O'HARE: My wife *calls* me everything.

Much of the dialogue is absurd. A customer talks about his face having healed up since his last visit for a shave. O'Hare acknowledges a dog that hangs around the shop, indicating the animal has been coming around since getting an ear that the barber accidentally cut off a patron.

There are also some outrageous visual gags. A heavily overweight man comes in to use the steam room and, hopefully, take off a few pounds. O'Hare forgets him in there until sirens start blaring to indicate overheated conditions. The barber quickly unlocks the door, and a skinny little man emerges.

In another vignette, a lady brings in her little girl wearing a party hat, disallowing the barber from cutting her hair. He removes that hat, and another hat is underneath—and another, and another...

The Barber Shop, like *The Pharmacist*, ends up with another stickup man coming into the shop. O'Hare runs away, the crook runs after him, so the barber hops on a bicycle. He circles around, meets up again with the criminal, gets hit from a fly ball from a nearby kids' baseball game, and both the barber and the crook go crashing down some steps, into the shop. O'Hare believes he is entitled to the reward until an observant cop reveals that the true hero was O'Hare's son, Ronald, the boy who hit the fly ball.

> POLICEMAN: Are you hurt, Mr. O'Hare?
> O'HARE: Not physically, no.

The film concludes with an amusing visual gag. O'Hare refers to his standup bass as Lena. A man comes in to sell him another, referring to it as Abe. O'Hare is not interested, but the man leaves the instrument at the barber shop, agreeing to pick it up after work; in the meantime, he leans Abe against Lena. When O'Hare later retrieves Lena, he sees a batch of violins on the floor, akin to a litter. "Lena, how *could* you?" he cries, after which he destroys the other bass and throws it out the door.

Harry Watson, one of the Watson family of child actors, enjoyed working with Fields. As he told biographer James Curtis:

> My dad, who was always on the set with us, said, "Mr. Fields used to be a juggler. He's the only man who could juggle nine balls at the same time. Why don't you go over and ask him to juggle something?" I went over, and he acted surprised when he

looked up at me. I said, "My dad says you're a good juggler." He had a pack of cigarettes in his hand—he had just emptied one—and he crumpled it up. He picked up a piece of carbon trim from the floor, about two inches long, and a pencil, and he started juggling. The stories about him not being nice to kids, I never found that to be true.[57]

Sennett would have been happy to produce more comedies with Fields, especially when *Variety* called them "the most consistently entertaining line of two-reelers currently coming to the trade."[58] However, one reviewer was not quite as enthusiastic about *The Barber Shop* as he was with Fields himself:

> This one isn't quite the equal of *The Pharmacist*, but it has sustained merriment growing out of Fields' fine knack for semi-eccentric character. Vaudeville comic that he is, Fields has the rare gift of creating his own comedy atmosphere, swiftly pronto, and right away, a trick the studio-trained clowns don't know. Nothing particularly brilliant about the collection of gags and gag situations that make up the two reels, except that they all hang upon the comedian's individual style of humor. Subject is bolstered with slapstick and hoke, and is warranted to register with pretty much any grade of audience for full value.[59]

Fields was on a winning streak, despite the fact that his studio was in receivership at the time. Paramount would fight its way out of bankruptcy, however, and come back stronger than ever. This would be Fields' home base for the next five years.

International House

Production and Distribution: Paramount
Executive Producer: Emanuel L. Cohen
Director: A. Edward Sutherland
Screenplay: Francis Martin and Walter De Leon, from a story by Neil Brandt and Louis E. Heifetz
Camera: Ernest Haller
Original Music: Howard Jackson, John Leipold, Ralph Rainger, Leo Robin
Songs:
"She Was a China Tea-cup and He Was Just a Mug"
Lyrics by Leo Robin, Music by Ralph Rainger
Sung offscreen by an unidentified man
Danced by Sterling Holloway, Lona Andre, Mary Jane Sloan, Gwen Zetter and chorus
"Thank Heaven for You"
Lyrics by Leo Robin. Music by Ralph Rainger
Sung by Rudy Vallee
"My Bluebird's Singing the Blues"
Lyrics by Leo Robin, Music by Ralph Rainger
Sung by Baby Rose Marie
"Reefer Man," Lyrics by Andy Razaf, Music by J. Russel Robinson

Sung by Cab Calloway and His Orchestra
Release date: June 2, 1933
Running time: 70 minutes
Cast: Peggy Hopkins Joyce (herself), W. C. Fields (Professor Henry R. Quail), Stuart Erwin (Tommy Nash), Sari Maritza (Carol Fortescue), George Burns (Doctor Burns), Bela Lugosi (General Petronovich), Gracie Allen (Nurse Allen), Edmund Breese (Doctor Wong), Franklin Pangborn (hotel manager), Rudy Vallee (himself), F. Chase Taylor (Snoopnagle), Budd Hulick (Budd), Cab Calloway (himself), Baby Rose Marie (herself), Lumsden Hare (Sir Mortimer), Harrison Green (Von Baden), Henry Sedly (Serge), Edwin Stanley (Mr. Rollins), Louis Vincenot (Mr. Brown), James Wong (Inspector Sun), Clem Beauchamp (newsreel cameraman), Ernest Wood (newsreel reporter), Etta Lee (maid), Wong Chung (health inspector), Gwen Zetter (tea pot in teacup number), Lona Andre (chorus girl in teacup number), Mary Jane Sloane (sugar bowl in teacup number).

This was another all-star ensemble piece, somewhat like *If I Had a Million*, but not quite as episodic. Although it had been released just prior to *The Barber Shop*, this writer chose to put the chapter on *The Barber Shop* earlier, because the cinematic aesthetic between it and the other Sennett two-reelers seemed more appropriate to the present study.

As *International House* opens, business rep Tommy Shaw (Stuart Erwin) is driving into Wuhu, China, by way of the desert, as the train lines are down. It is important that he make a bid on a new invention called the radioscope, for his company. Peggy Hopkins Joyce talks her way into being his passenger, as she believes several millionaires will be bidding on the radioscope, and she wants to snag another husband.

As she is very much a product of her era, and forgotten today, it is important to note that Peggy Hopkins Joyce was not an actress, but a noted socialite who had gone through several marriages, all to men of wealth, acquiring an impressive collection of furs and jewels along the way (something of a precursor to one of today's so-called "reality stars"). At one point during her journey with Tommy Shaw, the two are getting on each other's nerves. Tommy states, "I wouldn't enjoy this trip if you were Peggy Hopkins Joyce!" It is then that she reveals her identity to him.

When Professor Henry R. Quail (Fields) is first shown, he is loading up on several mugs of beer before taking off in his gyroscope, bound for St. Louis. When he lands this contraption in the middle of an assembly of guests at a hotel in China, he asks where he is.

Miss Joyce yells, "*Wuhu!*"

Quail responds, "Wuhu to you too, sweetheart." He then asks the hotel manager, "Hey, Charlie, where *am* I?"

The prissy manager (Franklin Pangborn) chirps, "*Wuhu!*"

Quail is taken aback. Plucking a flower from his lapel, he says sternly, "Don't let the posy fool you!"

From that point, Quail takes his place alongside Joyce, even ending up in her bedroom, much to the disapproval of her jealous ex-husband (played by *Dracula* star Bela Lugosi), who watches angrily from a hotel room across the street. The dynamic between Fields and Joyce takes advantage of the freedoms still allowed movies prior to the enforcement to the Production Code.

> PEGGY: Won't you join me in a glass of wine?
> PROFESSOR QUAIL: You get in first, and if there's room enough I'll join you.

Quail later looks in a keyhole as he passes a room and wonders aloud, "What *will* they think of next?" He then accidentally enters Peggy's room, and when she turns on a light, she finds him sleeping next to her. When the two escape together in a tiny Austin, the smallest car on the market at the time, this exchange occurs:

> PEGGY: I'm sitting on something!
> QUAIL: I lost mine in the stock market.
> (Peggy gets up to reveal a cat.)
> QUAIL: It's a pussy!
> PEGGY: Oh, I hope I didn't hurt it!
> QUAIL: So do I, my little tit-mouse!

The central idea of the film features an Asian inventor, Doctor Wong, demonstrating his radioscope to interested investors. This precursor to television can offer both picture and sound to virtually anything going on, anywhere in the world. Trying to show his test-audience a six-day bicycle race happening in New York, Wong stumbles upon a number of specialty numbers instead. This includes a song-and-dance bit featuring Sterling Holloway, a fun bluesy number by Baby Rose Marie (a child singer who would become quite popular in middle age as Sally Rogers on TV's *The Dick Van Dyke Show*), and a crooning Rudy Vallee. Fields disliked Vallee's music, and was allegedly responsible for the scene that shows Quail walking in as Vallee's song is being broadcast and asking, "How long has this dogfight been going on?" (Although Vallee responds to the screen, the exact nature of what he was responding to apparently wasn't made clear to him. When he later saw this scene and realized his song was presented as an object of ridicule, he felt he had been "double-crossed.") Certainly the most intriguing musical sequence was a wild jazz number by Cab Calloway, the lyrics of which tell the story of a "reefer man" who gets high and "goes flying through the sky." (When Fields was enjoying renewed

Trade ad for *International House* (Paramount, 1933).

interest from students on college campuses during the late 1960s, this particular sequence was especially popular.)

Along with the comedy offered by Fields, George Burns and Gracie Allen are delightfully funny with their usual wordplay, which was popular on radio at the time. Perhaps their best scene is when Burns, as the doctor, and Franklin Pangborn, as the hotel manager, take turns asking Nurse Gracie a series of questions.

> MANAGER: To what do you attribute your success?
> NURSE: Three things. First my very good memory ... and the other two things I forgot.
> MANAGER: Something *must* have happened to you when you were a baby.
> NURSE: No, but something happened to my brother when *he* was a baby. My father took him out for a stroll in the baby carriage, and when he came back he had a different baby and a different carriage.
> MANAGER: What did your mother say?
> NURSE: She didn't say anything—it was a better carriage.

Later on, Nurse Gracie answers the phone and states the doctor won't be back for some time because "he's on one of those eternity cases." Burns and Allen, like Fields, benefited greatly by being allowed to insert their own material in the script.

The scenes that most closely follow the slight narrative feature Tommy Shaw, a beleaguered business rep who, despite having received all necessary shots, comes down with childhood illnesses like measles, mumps, and chicken pox. These outbreaks seem to occur just as he's about to be married. This tepid subplot might seem less interesting than the offbeat musical numbers or the absurd comedy, but the actor who plays Tommy, Stuart Erwin, is an affable presence who plays this type of character perfectly. (Two decades later Erwin would be one of early television's first big stars with his own sitcom, *The Trouble with Father*).

Peggy Hopkins Joyce, even with her severely limited range and lack of charisma, received top billing, in the studio's attempt to make her another Mae West. She and Fields were already acquainted, as her risqué stage act appeared in the 1917 *Ziegfeld Follies* and *Earl Carroll's Vanities*. She had made her film debut in the 1926 film *The Skyrocket*, which caused the Wisconsin state legislature to introduce a bill allowing them to censor all subsequent movies entering the state. Peggy's notoriety, however, was, as indicated earlier, more for her acquiring rich husbands than her acting ability. This was not enough to parlay her lack of skills into any sort of lasting career. *International House* was her second—and last—film.

It was up to director Eddie Sutherland to put all of this footage into some semblance of a structure, and he manages to do so. The film is

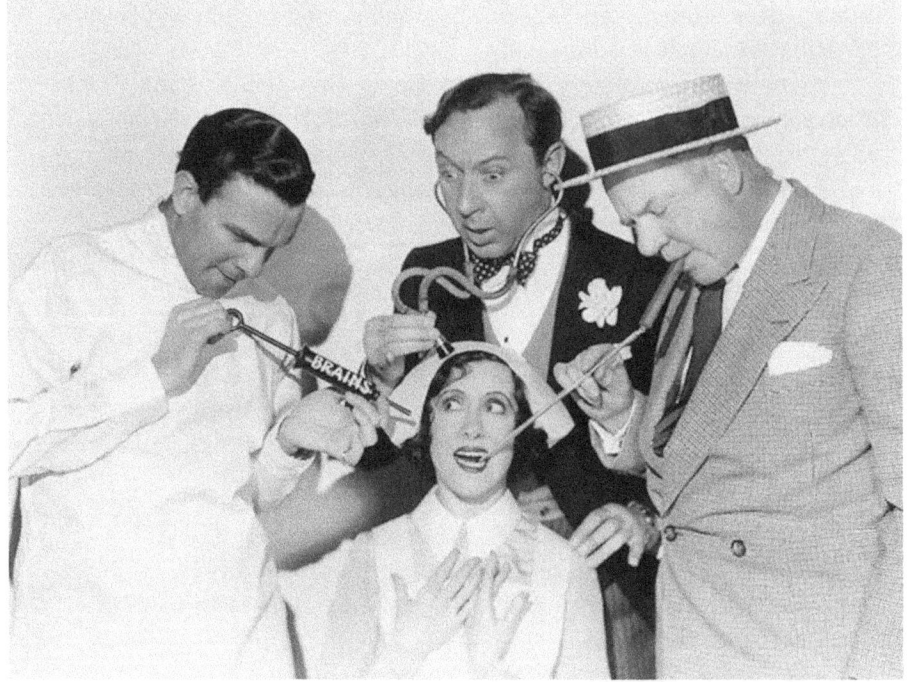

George Burns (left), Franklin Pangborn (center), and Fields surround Gracie Allen in this publicity still for *International House* (Paramount, 1933).

consistently entertaining and not so terribly uneven as its lack of structure would indicate. Sutherland was also not above using his directorial skill to help promote the film. There is footage existing of a supposed earth tremor during the filming of this movie, in which Fields and Pangborn react realistically to the situation. Years later, when this footage became available on the Internet, word got around that an earthquake actually hit Southern California during filming. Of course, the Internet also allows us to investigate whether an earthquake did—or did not—hit Southern California while *International House* was being filmed. It did not. The clip was merely a publicity stunt.

When *International House* was submitted to the Hayes Office, they made a list of several things that caused them concern. At this time, the office was merely operating in an advisory position, as the Production Code would not take effect for another year. In fact, in 1935, a year after the Code had been fully in force, they objected to Paramount's request to rerelease *International House*.

Word got out that the film was quite "blue," and this attracted curious moviegoers. As a result, *International House* became the W. C. Fields film seen by the most people thus far in his career. The fact that he also walked off with the picture, despite the formidable cast, made him something of a hot ticket. The studio offered him a contract, which he accepted. Fields received $15,000 for his work in *International House*, and would be paid substantially more for subsequent movies.

Moviegoers were happy with *International House* and, thus, so were distributors. Theatre owners wrote to *Motion Picture Herald*:

> I was surprised at the drawing power of this. The picture is pure nonsense, but very clever nonsense that our patrons seemed to enjoy. A picture with a lot of entertainment packed into it by well-known stars of radio, stage, and screen. This nonsensical presentation caused many laughs and [much] praise. The fact that we did better than usual the second night would indicate that it gave satisfaction.[60]

While Andre Sennwald, of the *New York Times*, raved:

> At the Paramount they are dispensing humor by the shot-gun method, and it should be said at once that *International House* has some direct hits. In a mad scenario the new film finds a generous amount of space for such diverse comics as W. C. Fields, Stuart Erwin, Burns and Allen and Stoopnagle and Budd, with a corner for Peggy Hopkins Joyce to dig gold in. Measured in laughs, this potpourri of unrelated talents is surprisingly good. How W. C. Fields, whose destination is Kansas City, finds his way into this lunatic ménage in a helicopter is something that cannot possibly matter after the picture has started on its unsteady course. With his regal and somewhat beery manner, his precious silk hat, his frozen face and his unlit cigar, he keeps his audiences in perpetual roars. His athletic argument with the hotel clerk, which brings most of the "International House" thundering about his ears, is the funniest thing in the picture, unless it be his clandestine rendezvous with Miss Joyce in her boudoir. Although the writing is uneven, a great deal of it is funny, and it is of particular help to Mr. Fields and to Burns and Allen.[61]

While waiting for production to begin on his next Paramount feature, in which he was to star, Fields spent time perfecting his golf game. This led to a cameo appearance in the Vitaphone short film *Hip Action*, which was the third entry in pro golfer Bobby Jones's short movie series "How to Break Ninety." Hollywood stars would appear for free in these films in exchange for getting tips on the game from Jones. *Hip Action* was released on June 24, 1933. Jones asks Fields to show him how he drives the ball. Fields does so, and Jones indicates that the comedian needs work on his "hip action." He proceeds to instruct Fields how to properly move his hips when he drives the ball.

Tillie and Gus

Production and Distribution: Paramount
Executive Producer: Emanuel L. Cohen

Tillie and Gus

Associate Producer: Douglas MacLean
Director: Francis Martin
Screenplay: Walter De Leon, Francis Martin, from a story by Rupert Hughes
Camera: Ben Reynolds
Editor: James Smith
Release date: October 13, 1933; rereleased: 1949 (Paramount)
Running time: 59 minutes
Cast: W. C. Fields (August Q. Winterbottom), Alison Skipworth (Tillie Winterbottom), Baby LeRoy (The King), Jacqueline Wells (Mary Sheridan), Clifford Jones (Tom Sheridan), Clarence Wilson (Phineas Pratt), George Barbier (Captain Fogg), Barton MacLaine (Commissioner McLennon), Edgar Kennedy (judge), Robert McKenzie (defense attorney), Ivan Linow (Swede), Master Williams (High Card Harrington), Herbert Evans (butler), Billy Engle (sailor), Walter Percival (Mr. White), Frank Hagney (jury foreman), Lew Kelly (Sourdough), James Butke, Lon Poff, Ferris Taylor (jurors), Irving Bacon, Harry Schultz (gamblers), Ed Brady, Blackie Whitford (men at bar), Cyril Ring, Brooks Benedict (card players), Eddie Baker (riverboat judge).

Tillie and Gus has Fields and Alison Skipworth operating as a team, similar to the dynamic used in *If I Had a Million*. Once again, their co-star status offers a comfortable cohesion, as each plays nicely off the other. The film further defines Fields' screen character, concentrating on his prowess as a shifty con man and bringing more attention to his antipathy towards children. However, in this film, his conning is used heroically, for the benefit of others.

The story deals with a young couple, Mary and Tom, with a baby boy they refer to as The King. They are left a pile of debts with the passing of Mary's grandfather and guardian. Skipworth and Fields, as the title characters, are relatives of the deceased man. They each receive a letter indicating they are among the beneficiaries in the will. When they arrive and discover all he left were debts, due mostly to the unscrupulous behavior of the will's executor, Phineas Pratt, they set out to turn the tables by fixing up a ramshackle boat they have inherited and entering it in a race against Pratt's boat.

Fields and Skipworth are introduced separately, the narrative indicating that they are an estranged couple. When they first see each other at the train station, on their way to the reading of the will, each pulls a gun on the other. Deciding instead to join forces for the sake of the younger couple, Tillie and Gus put their crooked ways to good use.

During the train sequence, the two demonstrate how they were, quite literally, partners in crime. When a poker game takes place on the train, Gus pretends to be a novice, while Tillie stands nearby and tells him, in

Fields, Baby LeRoy (The King) and Alison Skipworth in *Tillie and Gus* (Paramount, 1933).

code, what cards the others are holding. Spotting two jacks, she says, "I saw those two sailors the other day." This is a particularly delightful scene, one that helps further define their characters. They are obviously savvy people who realize they need to present themselves somewhat differently to the innocent relatives they are about to meet. Upon their arrival and discovery of the debts, Tillie and Gus lead Mary and Tom to believe they are missionaries.

Even though the movie is a programmer that runs under an hour, it has time for Fields to do a scene separate from the narrative, which turns out to be the highlight.

It features Gus trying to learn how to mix paint according to instructions on the radio. With all of the necessary materials in front of him, Gus carefully follows the directions as they are patiently spoken over the air. He fumbles as the radio announcer speaks more quickly than his actions can follow, making the scene amusing at the outset. But it becomes even funnier when, unbeknown to Gus, The King changes the station to an exercise program. Gus dutifully follows instructions where he raises his right knee, then his left, soon jogging in place. "*Whew*," he sighs, "there must be an easier way to mix paint." This very funny scene is connected to the movie by stating that Gus is mixing paint to give the boat a fresh coat as part of the restoration process.

The King is Fields' nemesis throughout the film. His irritation with the tot prompts his partner to ask, "Do you like children?"

"I do if they're properly cooked," he answers.

This was the first appearance of Baby LeRoy in a W. C. Fields film, but not the last. The dynamic between them is explored more fully in other vehicles, but the little boy's presence in *Tillie and Gus* definitely sets the stage for the eventual legend that W. C. Fields hated children. Fields *did* believe Baby LeRoy was stealing scenes from him, and considered the child merely a useful prop and certainly not a co-star. However, Simon Louvish, in his 1998 book *Man on the Flying Trapeze: The Life and Times of W. C. Fields*, wrote that, in later years LeRoy "could not recall the actor ever being mean to him."[62]

Much of the footage deals with the boat race between the old boat the family has inherited, the *Fairy Queen*, and Phineas Pratt's new boat, the *Keystone*, which is to take place on the 4th of July, amid much fanfare. Initially, Pratt tries to arrange to have the old boat condemned, enlisting the aid of the city commissioner. It results in this amusing exchange:

> COMMISSIONER: This boat was launched in *1881!*
> GUS: So is my wife, but she's still seaworthy.
> COMMISSIONER: She's probably got barnacles all over her. (pause) The *boat*, I mean.

The family insists they can have their boat ready by the 4th, and accept Pratt's challenge for a race.

The race starts with the *Fairy Queen* getting a good head start because Gus sabotaged the *Keystone* by sneakily tying it to the dock. However, when he unties the rope holding the firewood, all of the logs roll into the river. Since the boat is a steam engine propelled by a fire below, Gus must chop up portions of the boat to provide the necessary fuel. Gus also throws wooden boxes of fireworks down, resulting in an explosive spectacle as the boat sails triumphantly ahead.

More comical excitement is provided when The King goes overboard in a little bathtub, floating away from the boat. Gus tries to save him in a lifeboat, but it immediately sinks. He and Tillie then board a large raft and float over to The King, bringing him to safety. They must also rescue Pratt, who has fallen overboard. Once the race is won, Gus dunks Pratt underwater until he confesses his misdeeds to the sheriff, allowing Tom and Mary to claim their full inheritance, without debt.

At a running time of just under an hour, *Tillie and Gus* was intended to be part of a double feature in theatres, a relatively new concept at the time. Because the film is so short, there isn't a wasted second; it remains amusing throughout. The two young romantic leads are rather lackluster, but, in context, this is not a detriment. The focal point of the narrative is the team of Fields and Skipworth as the title characters. Fields exhibits a dry, sardonic bluster and intolerance overall, his general contempt for humanity resulting in his quest to con and outwit them. Skipworth comes off as a kindly grandmother type when, in fact, she is no different than the Fields character. The two make a mutually complementary team, not unlike Marie Dressler and Wallace Beery, the stars of such MGM hits as *Min and Bill* (1930) and *Tugboat Annie* (1933).

During the filming of *Tillie and Gus*, Fields was frequently at odds with the director, insisting on inserting several comic sequences of his own creation, including the paint-mixing business, and rewriting most of his dialogue. However, the success of this film, and the attention given to Fields' work overall, resulted in Paramount allowing him greater creative input thereafter.

Mordaunt Hall, of the *New York Times*, was quite pleased with *Tillie and Gus*:

> In a cheery absurdity billed as *Tillie and Gus*, one finds that clever clown, W. C. Fields, teamed with Alison Skipworth. The film is at the Rialto, which now can boast of being the house of uproarious mirth. Baby LeRoy helps greatly by his happy demeanor in decidedly exciting scenes of this hectic tale, which is attributed to Rupert Hughes. A good deal of this farce is given over to a hilarious race between two old-fashioned ferryboats. It is with the best of intentions that Gus and Tillie arrange to have the ramshackle Fairy Queen win from the rival craft, the Keystone. It is a mad race, for Gus does everything possible to wreck the Keystone. He even dons a diving suit and works under water boring holes in the Keystone's hull. The steering wheel of this ferry is fixed so that it comes off at the psychological moment and, when the wood for the Fairy Queen's fires falls overboard, Gus has the more or less ingenious notion of using boxes of firecrackers which happen to be in the cargo. This not only results in giving the necessary speed to the ferry, but the exploding rockets, Roman candles and whatnot fly from the Fairy Queen's smokestack to the rival boat. Insane as are the doings in this concoction, they succeed in being really funny. It is the sort of thing admirably suited to Mr. Fields' peculiar genius. There seems to be a novel gag in every few scenes.... Miss Skipworth rivals Mr. Fields in arousing laughter, but she, as Tillie, is more rational than is Gus.[63]

Theatre owners, reporting in *The Motion Picture Herald*, were also quite satisfied with the finished product:

I don't care where your old show is located, but don't rest a moment until you show your congregation this picture. It's a knockout, a rare gem. About the best ever. It is the talk of the village. It's a wow. Grab it, you will not be sorry.[64]

One ingratiating aspect of Fields' character here is an underlying kindness, a trait not often in evidence in his films. Gus (short for Augustus), along with Tillie, perceive the young couple as innocent as their baby, while Pratt is the sort of unscrupulous type they believe gives their fellow crooks a bad name.

Tillie and Gus shows Fields continuing to define his screen character for talkies. With Gus, he is able to exhibit sneakiness, irascibility, and a sardonic nature, all of which were, by now, pretty well defined. Some of the characteristics found in *Tillie and Gus* would forever be associated with W. C. Fields, even though this film is one of his least discussed efforts.

Alice in Wonderland

Production and Distribution: Paramount
Executive Producer: Emanuel L. Cohen
Associate Producer: Louis D. Lighton
Director: Norman Z. McLeod (Uncredited: William Cameron Menzies)
Screenplay: Joseph L. Mankiewicz, William Cameron Menzies.
Based on the books *Alice's Adventures in Wonderland* (1865) and *Through the Looking Glass and What Alice Found There* (1871) by Lewis Carroll
Camera: Bert Glennon, Henry Sharp
Music: Dimitri Tiomkin
Editor: Ellsworth Hoagland
Released December 22, 1933
Running time: 76 minutes
Cast: Charlotte Henry (Alice), Richard Arlen (Cheshire Cat), Gary Cooper (White Knight), W. C. Fields (Humpty-Dumpty), Cary Grant (Mock Turtle), Sterling Holloway (Frog), Edward Everett Horton (Mad Hatter), Roscoe Ates (Fish), Jack Oakie and Roscoe Karns (Tweedledee and Tweedledum), May Robson (Queen of Hearts), Alison Skipworth (Duchess), Leon Erroll (Uncle Gilbert), Louise Fazenda (White Queen), Ford Sterling (White King), Skeets Gallagher (Rabbit), Jackie Searl (Dormouse), Billy Bevan (Two of Spades), Lillian Harmer (Cook), Charlie Ruggles (March Hare), Baby LeRoy (Joker), Alec B. Francis (King of Hearts), Edna May Oliver (Red Queen), Ned Sparks (Caterpillar), Billy Barty (White Pawn), Joe Torillo, Harry Ekezian, and Meyer Grace (executioners), Jack Duffy (leg of Mutton), Patsy O'Byrne (Aunt), Colin Kenny (Clock), Polly Moran (Dodo bird).

Lewis Carroll's *Alice in Wonderland* has often been adapted to film. Its characters, fantasy element, and potential for visual effects are attractive elements for any filmmaker. The earliest version is from 1903, when filmmakers were beginning to explore the visual component to narrative cinema. The story continues to be adapted into the 21st century, including a 2010 movie version directed by Tim Burton.

This 1933 production was generally the vision of art director William Cameron Menzies, whose exotic sets for such films as *The Thief of Bagdad* (1924) and *Two Arabian Knights* (1927) were considered artistic triumphs in their time; he would later be responsible for the overall look of *Gone With the Wind*. There is a great deal of visual cleverness to his film of *Alice*, and some cinematic tricks that might have seemed rather innovative at the time of its release. However, from the vantage point of the 21st century, any interest in the aesthetics of this film is purely historical. It is otherwise a rather dull viewing experience.

W. C. Fields, who portrays Humpty-Dumpty, had absolutely no interest in participating in this movie, but, as he was now under contract, he had to appear due to the studio's insistence. None of the contract players, in fact, were particularly fond of appearing in this movie under the heavy makeup necessary for their roles, but it was especially difficult for Fields. Highly claustrophobic, Fields suffered a panic attack as the heavy Humpty-Dumpty makeup was applied to his face, and he began clawing the matter from his cheeks and eyes.

Beneath the Humpty-Dumpty makeup, Fields' delivery is angry and unaffected, clearly conveying his disdain for the role. To the end of his days, Fields would always name Humpty-Dumpty as the worst part he ever had to play. And who could blame him? The garish makeup takes a lot away from his performance. While we can obviously hear that it is Fields, we don't get the benefit of his facial expressions to augment what he's saying. Instead, his face is dead still, with only the Humpty-Dumpty mouth moving in and out of sync with the dialogue.

The script for *Alice in Wonderland* was extremely thick, weighing over seven pounds. Along with the dialogue and directions, each page featured elaborate drawings exhibiting Menzies's vision as to how each scene should be presented. He apparently directed alongside of credited director Norman Z. McLeod, making sure his visual sense was accurate. But while the film's visuals remain interesting, it plods along from station to station without managing to engage the viewer. The movie takes a long time to get started; much of the beginning is Alice (nineteen-year-old ingénue Charlotte Henry) wandering around her house before she even gets to Wonderland. There are times when the film captures the absurdity so prevalent in the original story, including bizarre effects and grotesque costumes and makeup. And it can be argued that the book itself is as

Fields was unhappy with his role (and his claustrophobia-inducing makeup) as Humpty-Dumpty in *Alice in Wonderland* (Paramount, 1933).

episodic as the film. What remains a mystery is why Paramount insisted on casting so many stars in this movie, then covering them with makeup to the point of unrecognizability.

This version of *Alice in Wonderland* pales alongside Walt Disney's 1951 animated feature. Actually, Disney was trying to get the rights to this story at the same time as Paramount. If he had, this movie likely would never have been made, and the first-ever feature-length animation might have been *Alice in Wonderland* rather than *Snow White and the Seven Dwarfs* (1937).

Alice in Wonderland was only in release for one week during the Christmas season of 1933, and it enjoyed little commercial success. The movie was popular enough with children, but not so with adults. Theatre exhibitors indicated strong attendance, but not a very good reaction from their audiences. Perhaps the only real fun one can get out of this movie in more recent times is the art direction by Menzies, the costumes and makeup by Wally Westmore and Newt Jones, and the music by Dimitri Tiomkin. Otherwise, this lavish production is little more than a curiosity.

Six of a Kind

Production and Distribution: Paramount
Executive Producer: Emanuel L. Cohen
Associate Producers: Douglas MacLean
Director: Leo McCarey
Screenplay: Walter De Leon and Harry Ruskin, based upon a story by Keene Thompson and Douglas MacLean
Camera: Henry Sharp
Editor: LeRoy Stone
Released February 9, 1934
Running time: 62 minutes
Cast: Charlie Ruggles (Whinney), Mary Boland (Flora), George Burns (George), Gracie Allen (Gracie), W. C. Fields (Sheriff "Honest John"), Alison Skipworth (Mrs. Rumford), Tammany Young (Busby), Bradley Page (Ferguson), Grace Bradley (Goldie), William J. Kelly (Gillette), Neal Burns (Gillette's secretary), Alfred P. James (Tom), Lew Kelly (Joe), Robert McKenzie (Good Time Charlie), Dick Rush (Steele), Leo Willis (Mike), James Burke and Pat O'Malley (detectives), Irving Bacon, Sam Lufkin (hotel clerks), Walter Long (holdup man), George Pearce and Florence Enright (tourists), Phil Dunham (drunk), William Augustin (Cop), Harry Bernard (eyeshade man), Kathleen Burke (Woman), Martin Faust (Porter), Verna Hillie (bank clerk), Lee Phelps (bit).

Six of a Kind is a delightfully wacky comedy and very much a product of its time. Despite the fact that Fields is featured in a supporting role, not part of the film's main ensemble, and doesn't even appear until nearly halfway through the movie, he steals the show.

The main stars of *Six of a Kind* are two comedy teams: Charlie Ruggles and Mary Boland, and George Burns and Gracie Allen. Fields himself is teamed once again with Alison Skipworth. And while the Ruggles–Boland team and the Fields–Skipworth team each feature two separate actors who worked well together, Burns and Allen were a bona fide comedy team (and married couple) already popular in radio, on stage, and in a few films. Fields had appeared with Burns and Allen in *International House*, while Boland and Ruggles appeared in one of the *If I Had a Million* episodes.

In *Six of a Kind*, Ruggles plays Mr. Whinney, a meager bank clerk who has been looking forward to going on a second honeymoon in California with his wife, Flora. To save expenses, Flora advertises for another couple to join them, and that is how George and Gracie get involved. A subplot has one of the bank employees embezzling a large sum of money and sticking it in Whinney's luggage, causing the administrators to believe that the timid clerk has absconded with the funds.

Most of the comedy deals with the incompatible couples attempting to travel together civilly. George and Gracie reveal they aren't married, so they all must sleep with the women in one room and the men in the other. Gracie's absurdities ("My name is Grace, but they call me Gracie for short") are in abundance. Plus, she insists on bringing her enormous Great Dane, Rang Tang Tang, along with them on the road trip.

The comedy is outrageous and amusing. Gracie's silliness annoys Whinney and Flora ("I have an aunt that sees with her mouth. She sees if the soup is hot."). George manages to con Whinney into washing the Great Dane down by the creek. When Gracie wants to take a picture of Flora, she asks her to back up until the woman falls backwards off a cliff and is saved by a branch sticking out of the mountain. When they are held up and robbed by two hoboes on the road, Whinney hides his watch under his hat. The criminals start to walk away after getting the group's money, when Gracie says, too loudly, "It's a good thing they didn't find your watch!" At one point, mild-mannered Whinney says to his wife, "I could just murder them and get it over with."

The comedy is steady, the pace is brisk, and all of the performers are funny and endearing. Whinney's mounting frustration, Flora's jittery confusion, Gracie's outrageous absurdities, and George's fast-talking sharpness allow the ensemble to successfully interact from each possible perspective. And this is *before* the subject of our study has made his first appearance.

When the group finally gets to Nuggetville, Nevada, they stay at the inn where Mrs. Rumford (Skipworth) is proprietor, along with the sheriff, "Honest John" (Fields).

The film concludes with all of these teams together at the hotel, the actual embezzler showing up and posing as a detective to acquire the money he planted in Whinney's bag, and Honest John's attempt to arrest the guilty party.

Despite the fact that *Six of a Kind* was well received by moviegoers, Fields was quite displeased at being part of an ensemble, being a supporting player, and, once again, part of a team. He was especially annoyed when Paramount planned a sequel, with the working title *"Three Pair."* This idea was jettisoned when studio heads noticed that critics and theatre owners all singled out Fields as the hit of the show. His hilarious one-liners, "I'm so thirsty I feel like the British army has been walking across my tongue in their stocking feet" and "I'm about as busy as a pickpocket in a nudist colony" delighted moviegoers and critics alike.

It was not the studio's intention for Fields to walk off with the picture. While the belief was that the chemistry between Skipworth and Fields was palpable and could assist the movie, it was really more of a spotlight for Ruggles and Boland and Burns and Allen, the latter having just signed a three-year contract with Paramount. James Curtis, in his biography of Fields, explained:

> The part of Sheriff "Honest John" was devoid of color, or, for that matter, the distinctive patterns of speech that only Fields could bring to the material. Working in a vacuum, the writers had sketched in a perfunctory version of the famous pool specialty, providing a germ of the monologue but little else, and a scene at a roulette wheel that gave all the laugh lines to Gracie Allen.[65]

Fields complained to the studio brass that his entrance was made too late in the film, and that they were trying to kill him in pictures.

At about this time, MGM noticed Fields' popularity and his chemistry with Alison Skipworth, and wanted to use him in a vehicle opposite Marie Dressler. Fields liked the idea of working with her and at the prestigious studio, especially since he would have star billing and the title role of "Fericke, The Guest Artist." The script, based on a German novel, would be written by the formidable comedy writers Ben Hecht and Gene Fowler, both of whom were friends of Fields. Paramount head Manny Cohen, concerned that Fields would be a bigger hit in a film by another studio, refused to loan him out for the role. Hecht and Fowler went on to other assignments, while Marie Dressler became seriously ill after filming *Dinner at Eight*, dying from breast cancer the following year. This ended any possibility of the film being produced. Fields never completely forgave Cohen.

When Fields finally agreed to honor his contract and appear in *Six of a Kind*, he ad-libbed and insisted on the inclusion, and exclusion, of certain scenes. First, the roulette-wheel sequence between him and Gracie Allen was cut. It was replaced with a scene in which George attempts to buy a sweater, thinking Honest John is the shop's proprietor. Because Burns excels as a straight man, all the laughs belong to Fields.

Fields then took over the pool game, played it as he had onstage, and replaced Alison Skipworth, who was originally to do the scene with him. Fields had always used William "Shorty" Blanche as his stooge in the *Follies* as well as in some silents. But after Blanche died in 1931, Fields looked for another sidekick. He eventually settled on Tammany Young, whom he'd known for some years and who had a small part in *Sally of the Sawdust*. Young was notorious in New York and Los Angeles for being a gate crasher,

Fields attempts to sell a hat to George Burns, in a very funny scene from *Six of a Kind* (Paramount, 1934).

successfully sneaking into sporting events and private parties, and bragging that he could crash any gathering, no matter how exclusive it may be. It is Young who asks the sheriff how he came to be known as "Honest John." The sheriff explains while shooting pool. It is here that Fields performs his celebrated pool routine from vaudeville. Naturally, the visuals of such a routine are better seen than described, but Fields handles the pool cue, and bangs around the pool balls, using various dexterous stunts while casually explaining how he earned his distinctive nickname: A man put his glass eye down on a bar, and rather than stealing it, John returned it to him.

Fields transcends his partnership with Skipworth in this movie. While in *Tillie and Gus* they pretty much shared their scenes equally, here Fields garners all the laughs, with Skipworth fading into the background a bit.

Fields and director Leo McCarey locked horns at first, but McCarey, a solid director with real vision, had the reputation of letting innovators like Stan Laurel and Charley Chase more or less direct themselves. He soon realized that Fields was brilliantly inventive as well, allowing him the same freedom on *Six of a Kind*.

Despite whatever tension may have initially existed on set, the veteran cast members had nothing but praise for one another. In an interview with a writer from *Screenland* magazine, Mary Boland said that Charlie Ruggles "has the keenest sense of the ridiculous and can create a humorous character—timid, bashful, oozing inferiority complexes of every kind. The audience holds out its hand in sympathy even while it laughs."[66] Ruggles, in the same article, recalled Boland's difficulty doing the scene at the cliff.

> Poor Mary, she almost passed out with nervous jitters. Walking backwards and at the count of four to plunge off the cliff into space was a tough job. They spent three days on that sequence and it began to look as if I would not have a wife to complete the journey to California.[67]

Filming for *Six of a Kind* concluded at the end of 1933, and Fields told the studio heads that he wanted to star in his *own* comedy vehicles, with *no* partners. He believed that, with sound, the screenplays that had failed to register with audiences during the silent era could be successfully remade as talkies. Fields, in fact, had been working on a screenplay for his own starring movie since wrapping *Tillie and Gus*. Shooting that screenplay would be his next project.

You're Telling Me

Production and Distribution: Paramount
Executive Producer: Emanuel L. Cohen
Associate Producer: William Le Baron
Director: Erle C. Kenton
Screenplay: Walter De Leon, Paul Jones, J. P. McEvoy, based upon the story "Mr. Bizbee's Princess" by Julian Street
Camera: Alfred Gilks
Editor: Otho Lovering
Release date: May 18, 1934
Running time: 66 minutes
Cast: W. C. Fields (Sam Bisbee), Larry "Buster" Crabbe (Bob), Joan Marsh (Pauline), Adrienne Ames (Princess Marie), Louise Carter (Mrs. Bisbee), Kathleen Howard (Mrs. Murchison), Dell Henderson (mayor), James B. "Pop" Kenton (Doctor Beebe), Robert McKenzie (Charlie Bogle), Nora Cecil (Mrs. Price), George Irving (Mr. Robbins), Alfred Delcambre (Phil Cummings), Fred Sullivan (Mr. Murchison), Jerry Stewart (Frobisher), George MacQuarrie (Crabbe), John M. Sullivan (Gray), James C. Morton (George Smith), Elise Cavanna (Mrs. Smith), William Robyns (postman), Harold Berquist (doorman), Tammany Young (caddy), Vernon Dent (fat man) Lee Phelps and Frank O'Connor (cops), Edward le Saint (conductor), Billy Engle, George Ovey, Albert Hart (loungers).

William Le Baron, the producer who had worked with Fields on some of his silent features, had suggested to the studio heads at Paramount that the comedian be resigned. Le Baron, who had also been instrumental in Paramount star Mae West's film success, had great faith in Fields. Fields had faith in Le Baron as well. The two would make several outstanding pictures together. First up would be *You're Telling Me*, a remake of *So's Your Old Man*. Fields surrounded himself with a cast of old friends, and started off the New Year of 1934 with the production. And just as the star was at least twice as funny with sound, *You're Telling Me* would be at least twice as funny as its predecessor.

Fields once again plays Sam Bisbee, a small-town druggist who enjoys inventing little things (one of his inspirations is a milk bottle with a nipple on either side—for twins). Sam's daughter Pauline wants to accept a marriage proposal from her boyfriend, Bob, a young man whose family members are the town's leading citizens. However, Sam's earthy ways are simply impossible as far as the boy's parents are concerned. Sam has invented a puncture-proof tire (in the silent it was a shatter-proof windshield). When he arranges for a demonstration, his car is towed while he meets the potential backers in their offices; when he returns for the demonstration, he shoots up the tires of what turns out to be a police car. He runs away, leaving his car behind, and takes the train home. Disgraced, he decides to commit suicide on the train by swallowing iodine.

Dialogue adds some much-welcome depth to the proceedings. The film opens with Sam coming home at midnight, more than a little tipsy, and when he is reprimanded by his wife, he insists it is only eight-thirty. However, when his daughter rolls in even later, Sam attempts to scold her in front of his wife, and without tipping her off as to the time, says: "How dare you come home in the middle of the ni—in the middle of half past eight!"

The use of dialogue does not mean Fields eschews physical comedy. Carrying home one of his puncture-proof tires, Sam sees a boy rolling a tire along the walk with a stick and decides that might be a more efficient way of transporting it. He attempts this, but the tire moves more rapidly than he anticipated, and he ends up having to run furiously to keep up with it, banging into a tree and knocking a youngster off his bicycle on the way. Another nice piece of physical comedy that embraces the pre–Code freedoms that would soon be verboten is when Sam arrives home and finds his wife speaking with Bob's mother. Things are progressing well, as Sam's wife is bred from society herself, so she tries to wave Sam away. Sam doesn't understand her signals, so he turns and looks down, to see if his pants zipper is open. It is quick, and subtle, with Fields playing it beautifully, but it is definitely something the Production Code would reject.

In *You're Telling Me*, Fields plays Bisbee as a much more tragic Everyman than he had in *So's Your Old Man*. Sam is indeed quite boorish, but innocently so. When he comes barging into the meeting between his wife and Bob's haughty society mother, bouncing his tire like a basketball and showing off a family album that includes strippers and convicts, he has no idea he's doing anything wrong. There is a warmth and a kindness in Sam Bisbee that makes him appealing, even as we laugh at his earthiness. This is especially borne out in the scene on the train.

As in the silent film, Sam cannot bring himself to swallow iodine. And when he unwittingly stumbles onto the private drawing room of the princess, and sees a bottle of iodine she had just used to treat a small scratch on her finger, he assumes that she is planning to commit suicide as well. With a real softness in his eyes, Sam tells her that someone so young and so pretty should never consider doing such a thing. The princess finds him amusing until he reveals that he himself was about to do the same thing. She asks why. He tells her. Fields plays this straight, and with the same warmth his character had exhibited earlier. But in these scenes, there is an underlying feeling beneath his boorish behavior. Now it is being displayed at the forefront. The princess is moved by his kindness and attention to her, as well as by this unfortunate man's situation. She is determined to do something about it.

Sam has to disembark at the next stop, some forty miles past his destination (time had gotten away from him while making this gracious young lady's acquaintance). Meanwhile, two local gossips who saw Sam and the woman on the train, have returned to town and spread rumors, which escalate to the point where Sam is said to have "picked up a chorus girl—they were throwing empty champagne bottles out the window as they went through town." Further improvements on the silent version occur when Sam decides to buy a pet for his wife as a peace offering, seeing that his friend has purchased a canary. "It will take a much bigger bird to square things with *my* wife," Sam says. In the next scene, he is leading a giant ostrich down the street on a leash, trying desperately to control the unmanageable animal. In the silent version, it was a pony. The ostrich offers a far more amusing visual.

The princess comes to town, tells the society people that she wants her friend Sam Bisbee and his family included because "he saved my life during the war." Sam, thinking she is putting on an act for his benefit, plays along. In the end, not only is everything patched up with his family, but the young lovers, Bob and Pauline, are allowed to marry.

The princess insists that Sam, not the mayor, christen the new country club by hitting the first golf ball on the club's course. Sam is flattered, but has never played golf before. This allows Fields to trot out his golf routine yet again. Tammany Young is the caddy, and actress Adrienne Ames (the princess) is the encouraging female who sympathetically listens to the frustrated golfer's mutterings.

While on the course, an executive who had been looking for Bisbee comes running up to him. He states that the backers found his car, tested the tires, and discovered they are indeed puncture-proof. They offer him a large sum for the rights. The princess intervenes, saying she will pay more to have the rights for her country. The subsequent dickering goes on until Bisbee is left a millionaire. The final shot of the movie shows Bisbee, now a wealthy man, seeing his family off on a trip while he stays home to "work." What we see is that he plans to sit in his palatial estate and drink with his buddies, indicating success has not changed him.

The situations in *You're Telling Me* are allowed more depth, the characters more substance, the gags are enhanced, and the dialogue supplements what had once been a pleasantly amusing silent feature and turns it into an enduring comedy classic. One of the reasons for the film's success is Erle C. Kenton's direction. Kenton had started with Mack Sennett's Keystone comedies, so he knew how to stage a slapstick scene. After Fields remarks that it would take a bigger bird than a canary to square things with his wife, Kenton cuts to a shot of the princess and her motorcade, headed to see Sam. When Kenton cuts back, Bisbee is coming out of the pet shop with a large, unmanageable ostrich in tow. The cutaway is perfect. The effect of the gag would be ruined if we saw Bisbee enter the shop and choose the ostrich. But Kenton also couldn't simply have the camera rest on the front of the building for the time it would take to make the purchase. And, cutting away to an expository scene would distract from the flow of the gag.

Kenton's choice of shots enhances many scenes. When a delighted Bisbee is about to read the letter he received from potential investors about his tires, it is just after he ruined the conversation between his wife and Bob's mother. He pulls out the letter, and Kenton cuts to a medium shot, with Fields in the center and the unhappy wife and daughter on either side. The wife leaves the scene at left as the daughter goes upstairs, leaving the scene at the right. Kenton has it framed so that Sam is surrounded by negative space, making him look truly alone. It is an impressive piece of cinematic staging.

Another inspired directorial choice occurs when Sam is in the princess's drawing room on the train. The gossips get off the train, and from the street, look in the window of the drawing room to see what's going on. Kenton shows this by presenting Sam and the princess in the foreground, and allowing us to see, in the background through a window, the two old gossips across the street staring judgmentally, even to the point of running along with the train as it starts off for its next stop. It is very funny and beautifully framed.

This is Fields' best film performance thus far. His deftness with his hands as he attempts to control his recently removed shoes and hat are not only funny, but amazing in its variety of ways the comedian can hold, set down, pick back up, put on, and remove these items as the scene progresses. His character shows a loftiness over his inventions, but a total obliviousness to his earthy behavior. Fields is consistently funny with his words and actions, but he also demonstrates a warmth and sympathy that never seem like an overt attempt at pathos. The scenes in which he tries to cheer up the princess, while also revealing his own troubles, show a side of Fields' character that had not been presented heretofore as clearly or effectively.

While the invention the film centers upon is the puncture-proof tire, we are also treated to such clever ideas as a funnel-like keyhole finder for drunks coming home too late, a chair that knocks out a burglar once he sits in it, and, perhaps most remarkably, a "nose-lifter upper," which helps one breathe and curtails snoring—something not unlike actual modern devices to assist those with sleep apnea.

The cast is delightful. Fields found a small part for his friend Elise Cavanna, who had played his wife in two of the Sennett shorts, and the woman he drags around the room in *The Dentist*. Another friend, Kathleen Howard, is wonderful as Bob's snooty mother. Fields would use her to even greater advantage in later films. Tammany Young is very good as the caddy during the golf sequence. Joan Marsh as the daughter is competent, but Buster Crabbe is quite stiff as Bob. In a 1980 interview with the author, Crabbe remembered:

> W. C. Fields wasn't a particularly friendly man. He didn't care about me, or anyone else for that matter. He would drink all day and never show it. He would never forget a line. I don't know how he did it. Sometimes he would ad-lib and it would be funnier than what the scenario writers had written in the script. The director stepped back and let him go, so he had more freedom than a lot of actors I worked with. Whenever he needed anything, he had Tammany Young to get it for him. Tammany was a very nice man, friendly to everyone.[68]

From left: Fields, Joan Marsh, Larry "Buster" Crabbe, and Adrienne Ames in *You're Telling Me* (Paramount, 1934), the sound remake of *So's Your Old Man*.

You're Telling Me is a deep and fulfilling movie experience. Critics, audiences, and exhibitors agreed. As one theatre owner told the *Motion Picture Herald*:

> One of the best W. C. Fields pictures to date because in addition to the fun that this star is noted for, they gave him a real story. This story was done before in the silent days, but it turns out to be swell entertainment in the talking form. This has wholesome fun, romance, and good story interest. One of the funniest pictures we have ever played. Everyone left happy.[69]

In past studies of Fields' work, *You're Telling Me* is given little attention. For years this film was tied up in litigation and unavailable for revival screenings or television broadcasting. Those issues have since been settled, and the film is readily available on DVD. It is interesting to note that one of the characters is named Charlie Bogle. Fields would later adopt that as a pseudonym for story and screenplay credit on some of his films, including his next one.

The Old Fashioned Way

Production and Distribution: Paramount
Producer: William Le Baron
Director: William Beaudine
Screenplay: Garnett Weston and Jack Cunningham, from a story by Charles Bogle (Fields). Contributing writers: J. P. McEvoy, Paul Jones, H. M. "Beanie" Walker, Hal Yates, Lex Neal, Walter De Leon, William R. Lipman, Frank Mitchell Dazey, Ralph Ceder, Claude Binyon.
Camera: Ben F. Reynolds
Release date: July 13, 1934
Running time: 71 minutes
Cast: W. C. Fields (The Great McGonigle), Joe Morrison (Wally Livingston), Judith Allen (Betty), Baby LeRoy (Albert), Jan Duggan (Miss Pepperday), Tammany Young (Gump), Nora Cecil (Mrs. Wendelschaffer), Otis Harlan (Mr. Wendelschaffer), Jack Mulhall (Dick Bronson), Samuel Ethridge (Bartley Neuville), Ruth Marion (Agatha), Richard Carle (Sheriff), Oscar Apfel (Mr. Livingston), Lew Kelly (Sheriff Jones), Clarence Wilson (Sheriff Prettywillie), Joseph Mills (Charles Lowell), Emma Ray (Mother Mack), Donald Brown, Tom Miller, Jeff Williams, William Blatchford (actors in "The Drunkard"), Dorothy Bay (maid), Georgie Billings (kid on train), Sam Flint (kid's father), Edward La Saint (train conductor), Sam McDaniel, Oscar Smith (train porters), Davison Clark (train passenger), Dell Henderson (manager of the opera house), Maxine Elliot Hicks (waitress), Lona Andre, Florence Lawrence, Marvin Loback, Billy Bletcher (audience members), Duke York (stage hand), Robert McKenzie and Pop Kenton (men playing checkers).

Paramount realized the success of Fields updating one of his older silent features, which had also been produced by the studio, and were pleased when he chose to do so again. This time his source material was *Two Flaming Youths*, one of his least successful early films. However, the plot was not used, only the idea of a traveling acting troupe headed by a shifty manager. Fields planned to update the material, using the working title, "Playing the Sticks"; it was ultimately released as *The Old Fashioned Way*.

Set in the late 19th century, during the days of touring melodramas, Fields is The Great McGonigle, stage performer and crooked manager of an acting troupe. The story deals with the troupe descending on yet another small town to perform the 1844 temperance play *The Drunkard*. A subplot deals with the romance between McGonigle's daughter, Betty, and a talented young actor in the troupe, much to the chagrin of boy's wealthy father. When he sees his son's adept performance, however, he changes his mind and tells him he may marry McGonigle's daughter, but *only* if they both keep their distance from the girl's nefarious father. Naturally,

Trade ad for *The Old Fashioned Way* (Paramount, 1934).

the loyal Betty refuses. McGonigle overhears this, after which he closes the show and announces that he is off to perform as a single in New York. It isn't true, of course, but he makes this sacrifice for his daughter's happiness. The film ends with McGonigle, now with a medicine show, hawking a useless tonic to would-be customers.

Fields' performances, even when playing someone as unscrupulous as McGonigle, continued to be as touching as they were funny. Director William Beaudine recalled:

> The audience was expecting a funny twist to this scene [in which he hugs his daughter goodbye]. And if Fields had made the slightest false step, the whole tragedy of his parting would have gone to pieces in a burst of laughter. But he didn't make that false step. He acted with the pathos of the true clown. He held his audience and conveyed to them the sadness of the old man's parting from the only person that meant anything in his life. That was a great bit of acting.[70]

McGonigle speaks with the Falstaffian flourish of an egotistical actor of the 19th century. He is shrewd, and unscrupulous. He is, in every sense of the word, a "trouper," practicing his art to often unappreciative audiences. Unable to support himself and his company by doing what he was born to do, he connives people like the wealthy widow Mrs. Pepperday. But he is also benevolent and loving toward his daughter, who understands him even while disapproving of his conniving ways.

This is also the film that features what is unquestionably the best encounter between Fields and Baby LeRoy, who is cast as Mrs. Pepperday's precocious child. During a dinner sequence, the unruly boy squeezes McGonigle's oversized nose, throws food at his face, and ruins his watch by dipping it in molasses. In retaliation, McGonigle gives the boy a swift kick in the seat of his pants after the other diners run to a window to see a "horseless carriage." Unfortunately, director William Beaudine was pressured by studio execs to water down the gag, making it acceptable to audiences. As Beaudine explained:

> The studio was in an uproar about that scene. They said, "You can't do that. People won't stand for it. You can't kick a kid!" It gets the biggest laugh in the picture.[71]

Reactive comedy also sets the tone for the scene where the delusional Mrs. Pepperday auditions for McGonigle. Seated precariously on a knitting kit that had been left on the couch, McGonigle forces himself to endure not only this uncomfortable spot, but the strident tones of Mrs. Pepperday. She warbles verse after verse of "Gathering Up the Shells (on the Seashore)," her singing leaving a great deal to be desired, but she *is* the wealthiest woman in town and McGonigle needs her money. As a result, he endures this ghastly performance and grants her one line in the play: "Here comes the prince!" The stage-struck woman rehearses this line at every spare moment, utilizing every possible inflection.

The twenty minutes of footage devoted to performing *The Drunkard* is an attempt to present the show as it would in its day, just as the reactions to such a show are done with accuracy. Director Beaudine cuts away from the action onstage to individuals in the audience, including an older man who is getting so worked up by the play that he's warned by his wife not to tax his heart. There is also some fun in seeing Fields play such an over-the-top villain in this segment. As a tribute to the old days of melodrama, it works. As a centerpiece to the movie, it does not.

That lengthy presentation notwithstanding, *The Old Fashioned Way* is a treat for Fields fans. In an early scene, McGonigle disembarks from a train that pulls in to a small town where his troupe is to perform, and believes he is being greeted by a brass band; this, of course, is for an actual luminary on the same train. We hear Fields' muttered asides ("The soup sounds good"), see his startled reactions to various happenings, and laugh at his character's conniving manner, particularly when he sneaks out of a rooming house without paying. The biggest treat of all for a Fields fan is the filmed record of his famous juggling act.

There have been snippets of Fields' juggling in previous films, but *The Old Fashioned Way* truly spotlights this area of the comedian's talents with a long showcase that includes many of his best routines. Fields juggles three balls, then four, bounces and catches them, and switches from hand to hand. He does another routine with cigar boxes that had been one of the highlights of his *Follies* act. The success of this scene resulted in Fields receiving several letters from young boys interested in learning to juggle. He answered every one.

Along with actors from an actual Los Angeles production of *The Drunkard*, Fields surrounds himself with old friends like Tammany Young as his loyal, ever-present valet, and hatchet-faced Nora Cecil as the distrustful owner of the rooming house where the troupe stays. Judith Allen and Joe Morrison are rather bland as McGonigle's daughter and her intended. It is Morrison's film debut and Paramount was hoping to groom the singer for better things. However, the fact that Fields allegedly engaged in a short-lived affair with Miss Allen (during a brief time when the five-times-married actress was between husbands) is how she got hired for the role. Jan Duggan, in her delightfully over-the-top performance as Mrs. Pepperday, worked well with Fields, and he would continue to use the actress throughout his film career.

While Paramount executives supported Fields' idea to update another of their silent features, and producer Le Baron allowed the star all but complete creative control, the studio's administration didn't think much of *The Old Fashioned Way*. Ever interested in the younger demographic, Paramount believed the film was, just as its title implied, old fashioned. They hoped the Fields name would attract enough moviegoers to break even. In their short-sightedness, they even let Fields' option run out without renewing it. Despite the studio's reservations, critics and audiences alike were delighted by *The Old Fashioned Way*. A writer for *Screenland* magazine—an admitted Fields fanatic—had this to say:

> If you are, as I am, a W. C. Fields complete push-over, then rush to see his latest. It is also his funniest. If for some weird reason you are still immune to the Fieldsian fascination, let me beg that you give him one more chance. If *The Old Fashioned Way* doesn't make you howl, scream, giggle, gasp, or at least chuckle and chortle, then I am really disappointed in you.[72]

In an issue of *Motion Picture Herald* an article lists top box-office champions for the month of August 1934. *The Old Fashioned Way* rests loftily on that list, along with MGM's *Treasure Island*, and the Warner Bros. musical *Dames*.

Fields had written the original story for *The Old Fashioned Way* (under the pseudonym Charles Bogle), and it was very much his project. So, when Paramount decided to renew his contract based on this success, Fields knew he was in a position to make some demands. The year 1934 was a time when Paramount was rebounding financially, getting rid of highly paid actors whose films were not netting satisfactory results, and keeping those who did. Along with Fields, those who had shown their worth included Bing Crosby, Mae West, Gary Cooper, and Cary Grant.

The same execs who feared *The Old Fashioned Way* was out of date, were the same ones who asked Fields to make a cameo in an actual melodrama. Fields balked, but when Paramount agreed to his contract renewal demands, he grudgingly accepted.

Mrs. Wiggs of the Cabbage Patch

Production and Distribution: Paramount
Producer: Douglas MacLean
Director: Norman Taurog
Screenplay: William Slavens McNutt, Jane Storm (Uncredited: Jack Mintz, Grover Jones), based upon the 1901 book by Alice Hegan Rice.
Camera: Charles Lang
Editor: Hugh Bennett
Release date: October 19, 1934
Running time: 80 minutes

Cast: Pauline Lord (Mrs. Wiggs), W. C. Fields (Stubbins), ZaSu Pitts (Miss Hazy), Evelyn Venable (Lucy), Kent Taylor (Bob), Charles Middleton (Bagby), Lillian Elliot (Mrs. Bagby), Donald Meek (Mr. Wiggs), Jimmy Butler (Billy), George Breakston (Jimmy), Edith Fellows (Australia), Virginia Weidler (Europena), Carmencita Johnson (Asia), George Reed (Julius), Mildred Gover (Priscilla), Arthur Housman (Dick Harris), Walter Walker (Dr. Barton), Sam Flint (Jenkins), James Robinson (Mose), Edward Tamblyn (usher), Al Shaw and Sam Lee (stage comedians), Del Henderson (house manager), George Pearce (minister).

W. C. Fields had felt backed into a corner when it came to making a cameo appearance in the hoary melodrama *Mrs. Wiggs of the Cabbage Patch*. He believed his involvement with this project would be detrimental to his now-successful film career, and that the only reason for his participation was to ensure that Paramount would see a return at the box office. The more he thought of it, in fact, the more incensed he became. He even considered not signing a new contract with the studio and becoming an independent, along with Bing Crosby and Mack Sennett, using United Artists as a distributor. But, in the end, practicality won out.

The story has Mrs. Wiggs facing eviction, her husband having gone off years earlier to search for gold in the Klondike. She owes money on the shack where she lives with her five children, the oldest of whom works to help out with finances, while Mrs. Wiggs takes in laundry. Things get especially tight once the eldest son contracts tuberculosis and can no longer work. Social worker Alice helps out by bringing them food on Thanksgiving.

W. C. Fields plays Stubbins, a suitor for Tabitha Hazy, the Wiggs's husband-hunting neighbor. However, Miss Hazy can't cook, so Mrs. Wiggs cooks a nice meal for which Tabitha can take credit. When he discovers the ruse, he refuses to marry the spinster, and she throws him out. The film ends with Mr. Wiggs returning with enough money to make the family solvent once again.

Mrs. Wiggs of the Cabbage Patch had been filmed in 1914, again in 1919, and would be once again in 1942. Even by 1934 the story creaked. A scene like the one in which Mrs. Wiggs describes a vaudeville show to her son Jimmy, while the child slowly fades away and dies, is a good representation of what this movie has to offer. Stage actress Pauline Lord is making her film debut in the title role, and was reportedly confused by the entire process of acting for the camera. Broader gestures, necessary for the stage, needed to be toned down. Facial nuance was caught, no matter how subtle. It was not a good experience for her. She made one other film before leaving movies and returning to the stage. Despite this, it is good that we have a filmed record of her work.

In *Mrs. Wiggs of the Cabbage Patch* (Paramount, 1934), Fields and comedienne ZaSu Pitts had a hilarious scene together in this otherwise maudlin story.

W. C. Fields does not appear until the film's final twenty minutes. By all accounts, the actor was difficult to work with on this shoot, although in fairness to Fields, the rustic location conditions for the movie were quite bad. The children in the cast were warned not to wander from the set due to rattlesnakes. Fields was assigned an onset tent containing a cot and an end table. Even toilet accommodations were relegated to holes dug in the ground for cast and crew. Fields reportedly sat in his tent drinking when not actually filming, his only companion being Tammany Young.

About her famous co-star, actress Evelyn Venable recalled: "He was always fried before noon. When we started shooting at eight a.m. he had his drink already half gone."[73] Edith Fellows, one of the children in the movie, recalled for biographer James Curtis that the comedian was "a very strange man," who asked her to drink something to "keep the rattlesnakes away." It looked like water, but was actually gin.[74] The teacher on the set warned Fields to stay away from the children unless he was doing a scene with them. However, Carmencita Johnson, another of the film's child actors, told Curtis that Fields overheard her say how much she liked cantaloupes, and had Tammany bring her to his tent where she could pick as many fresh cantaloupes as she wanted from several Fields had on ice. "I only took one," she said, "because I was very well behaved, said thank you, and left. That was a very sweet thing for him to do."[75]

Despite being unhappy with the accommodations, Fields still wanted to come off as well as he could in the movie. He instructed the prop men to build a three-foot wire fence for his scene, and improvised a bit where he gets tangled in it as he goes to call on Miss Hazy. This bit of business turned out to be the funniest thing in the film. Fields also liked and respected ZaSu Pitts, so he was comfortable when playing scenes with her. The film was completed and released in October of 1934 to some good notices and decent box office, the studio's ploy to include Fields having resulted in reasonable success. Reviews pointed out that Fields and Pitts were the hit of the movie, despite their limited footage together. Andre Sennwald stated in the *New York Times*:

> The patient and doleful Miss Hazy has become the fluttering ZaSu Pitts and, for no more pious reason than to make you roar, she has been provided with a suitor in the outlandishly funny person of W. C. Fields.[76]

A theatre owner in Oregon reported to the *Motion Picture Herald*:

> The biggest midweek business we have ever enjoyed and the patrons ate it up. If there ever was a small town picture here it is, and the whole family can come too. May not be Broadway's idea of entertainment, but it's got Main Street written all over it.[77]

However, in a letter to his friend Jim Tully, Fields stated:

> I saw [the movie] for the first time a few nights ago in North Hollywood ... when I came on the screen I stunk so badly the police came in with the impression that someone had been throwing stink bombs around.[78]

Despite any misgivings, substandard location conditions, or problems with the cast and crew, W. C. Fields is hilarious in this movie. There's nothing likeable about his character, but he has great lines, and wonderful bits of business (such as a scene at the dinner table where he cuts off half the mince pie for himself). He has great chemistry with Pitts, and the fact that each enjoyed working with the other is evident. The scene is an odd departure from the main story, disrupting its rhythm, but, judging by the box-office take, it served its purpose.

Appearing in the film did not turn out to be detrimental to W. C. Fields' career as he had predicted. But Fields told the Paramount brass in no uncertain terms that cameo appearances in films like *Alice and Wonderland* and *Mrs. Wiggs of the Cabbage Patch* were a thing of the past. He was far too busy creating what many would consider to be his masterpiece.

It's a Gift

Production and Distribution: Paramount
Producer: William Le Baron
Director: Norman Z. McLeod
Screenplay: Jack Cunningham, Charles Bogle, J. P. McEvoy
Camera: Henry Sharp
Release date: November 30, 1934
Running time: 68 minutes
Cast: W. C. Fields (Harold Bissonette), Kathleen Howard (Mrs. Amelia Bissonette), Jean Rouverol (Mildred Bissonette), Julian Madison (John Durston, Mildred's fiancé), Tommy Bupp (Norman Bissonette), Josephine Whittell (Mrs. Dunk), Diana Lewis (Miss Dunk), Baby LeRoy (Baby Dunk), Tammany Young (Everett), Morgan Wallace (James Fitchmueller), Charles Sellon (Mr. Muckle), Patsy O'Byrne (Mrs. Frobisher), T. Roy Barnes (insurance salesman), Guy Usher (Bosterly), Dell Henderson (Abernathy), Helene Chadwick (Mrs. Abernathy), Jerry Mandy (vegetable man), Jack Mulhall (butler), William Tooker and Edith Kingdon (old couple in limo), Jane Withers (girl wanting to play hopscotch), Don Brookins, Art Green, Walter Trask, Chill Wills (Avalon boys).

Generally considered the best of W. C. Fields' feature films, *It's a Gift* reworks the structure of his silent feature *It's the Old Army Game* and once again resurrects several comedy routines that Fields had done in the *Follies*.

It's a Gift features Fields as Harold Bissonette, a put-upon Everyman, who wants to leave his dull life as a storekeeper and have his own California orange grove. The very first scene establishes the imminent passing of Harold's uncle Bean, via a telegram, then moves right into a shaving sequence that features no dialogue. Harold is trying to shave in the bathroom mirror while his teenage daughter is cleaning up and primping. He tries to see over her, and around her, but to no avail. He tries using a handheld mirror by having it dangle from a light fixture, but it keeps moving. As he makes one final attempt, lying backward over a chair, his wife walks in. The daughter has left by now, and his exasperated wife asks why he is shaving in so ridiculous a manner. Fields once again shows his adeptness at physical comedy in this scene, making even clumsy movements seem graceful. He told actress Jean Rouverol, playing his daughter Mildred, to simply go about her business as she does in real life (brushing her hair, applying makeup, etc.). She did, and Fields worked his comedy around her natural performance. Jean Rouverol had been rehearsing for Max Reinhardt's Hollywood Bowl presentation of Shakespeare's *A Midsummer Night's Dream*, and was taken from the cast and placed in *It's a Gift*, her first film, due to an obligation with Paramount Pictures. She was replaced onstage by her understudy, Olivia de Havilland, who later went on to appear in the film version for Warner Bros., also securing a movie contract that led to stardom. Miss Rouverol was not happy "going from Shakespeare to this drunken vaudevillian. I wasn't sophisticated enough, or knowledgeable enough, or even smart enough, to realize I was working with one of the great comic geniuses of the twentieth century."[79]

The first few scenes set up the character of Harold perfectly. He has a haughty, nagging presence for the wife, a particularly strident little boy for his son, and the daughter who selfishly exhibits no regard for her father's needing to shave before work. The scene concludes with Harold slipping on one of his son's errant roller skates and falling hard on the floor. His wife reacts to this by saying, "Be careful with those skates—I just had them fixed!"

Harold's home life has been established as one that dismisses his presence, and his needs, as unimportant. It is all done with humor. Every one of these scenes elicits laughter, and Fields plays the character as put-upon, but still somewhat defiant. His "ah shut up" to his bratty son, his dismissive reaction to his wife's nagging, and his remoteness from his daughter's refusal to leave her boyfriend and move to California, show him as living in his own world, blocking out that which he finds distasteful. When he proclaims to his daughter that *he* is master of the house, he has to do so quietly so his wife doesn't hear him. He leaves the house as she continues to nag.

He fares no better at work. Our look into this business for this one day shows him being yelled at by an impatient customer requesting

Charles Sellon (left) and Fields in the classic *It's a Gift* (Paramount, 1934).

cumquats, a cranky old blind man who comes into the store and proceeds to break glassware and make angry demands as Harold fulfills his request for a pack of gum ("I'm not gonna lug that with me! Send it!"), and a toddler who turns on the molasses faucet and fills the store with the sticky substance (the child's mother angrily reacts with "How dare you pour molasses on the floor and ruin his shoes!"). Harold is forced to respond at different levels for different people. He must be patient with his nagging wife and his troublesome customers. He is more demanding with his dimwitted assistant, whom he fires, blaming him for the destruction the toddler has caused. The store scene is one of the movie's many highlights.

Harold is a pleaser. His patience with even the most troublesome customers is admirable, but it's also part of what makes the sequence in the grocery store so funny; for example, when he repeatedly tells the blind man to move away from the glass, there's just that little undercurrent of strain beneath his otherwise pleasant tone.

In another highlight, Harold leaves his nagging wife, who continues her tirade, and decides to sleep on the porch swing outside. Constant

Tammany Young (left) was Fields' favorite stooge and right-hand man during this period. By all accounts, Young was a kind and gentle person. This still was taken on the set of *It's a Gift* (Paramount, 1934).

interruptions ensue, from the jingling of a milk man's glass bottles ("Please stop playing with those sleigh bells"), to a vegetable man loudly hawking his wares. The insurance salesman looking for Carl La Fong is perhaps the funniest portion of this sequence, the man boisterously trying to sell Harold a policy ("You could retire at ninety, with full benefits"). This awakens Harold's wife inside ("If you and your friend are going to stand out here and tell ribald stories..."). A frustrated Harold chases the man away with a meat cleaver. The toddler upstairs drops grapes into the sleeping Harold's mouth. The upstairs teen girl bounds loudly down the stairs then hollers a conversation up to her mother. Harold's fuming, frustrated reaction enhances the humor of the scene.

The "back porch" routine, of course, is from "The Comic Supplement," which Fields had written with satirist J. P. McEvoy, and had perfected onstage for years. The silent version in *It's the Old Army Game* was amusing enough, but in *It's a Gift* the addition of dialogue enhances its effect, as do the nonverbal sounds (e.g., an annoyingly squeaky clothesline mistaken for a mouse, and a coconut bouncing down the stairs).

While these first scenes establish the characters, the body of the film is transitional, showing the family en route to California. The narrative continues to be interrupted by episodic sequences. First, a pleasant stop at a hobo camp, allowing the viewer to take something of a breather after the wildly funny scenes that preceded it. This is followed by a picnic the family decides to have, not realizing the land they are on is private property (the premise of another tried-and-true sketch). Even if they *had* been in a public park, their behavior is atrocious. They break a statue, rip apart a feather pillow causing its contents to spread all over the grounds, and casually leave wrappers and debris throughout their picnic area.

They continue on their way, passing many beautiful orange groves ("I hope our orange grove is half as nice as this," Mrs. Bissonette says pleasantly, receiving a contented smile from her husband) and finally arrive at the property Harold had purchased, unseen. It is worthless. The land is empty of any living vegetation, its soil hard and dry. The house is a small, unlivable shack. Fields is allowed to play some level of pathos in this scene, sitting alone (with the exception of the family dog) and dejected on the front porch of the shack as his family angrily walks away. There are a few moments of unhappiness before a nearby rancher hurries over and states, "You're lucky and you didn't know it."

"Well, I wasn't absolutely sure about it," he responds, deadpan.

The rancher—a Mr. Abernathy—then tips Harold off to the fact that some land developers have designs on his property for a race track. Harold's wife doesn't hear what the rancher says, but walks up as a team of real estate investors offer to take the property off Harold's hands for $5,000. Harold refuses. They raise the offer to $10,000. Still no. Then $15,000, and Harold stands firm. His wife is apoplectic. When accused by one of the haughty businessmen of being drunk, Harold responds, "Yeah, and you're crazy. I'll be sober tomorrow, but you'll be crazy the rest of your life." It is Harold who sets the price: $44,000—$4,000 of which would be paid as commission to Mr. Abernathy—and a premium California orange ranch.

"It's a *holdup*!" the businessman objects. "But it's a deal."

The film ends with Harold and his family living comfortably and peacefully on their new orange grove.

This film's story is thin—primarily a series of comic episodes. Its structure, though, is a refreshing change from most other comedy features; instead of using comedy to help tell a story, the entire focus is on a relentless series of jokes and gags, with the story serving the purpose of advancing the film from one comedy sequence to the next.

Considerable changes were made from script to screen. There was a sequence in the script where Harold hurriedly drives a woman to the maternity hospital, but that disrupted the flow of the narrative and was removed. Fields would resurrect it as the climax to his later film *Never Give a Sucker an Even Break*. The youngest child was originally going to be a girl, but was changed to a boy. And there was also a sequence where child actress Jane Withers follows Harold on his way to the store and plays hopscotch with him. All that remains with her is a quick bit where she runs up to him and says, "I have a piece of chalk, you wanna play hopscotch?" and he shoos here away. Fields never forgot her, though. A year later Withers got her first big role at Fox, and Fields had a bouquet of roses delivered to her on the set.

The store sequence was rehearsed carefully and a great deal of business was added during filming, while some bits were cut from the film. When veteran actor Charles Sellon, as Mr. Muckle, the blind man, comes crashing through the door, breaking the glass with his cane, Fields was to run up to him just upon impact. Nearly an entire day was spent perfecting that one shot. A scene where Muckle steps in a crate of eggs was filmed but later cut. Fields wrapping the stick of gum was another bit of business not in the script that took a great deal of time to get just right. Fields, the cast, and the director were patient with one another other, and with the process. Many ideas came about during filming that improved each scene a great deal (e.g., actor Morgan Wallace, the demanding customer who kept loudly asking for cumquats, was first instructed to request granulated sugar. "Cumquats" is much funnier). The sets are very impressive and serve the comedy well, particularly the grocery store and back porch scene. The final sequence, depicting the wealthy Bissonette family in luxurious surroundings, was shot at Fields' own property.

As with the store sequence, other comic bits were reworked during filming. In the scene where Harold drives the family jalopy into the private property for the picnic and hits a statue of Venus de Milo, his wife angrily castigates him. Harold responds, "It was already broken—look at the arms." It was not until they shot the scene that Fields ad-libbed the line that is ultimately used: "She ran right in front of the car!"

It's a Gift was W. C. Fields' biggest hit to date and his best received film by moviegoers and critics. Exhibitors, reporting in the trades, proclaimed:

- The lines were so fast in this one that a fellow got tired laughing!
- This is one swell comedy!

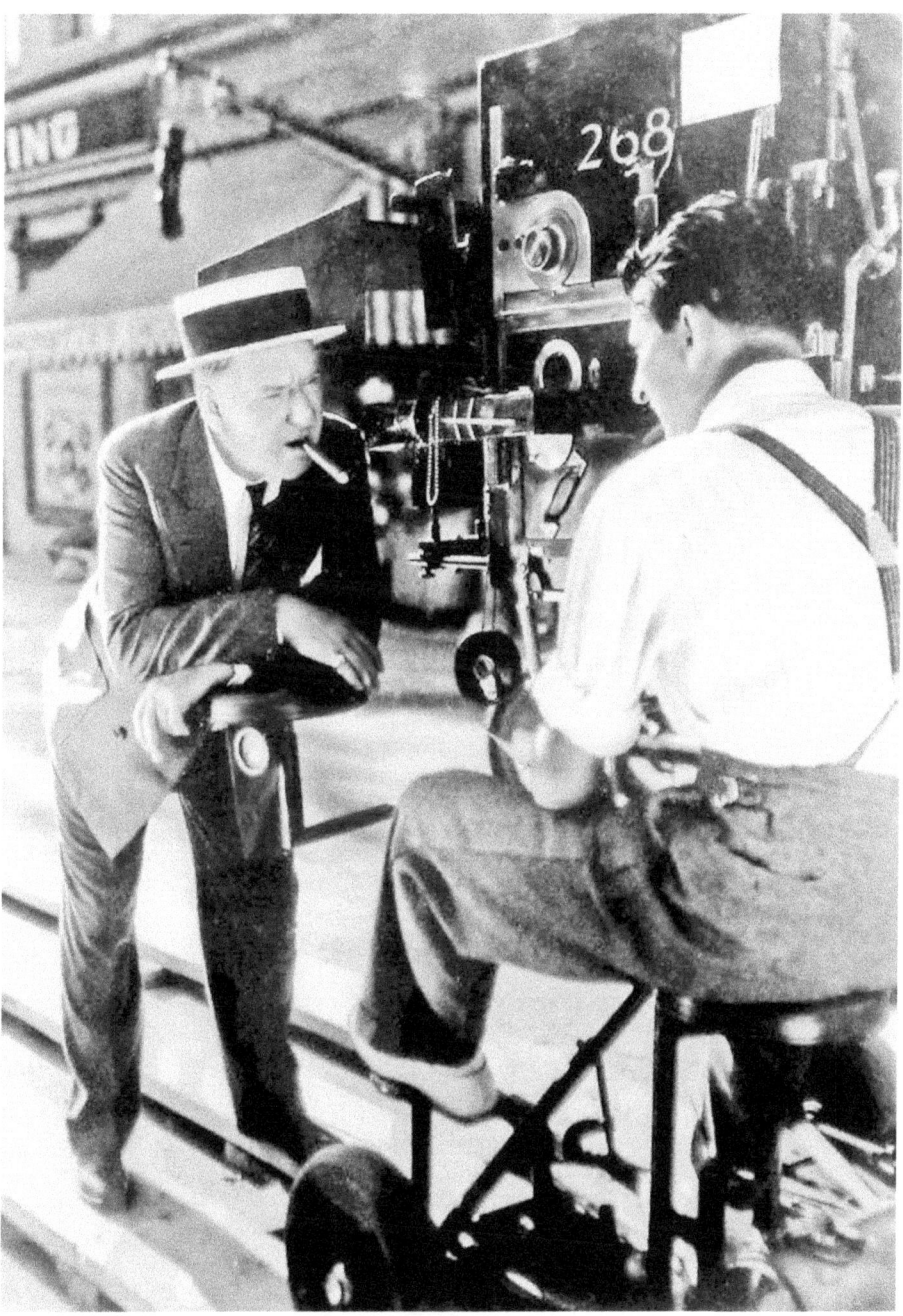

Fields and cameraman Henry Sharp discuss the upcoming shot on the set of *It's a Gift* (Paramount, 1934).

- Good old W. C. Fields turns in another good show for us ... the patrons howled with laughter![80]

Andre Sennwald. in *The New York Times*, made mention of Fields' exceptional supporting cast:

> The great man's assistants in the new comedy provide him with excellent foils. As the nagging wife Kathleen Howard is so authentic as to make Mr. Fields' sufferings seem cosmic and a little sad despite their basic humor. As the thick-witted grocery clerk, Tammany Young is an effective lunkhead, and Charles Sellon, as the blind man, is quite as irresistible as he was last month as the wheel-chair invalid in "Bright Eyes." The fact is that Mr. Fields has come back to us again and *It's a Gift* automatically becomes the best screen comedy on Broadway.[81]

Fields would forever be pleased with the cooperation he received during the filming of this movie. He was loyal to those whose work he knew and trusted. The actors, technicians, and gag writers were grateful to him for this.

Someone else whose work Fields had long respected was Charles Dickens. In his next film, that great storyteller would, in essence, be his screenwriter.

David Copperfield

Production and Distribution: Metro-Goldwyn-Mayer
Producer: David O. Selznick
Director: George Cukor
Screenplay: Howard Estabrook, Hugh Walpole
Based on the 1850 novel *The Personal History, Adventures, Experiences, and Observation of David Copperfield, the Younger of Blunderstone Rookery (Which He Never Meant to Publish on Any Account)* by Charles Dickens
Camera: Oliver T. Marsh
Release date: January 18, 1935; rereleased: 1939, 1962 (MGM)
Running time: 130 minutes
Cast: W. C. Fields (Micawber), Freddie Bartholomew (David, as a child), Frank Lawton (David, as a man), Elizabeth Allen (Mrs. Copperfield), Jessie Ralph (Nurse Peggotty), Lionel Barrymore (Dan Peggotty), Maureen O'Sullivan (Dora), Madge Evans (Agnes), Edna May Oliver (Aunt Betsy), Lewis Stone (Mr. Wickfield), Roland Young (Uriah Heep), Basil Rathbone (Mr. Murdstone), Elsa Lanchester (Clickett), Harry Beresford (Doctor), Hugh Walpole (Vicar), Herbert Mundin (Barkis), John Buckler (Ham), Fay Chaldecott (Em'ly, as a child), Florine McKinney (Em'ly, as a woman), Una O'Connor (Mrs. Gummidge), Violet Cooper (Jane Murdstone), Jean Cadell (Mrs. Micawber), Lennox Pawle (Dick), Renee Gadd (Janet), Marilyn Knowlden (Agnes), Ivan Simpson (Littmer), Hugh Williams (Steerforth), Mabel Colcord (Mary Ann), Dennis Chaldecott (Micawber's son), Yorke Sherwood (Quinion), Sonny Ray (Mickey), Arthur Treacher (Donkey Man).

For the film adaptation of Charles Dickens's *David Copperfield*, Metro Goldwyn Mayer gathered most of the leading stars on their roster and placed them in director George Cukor's more than capable hands.

Producer David O. Selznick realized the depth of Dickens's novel and felt it would be more effective as two separate films. This idea was nixed, which meant that, in order to tell the story from beginning to end, the text would have to be cut substantially. The result is a truncated version of *Copperfield*, omitting several characters from the book (including David's good friend Thomas Traddles).

Louis B. Mayer, head of MGM, wanted his own child star Jackie Cooper to be cast in the title role, but producer Selznick wanted a British actor. Freddie Bartholomew was flown in from England under the supervision of his aunt, and played the role. He was so well received he ended up with an MGM contract.

Charles Laughton had already been cast as Micawber, amid much publicity. However, Laughton was unhappy with the role, feeling he was unsuited to play it, and was released after two days of filming. Selznick liked the idea of replacing Laughton with W. C. Fields, but had to arrange for a loan-out from Paramount. This would also halt that studio's production of *Mississippi*, which would pair Fields with Bing Crosby. However, Selznick was desperate, having been working on the film for over a year in pre-production. MGM agreed to put up money for whatever financial losses the halting of *Mississippi* caused (including lead actress Joan Bennett's salary) in order to secure Fields' services.

For one of the very few times in his movie career, W. C. Fields stuck to a script; so great was his respect for Dickens's prose that he refrained from ad-libbing. That does not mean, however, that the film is completely faithful to the character of Micawber, who was described by the author as bald. Charles Laughton agreed to have his head shaved for the part, but Fields refused to do so, citing, with photographic evidence, other hirsute actors who had essayed the role. Fields also did not speak with a British accent, using instead his regular delivery to speak the lines. Some critics pointed this out, but all agreed his was among the most believable performances in the movie.

David Copperfield was an enormous success with critics and audiences upon its release in January of 1935. A critic for *Variety* wrote that it was "almost always excellent."[82] *The New Yorker* called it "one of the superb things of the movies" and that Freddie Bartholomew offered "one of the prettiest performances ever given on the screen by a youngster."[83] The film was made for just over $1 million dollars, grossing nearly $3 million worldwide.

Micawber (Fields) with young David Copperfield (Freddie Bartholomew) in the 1935 film adaptation of Charles Dickens's favorite novel. *David Copperfield* **(Metro-Goldwyn-Mayer, 1935).**

Literary works adapted by Hollywood in its golden age do not always age well. This is the case with *David Copperfield*. At the time of its original release, however, it was nominated for Best Picture of 1935; it lost to another MGM literary adaptation, *Mutiny on the Bounty*, starring Clark Gable and (oddly enough) Charles Laughton.

Fields was pleased with his role in the film, happy to have had the opportunity, and realized that such a prestigious film would only increase his star power. He enhanced his performance with bits of comic business, some of which did not make the final cut, but his role remains among the most popular in the movie. Indeed, it is the only reason it is remembered today.

By the end of 1934, Fields had completed starring roles in three features, a cameo appearance in another film, and the supporting role in *David Copperfield*. The Great Man was showing some signs of fatigue, but the fact that he was a rising box-office star in his mid-fifties kept him going. At least for now.

Mississippi

Production and Distribution: Paramount
Producer: Arthur Hornblow, Jr.
Director: A. Edward Sutherland
Screenplay: Francis Martin, Jack Cunningham, from a story by Booth Tarkington; adapted by Herbert Fields, Claude Binyon, and Dore Schary
Producer: Arthur Hornblow, Jr.
Camera: Charles Lang, Karl Struss
Editor: Chandler House
Release date: March 22, 1935
Running Time: 73 minutes
Cast: Bing Crosby (Tom Grayson), W. C. Fields (Commodore Jackson), Joan Bennett (Lucy), Queenie Smith (Alabam), Gail Patrick (Elvira), Claude Gillingwater (General Rumford), John Mijan (Major Patterson), Fred Kohler (Captain Blackie), Paul Hurst (Hefty), Theresa Maxwell Conover (Miss Markham), John Larkin (Rumbo), Libby Raylor (Lavina), Harry Cody (Abner), Stanley Andrews, King Baggot, Mahlon Hamilton, George Lloyd, Francis McDonald, Al Richmond, Eddie Sturgis (gamblers), Warner Richmond, Matthew Betz, Lew Kelly (men at bar), Jean Rouverol (Lucy's friend), Fred Toones (Leadsman), Dennis O'Keefe, Mabel Van Buren, Bill Harwood, Mary Ellen Brown (party guests), Ann Sheridan (schoolgirl), The Cabin Kids (The Inky Kids).

When W. C. Fields was first assigned to appear in *Mississippi*, the romantic lead was to be played by singer Lanny Ross. However, when Ross was replaced by Bing Crosby, Fields had to take second billing. Despite his having achieved great popularity, Fields was still not as big a star as Crosby, who had hit records and a popular radio show. In 1934, Crosby was instrumental in saving the record business. Jack Kapp, founder of Decca Records, wanted to lower the price of records from a dollar to 35¢, and negotiated with Crosby to take a royalty for records sold, instead of a flat fee. Crosby's popularity made this situation work on all levels, saving the recording industry; otherwise, by some estimations, the Great Depression could have wiped out phonograph records. Thus, Bing Crosby was a greater box-office draw than Fields.

Fortunately, the director was Eddie Sutherland, with whom Fields had worked in the silent movie days. While they had some friction years earlier, they were now friends. Fields was difficult on the set of *Mississippi*, but it does not show in his spot-on performance. And Sutherland, who understood the comedian's process, stood back and allowed him to ad-lib freely.

In his opening scene, Fields establishes his Commodore Jackson

One-sheet for *Mississippi* (Paramount, 1935). Fields was not pleased with taking second billing to Bing Crosby.

character as a blustery braggart who masks his cowardice with tales of his exploits as an Indian fighter. An exchange goes like this:

> SKEPTICAL PASSENGER: You're an Indian fighter?
> COMMODORE: My last encounter with the redskins was over thirty-five years ago. I whipped out my revolver—
> SKEPTIC: Revolvers weren't invented thirty-five years ago.
> COMMODORE: The Indians didn't know that. Doesn't matter, I threw it away. I had just swum the rapids with a canoe under one arm and a goat in the other.
> SKEPTIC: How could you swim with your arms full?
> COMMODORE: I had very strong legs.
> LADY PASSENGER: You must have been full of fire in your youth.
> COMMODORE: I had to carry fire insurance until I was forty.

The Commodore goes on to brag about being faced by an entire Indian tribe, and his having to pull out a knife and cut his way "through a wall of human flesh."

Crosby's character of Tom Grayson is branded a coward due to his pacifism. He backs down from fights and refuses duels purely on principle. As a result, his fiancée breaks off their engagement, but her younger sister makes her interest known. It is up to the Commodore to make Grayson appear braver once he hires the singer to perform on his ferryboat. He gives him a few tricks that had worked for him in the past, such as forcefully commanding someone to sit down. He also bills him as "The Singing Killer," and regales others with stories of the young man's fighting prowess. As a result, Grayson's reputation grows considerably.

The film, overall, is rather dull and ordinary. The Rodgers and Hart songs that Crosby performs are not suited to his style. They were specifically written for a singer like Lanny Ross, but not altered for Crosby. While Bing does what he can with the material, and the songs themselves are okay, they are far from memorable.

It is Fields who steals the movie, and his comic bits that sustain it. Along with his aforementioned dialogue sequences, one comic bit with only scant dialogue features the Commodore playing cards with a group of gun-wielding gamblers. When he draws five aces, he tries to throw a couple away, but picks up a couple more. Two men present four aces in their hand, and one shoots the other, accusing him of cheating. The Commodore claims a pair of deuces to avoid such a reaction.

This sequence was originally rather short, but Fields kept adding bits of business to extend it. He yells at someone, the other card players look in that direction, and he throws an ace behind his back as they do. Then he draws another ace, and does a comical double-take. He asks for a drink and places it on a card, causing it to stick to the bottom of the glass. He moves the glass away with the card stuck to the bottom, draws another, and reacts to yet another ace. This sequence allows Fields the opportunity to control the scene completely. It cuts from a medium shot of the card players, to a close-up of the card Fields draws, to a close-up of Fields' reaction. It is one of the comic highlights of the movie.

Fields has several routines that are simply woven into the fabric of the story. At one point he hears a pianist playing a tune and inquires as to its title.

> PIANIST: "Swanee River." It's brand new.
> COMMODORE: No good. It'll be forgotten in two weeks!

Fields then spends the remainder of the film occasionally humming it to himself.

Another great line deals with marriage. The Commodore insists, absurdly, that marriage is acceptable for a woman, but not a man. "Women are like elephants," he philosophizes. "I like to look at them, but I wouldn't want to own one."

Basically, *Mississippi* is a weak musical-drama that is bolstered by a delightful comic performance by W. C. Fields. When it was previewed, it was obvious that W. C. Fields handily stole the picture. Bing Crosby was so incensed at the second-billed actor walking away with his movie that he complained loudly to the Paramount brass. His demands included having some of the comedy cut from the film, and a few more songs added. Paramount complied, even asking Rodgers and Hart to compose another number and send a demo from the East Coast. Fields was disappointed at his scenes being cut and threatened to sing in his next movie just to get back at Crosby.

Crosby had not quite developed the cool, wisecracking style he exhibited in his later films opposite Bob Hope, and comes off as rather bland in a role that had been written for another actor and another singer. He was currently a major recording star and this parlayed into movie stardom that began in short subjects and grew rather quickly. At the time *Mississippi* was being filmed, in early 1935, Crosby was just coming off a year where he ranked as the number-one box-office star in movies. Crosby would continue to be so popular in movies that, based upon tickets sold, he remains, in the 21st century, the third-most popular movie star of all time (after Clark Gable and John Wayne). But at the time he made *Mississippi*, he was still figuring out how he could transition from a singer who acts into an actor who sings.

Some period critics were satisfied with *Mississippi*. The *New York*

Times stated, "Amid an atmosphere of magnolia, crinoline, and Kentucky whiskey, the boozy genius of Mr. Fields and the subterranean croon of Mr. Crosby strike a happy compromise."[84] *Motion Picture Herald* stated, "The film is a melodramatic and sometimes tense romance. Fields' comedy, in both dialogue and action, is good for its full quota of laughs."[85] However, the critic for *Variety* was disappointed: "Paramount obviously couldn't make up its mind what it wanted to do with the film; it's rambling and hokey. For a few minutes it's sheer farce; for a few moments it's romance. And it never jells.... Fields works hard throughout the film and saves it, giving it whatever entertainment value it has."[86]

While the individual music and comedy sequences are enjoyable, the tone of the entire film varies wildly and does not seem to know what it wants to be. The chemistry between the two stars is nonexistent.

Despite his misgivings about this project, W. C. Fields was enjoying the stardom his hard work had finally achieved, including his role in *David Copperfield*, a prestigious picture that received even more attention than his popular comedies. In fact, moviegoers were reporting that audiences were bursting into spontaneous applause when Fields appeared onscreen. This gave the comedian even more clout to negotiate his next project at Paramount.

Man on the Flying Trapeze

Production and Distribution: Paramount
Producer: William Le Baron
Director: Clyde Bruckman (Uncredited: W. C. Fields)
Screenplay: Jack Cunningham, Ray Harris, Bobby Vernon
(Uncredited: Clyde Bruckman, Roy Briant), from a story by Charles Bogle and
  Sam Hardy
(Uncredited: Jack Cunningham, Frank Griffin)
Camera: Alfred Gilks
Editor: Richard C. Currier
Released August 3, 1935
Running time: 66 minutes
Cast: W. C. Fields (Ambrose Wolfinger), Mary Brian (Hope Wolfinger), Kathleen Howard (Leona Wolfinger), Vera Lewis (Mrs. Cordelia Neselrode), Grady Sutton (Claude Neselrode), Lucien Littlefield (Mr. Peabody), Oscar Apfel (Malloy), Lew Kelly (Adolph Berg), Willie the Weasel (Tammany Young), Walter Brennan (Legs Garnett), Harry Ekezian (Mishabob), Tor Johnson (Tosoff), Arthur Ayelsworth (Judge), David Clyde (Wallaby), Carlotta Monti (secretary), James Burke, Edward Gargan (patrolmen), Helen Dickson (Miss Dickson), James Flavin (Henry), Sam Lufkin (ticket taker), Mickey McMasters (referee), Micahel Visaroff (man in jail cell),

Joe Sawyer (ambulance driver), Charles Morris (turnkey), Heinie Conklin (street cleaner).

For his next movie, Fields wanted to do a sound version of *Running Wild*, having been pleased with the success of other sound versions of his silent features. Paramount continued to be supportive of this process, delighted that past failures were being updated into current hits. Each new vehicle was a second chance for Fields to effectively present his comic ideas.

Man on the Flying Trapeze is a brilliant study in absurdity, right down to its incongruous title, based upon the popular 1867 song "The Daring Young Man on the Flying Trapeze." And while Paramount released a Popeye cartoon based upon the song a year earlier, the Fields film has nothing to do with a trapeze, a circus, or anything remotely connected with the tune. Fields simply liked the title. (In England, it was released as *The Memory Expert*).

Fields is Ambrose Wolfinger, a working man whose home life is a nightmare: his wife, Leona (Kathleen Howard), is constantly exasperated with him, and living with them are Leona's disapproving mother, Mrs. Neslerode (Vera Lewis), and her good-for-nothing son, Claude (Grady Sutton). Ambrose does, however, have a supportive and loving daughter—a product of his first marriage—prophetically named Hope (Mary Brian, reprising her role from *Running Wild*), who unfailingly stands up for her father against the surly members of the household.

The movie opens with Leona lying in bed, waiting for Ambrose to finish brushing his teeth. In fact, Ambrose is in the bathroom noisily running his toothbrush over the shelf of the medicine cabinet while sneakily taking a shot from a bottle of liquor he had stashed away. The parameters of the couple's relationship are immediately established by the wife's haughty manner ("will you *please* go to bed!") and Ambrose's sheepish "Yes, dear, right away, dear" response. Ambrose takes a maddeningly long time to get into bed. Already clad in his pajamas, he blows into each of his socks and carefully rolls them up, while Leona fumes. It is all delightfully off-kilter, and effectively introduces each character.

The absurdities continue when two burglars sneak into the basement with the intention of robbing the house. They happen upon Ambrose's applejack, partake in some, and are soon tipsily singing "On the Banks of the Wabash, Far Away." Leona awakens Ambrose with the absurd line, "There are burglars singing in our cellar!" He groggily responds, "What

Opposite: **Trade ad for** ***Man on the Flying Trapeze*** **(Paramount, 1935).**

Mary Brian and Fields on the set of *Man on the Flying Trapeze* (Paramount, 1935).

are they singing?" He takes his time putting his socks back on (putting two on one foot, and believing the other to be lost) while his wife continues to urge him to hurry. Meanwhile, Ambrose reacts to the hour of the night ("Couldn't they have robbed us later in the morning? … Maybe I could sleep for an hour and go down there") and comments on the burglars' lack of musical ability ("Oh, what awful voices"). He grabs a pistol, insisting it isn't loaded, but when he demonstrates, it fires a live round. Leona faints, prompting Ambrose to ask unconcernedly, "Did I *kill* ya?" The noise awakens Mrs. Neselrode, Claude, and Hope.

The ensemble is now onscreen, as is the family dynamic. Claude is a grown man, stocky and over six feet tall, but he is protected by his mother as though he were a child. When Ambrose asks him to assist in confronting the burglars, Mrs. Neselrode says to Claude, "I know you have the courage of a lion. But if you want your poor mother to die of a heart attack, you go in that basement." Claude assures her he will not. Hope, a diminutive young woman about five feet tall, offers to go instead, but Ambrose refuses. "Sure," Mrs. Neselrode says, "if it's your own family, it's a different story!"

The absurdity continues when a policeman, summoned to the scene, joins the would-be burglars in a drink, then in song. Ambrose trips and falls down the stairs, and joins them as well. He accompanies the police, and the burglars, to night court so he can testify against them. He ends up going to jail for making applejack without a license, while the burglars go free (they didn't actually steal anything). Hope drives down to the station and posts bail for her father.

The character of Ambrose is not like Harold in *It's a Gift* or Sam in *You're Telling Me*. Sam's wife is more put-upon and beleaguered than nagging. Harold's wife (also played by Kathleen Howard) is nagging, but Harold has his inventions, his friends, a means of escape into his own world. Ambrose is the ultimate sympathetic victim. He comes down to breakfast the following morning, after having had no sleep, and discovers all the food is gone except for some cold toast. Yet he works to support these people, as does Hope, while Claude is so lazy he takes a regular nap after breakfast. He is also a thief. He is seen stealing an expensive ringside ticket to a wrestling match from Ambrose's shirt pocket while the head of the house readies himself for a day at the office.

Although the emotional impact of the central character is significant here, the film never stops being a comedy. The breakfast table sequence has a certain poignancy, with Ambrose never getting any of the food his hard work pays for ("I've been eating cold toast for eight years. I've grown to like it). Mrs. Wolfinger, scanning the newspaper, reads a ridiculous rhyming poem aloud, insisting Ambrose pay attention. Meanwhile, he loudly crunches his burnt toast, drowning out what she says. When Claude proudly announces he "found" a ringside ticket to a wrestling match, Fields offers one of his wonderful double-takes. But when Ambrose searches in his jacket pocket for the ticket, his face falls as he realizes he's been robbed. The final definition of the character occurs in the very next scene when Hope and Ambrose are in the car, headed to work. Hope asks about the ticket to the wrestling match, calling Claude "a lazy, fat, overfed, monkey" to which Ambrose responds generously, "He isn't that fat."

The dialogue continues:

HOPE: I know you wouldn't have remarried if it wasn't for me.
AMBROSE: What are you talking about?
HOPE: When I was a little girl I overheard you saying to a friend that you never would have married if it wasn't that Hope needed a mother.
AMBROSE: Do me a favor. Never repeat that as long as you live. I must have been drinking.
HOPE: No, Dad. You weren't drinking.

Kathleen Howard and Fields pose for a shot on the set of *Man on the Flying Trapeze* (Paramount, 1935). Howard, a former opera singer, had great respect for her innovative co-star.

This exchange, only seconds long, is performed seriously, perfectly encapsulating the characters. The look on Fields' face is one of thoughtful sadness. It is quite moving.

With the family dynamic firmly established, Ambrose is then shown in the workplace, where he has control of his own situation as the firm's "memory expert." He keeps a large, sloppy pile of papers on his roll-top desk that is confusing to all but him. He remembers every client's dossier by heart, so whenever one visits, he is called into the office of the firm's president ahead of time to offer such details as family matters, so the president can be prepared to make a good impression on the client ("How is your son, the tennis pro?"). Wolfinger is an underling at work, but, at the very least, he is left to his own filing system and feels needed in a way he does not at home.

Ambrose, in order to get the day off to see the wrestling matches, indicates that his mother-in-law died from drinking "bad liquor." He gets the day off, but since he had his ticket stolen by Claude, he must stand in line to get a general-admission seat. Those sell out before he gets to the ticket window, so he tries to watch the match through an opening outside of the arena. However, when one wrestler tosses another out of the ring, he flies out the door, knocking Ambrose into the street. Claude sees him in the gutter and believes he is in a drunken stupor with his secretary, who is attending the matches separately and goes to Ambrose's aid once she sees him injured. Meanwhile, wreaths of flowers start arriving at the Wolfinger residence, along with cards and letters of condolence. An obituary even appears in the evening paper. Mrs. Wolfinger calls her husband's workplace to find out what is going on, and the firm's manager discovers Ambrose's ruse to get out of work. Ambrose is fired.

There are a couple of comic highlights in this film that need to be addressed. First, there is a brilliant scene in which Ambrose moves his car as a courtesy, but discovers himself to be in a No Parking zone. He is given a ticket by two different patrolmen, simultaneously. When he prepares to move his car, he discovers he is hemmed in, so he waits. While waiting, he gets *another* ticket from a *different* patrolman. The sheepish Ambrose is not forceful enough to convey that he is being repeatedly ticketed for the same offense. This scene dovetails into another, wherein one of the car's wheels gets away from him, causing him to run down the street after it. Ambrose is seen running down railroad tracks, barely avoiding oncoming locomotives. (The use of rather obvious rear-screen projection, a technique that had been introduced about the time that talkies arrived, was used to better effect in *The Fatal Glass of Beer*, when it was apparent that Fields was parodying the unevolved technology.)

The other highlight is at the Wolfinger residence, where Ambrose will soon accept responsibility for his misdeeds. Mrs. Wolfinger and Mrs. Neselrode are already upset over the steadily incoming flowers and tributes, along with the lie about the mother-in-law's sudden death from alcohol poisoning. Claude has come home and insists he saw Ambrose drunk and lying in the gutter with his secretary. Hope is waiting for her father to get home, wanting to hear *his* side of the story. When Ambrose returns, he tells the truth, indicating he is only guilty of taking the day off from work and using Mrs. Neselrode's death as an excuse. Claude argues back, Hope argues with him. Claude threatens to hit Hope. And Ambrose knocks out Claude.

This triumphant moment might be somewhat less comic than the denouement in *Running Wild*, but it is somehow more gratifying. Ambrose has taken abuse for a long time, and his genuine reaction is one of the film's many emotionally powerful moments. It dovetails into comedy when Ambrose also takes a wild swing at his elderly mother-in-law.

Ambrose is contacted by his firm at the new house that he has moved into with Hope, just as he is ready to go to the office and beg for his job back, at less pay. Hope answers the phone, hears that it is the firm, and, realizing she can negotiate better than her father, states that he is in the shower. Ambrose, sitting nearby, looks confused, and turns toward the bathroom. "*Who's* in the shower?" he keeps asking, while being shushed by his daughter. Hope realizes how desperate the firm is to get her father back, so she fibs that he has an offer from a rival firm. It is then that his old firm agrees to match the offer, also offering him four-weeks paid vacation every year.

The film ends with a gag. Ambrose wants to reconcile with his family. His wife is contrite, but her mother and brother maintain the same attitude. The last shot shows Ambrose, his wife, and Hope sitting in the front seat of his new car, with Claude and Mrs. Neselrode in the rumble seat. It starts to pour as they make their way down the road, all completely ignoring the fact that the two seated outside are being drenched.

Man on the Flying Trapeze is one of W. C. Fields' most serious comedies as well as his most introspective. Other studies and biographies have pointed out that Fields' own life was reflected in his characters. Claude represented his son, W. C. Fields, Jr., who went by the name of Claude. And although he was, at the time of this film, a thirty-two-year-old lawyer, Fields still looked upon him as a pampered mama's boy. The mother-in-law represented one aspect of Fields' wife, including such lines as "When I was a young and pretty girl, I vowed to my dear mother, lips that touched liquor would never touch mine." Hope symbolized the loving daughter Fields always wanted but never had. An amusing little in-joke is that Ambrose's secretary was played by Fields' real-life mistress Carlotta Monti. The reading she gives of her brief monologue is hilarious in its intensity.

Despite the pathos and underlying seriousness, the comedy continues throughout. Even in the scene where Ambrose is relating how his mother-in-law died, when his manager says, "It must be hard to lose your mother-in-law," Ambrose replies, "Practically impossible." As moving as this film can be, it balances with the comedy perfectly, which keeps the film moving at a good pace. Ambrose has his faults, of course, but he's automatically likeable because everyone else around him, with the exception of his daughter, is so much worse. And their behavior justifies his obvious disdain for them.

Clyde Bruckman, who had worked closely with Buster Keaton on some of his landmark silent comedies including *The General* (1927), and developed a strong reputation as a writer and director, was, by this time, a raging alcoholic. Since liquor flowed quite freely on a Fields set, it exacerbated Bruckman's problem. Fields liked Bruckman, having worked with him on the Sennett shorts, and had requested his services for this film. He was quite understanding and forgiving, but had to take over the direction reins himself. It was the only time Fields directed one of his own movies, and it is unfortunate we don't know which scenes he specifically shot; thus, we cannot properly assess his vision as a filmmaker. *Man on the Flying Trapeze*, however, maintains its aesthetic sense throughout.

The performances are exquisite, from seasoned character actors like Lucien Littlefield and Oscar Apfel, to the ensemble cast Fields personally chose to play his family. He was quite fond of Grady Sutton, having met him on the set of *The Pharmacist*. He asked that Sutton be cast in his movies whenever possible. Mary Brian lived across the street from Fields, and she was actually offered this part by his yelling to her from his front yard. Vera Lewis, as the mother-in-law, had been in films for twenty years by the time of this movie, and had made a name for herself in several roles as a judgmental fussbudget. Fields especially liked the fact that, off the set, she was the polar opposite of her screen persona—a warm, kind lady who laughed easily and enjoyed working with comedians. Kathleen Howard, who played Mrs. Wolfinger, entered films after a dozen years as an opera singer, and told the *Los Angeles Times* that the biggest challenge in working with Fields was not spoiling a take with laughter.

Critics of the time were mixed in their reception to the film, although not to its star. Andre Sennewald, in the *New York Times*, wrote:

> "Man on the Flying Trapeze," although it is marred by that cheapness of manufacture which we have come to expect in Mr. Fields' pictures, provides some of the richest humor that has reached the screen in months. If you are properly versed in the W. C. Fields tradition, you will know at once that the Charles Bogle who is credited with co-authorship of the story is really the modest star himself. The photoplay is less a connected narrative than a string of episodes describing a typical day in the life of Mr. Ambrose Wolfinger, a browbeaten husband and minor office worker. It is one of the faults of the film that some of the situations are dragged out past the saturation point, and there is a distinctly inappropriate scene in which Mr. Fields goes in slapstick pursuit of an automobile tire. But the comedy is frequently hilarious, and it always possesses those overtones of pathos and futility which we Fields idolaters recognize as his cynical comments on the world around him.[87]

It is worth mentioning that, in 1946, Andy Clyde made a two-reel comedy at Columbia entitled *Andy Plays Hookey*, which is essentially a remake of *Man on the Flying Trapeze*. By that time, Clyde Bruckman was working at Columbia and was notorious for lifting ideas from earlier films he had directed, even if he had no claim to the material. The car-parking sequence in *Man on the Flying Trapeze* can be found in the 1940 Buster Keaton Columbia short *Nothing but Pleasure*. Bruckman would later be sued by Harold Lloyd for stealing ideas from his older films, and would eventually be deemed unemployable. He committed suicide in 1955, leaving behind the note: "I have no money to pay for a funeral."[88] Keaton paid those final expenses.

When the filming of *Man on the Flying Trapeze* concluded in May of 1935, the stress of the production left Fields quite ill. He suffered from back trouble during much of the shoot, and had been eating and sleeping poorly. Having to take charge of so many aspects of the movie, from daily story conferences to assisting with the direction, as well as acting and having to be funny in nearly every scene, further weakened him. Once the film was "in the can," he retreated to a sanitarium to recuperate, but his emotions were attacked again when his friend Will Rogers was killed in a plane crash in August. Then, in October, Sam Hardy was stricken on the set of an Eddie Cantor film, and died. It was all too much for Fields, who remained unable to work for the rest of 1935, despite having signed a new contract with Paramount. That contract called for three films over a twelve-month period, beginning January 1, 1936. For this he would receive $100,000 per film and 10 percent of the gross receipts.

Fields spent most of his time lying in bed, staring at the ceiling, and worrying about lost time and money. This simply added more stress and didn't allow him to recover. Soon, the talk around Hollywood was that *Man on the Flying Trapeze* could very well be W. C. Fields' last film.

Poppy

Production and Distribution: Paramount
Executive Producer: William Le Baron
Associate Producer: Paul Jones
Director: A. Edward Sutherland
Screenplay: Waldemar Young and Virginia Van Upp, based upon the play by Dorothy Donnelly; contributions by Jack Cunningham and Bobby Vernon.
Camera: William C. Mellor
Editor: Stuart Heisler
Released June 19, 1936
Running time: 73 minutes
Cast: W. C. Fields (Eustace McGargle), Rochelle Hudson (Poppy), Richard

Cromwell (Billy Farnsworth), Catherine Doucet (Countess DePuizzi), Lynne Overman (Whiffen), Granville Bates (mayor), Maude Eburne (Sarah Tucker), Bill Wolfe (Egmont), Adrian Morris (Bowman), Rosalind Keith (Francis Parker), Ralph Remley (carnival manager), Tom Kennedy (hot dog vendor), Tammany Young (Joe), Helen Holmes (dowager), Malcolm Waite, Dick Rush, Doc Stone (deputies), Dewey Robinson (calliope man), Charles McMurphy (constable).

After being laid up for nine months, W. C. Fields felt ready to do another movie, but among the various ideas that had been considered, none seemed feasible for a man in his condition. The choice was to instead do a sound version of his first big stage success, having already been filmed as the silent feature *Sally of the Sawdust*. However, due to Fields' condition, *Poppy* is one remake that isn't quite as good as the original version.

W. C. Fields was in such poor health during the shooting of *Poppy* that he had to rely heavily on his stunt man, John Sinclair. There are long stretches in the film when his character in not onscreen at all. This had been the case with *Sally of the Sawdust*, but that was due to the director D. W. Griffith wanting to spotlight his protégée, Carol Dempster, who was in the title role. Director Sutherland had no interest in doing the same for Rochelle Hudson, the current Poppy, but did explain the problems filming W. C. Fields: "I don't think Willie was in 25 percent of this picture."[89]

Fields was so unsteady on his feet, especially during the initial weeks of shooting, that Sutherland lined up several people lying on either side of him out of camera range to catch him if he fell over. "We completed *Poppy* here, weeks behind schedule," Sutherland would recall. "But I shudder to think of how many weeks behind we might have been if Bill Fields had not insisted upon working day after day when he should have been home in bed."[90] During the filming of *Poppy*, Fields had his friend Tammany Young on the set helping him through the more difficult situations. Young also had a small part in the movie.

The opening of *Poppy* shows the title character along with her foster father, Eustace McGargle (Fields), sitting on a park bench, broke and hungry. Unlike *Sally of the Sawdust*, we get no establishing backstory in which Poppy's mother dies, but not before insisting that McGargle look out for her daughter's welfare. There are, however, some very funny bits in *Poppy*. One has McGargle going into a bar with a dog. Using ventriloquism, he makes it appear that the dog can talk. The bartender is flabbergasted and offers to buy the dog from him. McGargle reluctantly sells him, then throws his voice again to make the dog say, "Because you sold me, I will

Bill Wolfe (left), Fields and Catherine Doucet in *Poppy* (Paramount, 1936).

never speak another word." McGargle's parting words are, "He's a stubborn rascal; I'll bet he means it." The scene concludes with the bartender frantically yelling at the dog to "speak" as the canine yawns, completely ignoring him.

Another fun scene occurs once McGargle and Poppy join a carnival and begin selling an elixir for a dollar a bottle. A crowd of stereotypically slow-witted fairgoers are attracted by McGargle's spiel and one decides to ante up. He gives McGargle five dollars, expecting change. McGargle instead gives the man five bottles. The man protests. McGargle firmly states "No more!"

Fields' character is still the good guy protagonist of the narrative, despite being crooked in his approach to attaining any kind of success. McGargle also raises money with a classic shell game, where he hides a nut under one of three shells, then moves them around, asking customers to guess under which shell the nut can be found. McGargle dupes customers by sneaking the nuts into his hat. Later, when visited by dignitaries, including the mayor, he abruptly changes his tone and acts as though he is giving a sermon on the evils of gambling. But when he tips his hat, the nuts are revealed, stuck to his head.

It is the mayor's son with whom Poppy falls in love. The boy's parents do not consider the daughter of a carnival barker to be suitable marriage material, however. It then falls to McGargle, working in tandem with a lawyer, to change their minds by passing off his charge as a countess who is heir to a great fortune. The lawyer double-crosses McGargle, but a kindly woman, Sarah Tucker, points out the uncanny resemblance Poppy has to an actual countess, now reportedly deceased. In the end it is revealed that Poppy is indeed the rightful heir. She also learns that McGargle is not her real father (or "Pop," as she calls him), but that she was entrusted to his care upon her mother's passing. Poppy still intends to share her wealth with McGargle, who imparts the advice, "Never give a sucker an even break."

One writer for the *New York Times* was pretty unimpressed with *Poppy*, as the following attests:

> Other than as a pretext for William Claude's return, the Paramount's new film is painfully frail. "Poppy," as you probably have forgotten, was the occasion years ago of Mr. F.'s talking début on the stage [sic]; previously he had been a "dumb" act in vaudeville. Then it served as the basis for his film, "Sally of the Sawdust," made by D. W. Griffith. If this suggests that the tale is Homeric, be warned: it's as thin as a whisper.[91]

Poppy should have been quite an improvement over the silent version, especially with the addition of the aforementioned comedy bits that could only be done effectively with dialogue. But Fields' condition, the obvious use of a stuntman (especially during slapstick sequences, such as a fall he takes while playing croquet), a pretty far-fetched plot, and a supporting cast that wasn't as strong as in previous films, all added up to a movie that was, at best, average. Fields realized that his condition would also be a hindrance to the precise timing and coordination necessary for him to perform his juggling as well as he should, so there are no juggling sequences in *Poppy* as there had been in the stage and silent film versions.

One interesting standout in this movie was Bill Wolfe as the man bilked out of five dollars. Fields picked him out of a casting call, and his scrawny appearance, gaunt face, and his lack of proficiency with dialogue, appealed to the comedian's sense of the absurd. Wolfe would appear frequently in Fields' subsequent productions, in small "decorative" parts, where his odd appearance enhances the visual aspect of a scene.

Despite his wobbly condition during the filming of *Poppy*, Fields benefited from the experience. Rather than lying in bed, the activity of working on a movie, despite any limitations, was rejuvenating. Upon its completion, Fields felt better than he had in months. Sadly, as he started to recover, his dear friend Tammany Young, who was always at his side helping him out, died in his sleep at the age of forty-nine. A despondent Fields again stopped eating and sleeping. His condition rapidly became worse, and his back trouble once again flared up. He would be off the screen for the entirety of 1937.

Because of Fields' inability to work, Paramount stopped paying him. Fields realized he had to work somehow, and he looked into the possibility of doing something less taxing, where he could conserve his energy while attempting to recover. Even though he had always been rather dismissive of radio as a form of entertainment, his mind had recently been changed. While he was laid up, there was little else for him to do but listen to it. He discovered that he enjoyed the programs of old friends from the *Follies*, like Eddie Cantor and Fanny Brice, and thought that, even in his current condition, he could somehow work in this medium until he recovered well enough to return to movies. Fields got the word out that he was looking for opportunities on the airwaves.

The Big Broadcast of 1938

Production and Distribution: Paramount
Producer: Harlan Thompson
Director: Mitchell Leisen
Screenplay: Walter De Leon, Francis Martin, and Ken Englund (Uncredited: W. C. Fields, Patterson McNutt), based on a story by Fredrick Hazlitt Brennan; adapted by Howard Lindsay and Russel Crouse
Camera: Harry Fischbeck
Editor: Chandler House, Eda Warren
Songs:
"This Little Ripple Had Rhythm" (1937)
Music by Ralph Rainger
Performed by Shep Fields and His Rippling Rhythm Orchestra
"Don't Tell a Secret to a Rose" (1937)
Music by Ralph Rainger, Lyrics by Leo Robin
Sung by Tito Guízar
"Noche De Ronda" (1935), Written by Maria Teresa Lara
Sung by Tito Guízar
"You Took the Words Right Out of My Heart" (1937)
Music by Ralph Rainger, Lyrics Leo Robin
Sung by Dorothy Lamour
"Thanks for The Memory" (1937), Music by Ralph Rainger, Lyrics Leo Robin

Sung by Bob Hope and Shirley Ross
"Mama, That Moon Is Here Again" (1937), Music by Ralph Rainger, Lyrics
    Leo Robin
Arranged by Fletcher Henderson
Sung by Martha Raye
"The Waltz Lives On" (1937), Music by Ralph Rainger, Lyrics by Leo Robin
Performed by Shirley Ross, chorus, and dancers
"Charleston" (1925), Music by James P. Johnson. Lyrics by Cecil Mack
Performed by chorus and Ben Blue with dancers
"Truckin' (They're Going Hollywood in Harlem") (1935)
Written by Rube Bloom, Lyrics by Ted Koehler
Performed by Martha Raye and dancers
The cartoon sequence accompanying the "Rippling Rhythm" sequence was
    directed by Leon Schlesinger
Release date: February 11, 1938
Running time: 91 minutes
Cast: W. C. Fields (T. Frothingill "T. F." Bellows/S. B. Bellows), Martha Raye
    (Martha Bellows), Dorothy Lamour (Dorothy Wydnham), Shirley Ross
    (Cleo), Lynn Overman (Scoop), Bob Hope (Buzz), Ben Blue (Mike), Leif
    Erickson (Hayes), Patricia Wilder (Honey Chile), Grace Bradely (Grace
    Fielding), Rufe Davis (turnkey), Lionel Pape (Lord Droopy), Virginia Vale
    (Joan), Russell Hicks (Captain Stafford), Lorna Gray (divorcée) Irving
    Bacon (prisoner), Monte Blue (passenger), Shep Fields (bandleader),
    Bernard Punsly (caddy), Edgar Norton (T. F. Bellows's secretary), James
    Burtis, Sherry Hall, Jimmy Conlin (reporters), Lola Jensen, Evelyn Hard-
    ing, Louise Allen, Muriel Barr, Carol Adams, Marine Burton, Paula De
    Cardo, Eleanor Counts, Dorothy Dayton, Esther Pressman, Yvonne Duval,
    Nora Gale, Geraldine Fissette, Lola Jensen, Vivian Wilson, Colleen Ward,
    Ercelle Woods, Marion Weldon, Amzie Strickland, Suzanne Ridgeway,
    Katharine Snell, Alma Ross, Bobbie Sheehan, Eleanor Peterson (chorus
    girls).

Radio seemed a natural medium for W. C. Fields. His raspy voice, with its distinctive side-of-the-mouth delivery, was instantly recognizable to Americans who regularly went to the movies. And, in the 1930s, that included just about everyone.

Fields first appeared on radio for a special NBC program honoring Paramount's chairman of the board, Adolph Zukor, in January of 1937. He was not in attendance at the celebration, as he had to broadcast from his sickbed at home. However, subsequent discussion as to his interest in, and potential for, radio broadcasting did continue. For Fields to succeed in this medium, he had to invent a new character. His put-upon Everyman, although quite effective in sound movies, would not work as effectively in radio. He would need characters to play off, situations to work in, and exaggerate his already colorful personality.

Radio writer Dick Mack had recently been hired to write material for ventriloquist Edgar Bergen's wooden sidekick Charlie McCarthy. Bergen and McCarthy were wildly popular on the airwaves, despite the absurd notion of a ventriloquist performing on a non-visual medium. Mack concluded that Fields was a great reactive comic and could respond well to Charlie verbally. Intrigued by the prospect of playing off the wisecracking, tuxedo-clad McCarthy, Fields applied for membership in the American Federation of Radio Artists in March, and, by May, he was making his first appearance on *The Chase and Sanborn Hour* with such guests as Don Ameche, Dorothy Lamour, and the show's headliners, Bergen with McCarthy. Fields was the biggest star on the program, earning the highest salary. The idea of the comedian trading barbs with the quick-witted dummy worked. Listeners delighted in their silly repartee. Critics and columnists took notice as well.

Before May ended, NBC announced a radio contract with W. C. Fields for the next twenty weeks. The income was helpful, the work was something he could do without taxing his shaky health, and his appearances garnered huge ratings. By his second appearance on *The Chase and Sanborn Hour*, the program had eight million listeners, and the audience only continued to grow. The banter between W. C. and Charlie further enhanced Fields' reputation for loathing children. Fields drawled threats like "I'll take you piggy back on a buzz saw" and Charlie would ask, "are you eating a tomato or is that your nose?" And the audiences loved it. Soon, Fields was featured on the cover of radio magazines, while he and Charlie generated more revenue by appearing in ads for RCA.

The steady work was a tonic to Fields. His strength gradually increased, he gained back some of the weight he had lost (and then some), and his health slowly improved. Paramount wanted to capitalize on the fact that their star player was now performing for the largest audience of his career, and Fields believed he was well enough to make another movie. And while he had the starring role in *The Big Broadcast of 1938*, playing two parts, this musical-comedy was filled with a number of scenes in which he did not appear. Thus, it was less demanding for him than a tour de force like *It's a Gift*.

In *The Big Broadcast of 1938*, Fields portrays brothers S. B. and T. F. Bellows. T. F. has acquired a $40 million ocean liner, the S. S. *Gigantic*, and is about to race a smaller ship, the S. S. *Colossal*, from New York to Cherbourg, over a three-day period. T. F. arranges for S. B. to be a passenger on the *Colossal*, believing he will cause enough disruptions to

While recovering from a serious illness, Fields made successful appearances on radio, c. 1937.

hamper them in the race. After a golf game, S. B. is late, and arranges to be dropped off on the ship by plane. However, he ends up on the *Gigantic*, along with his daughter, who seems to be a victim of perpetual bad luck. Meanwhile, a radio personality, Buzz Fielding (Bob Hope, in his feature film debut), is hosting a live show from the *Gigantic*, with his ex-wives and girlfriends among the passengers. Hence, Fields' first movie after year's absence from films, during which he became a hit on the radio, is about a transatlantic broadcast.

While *The Big Broadcast of 1938* has a pleasant, breezy manner, it is a rather insubstantial film. It was not really an appropriate vehicle for Fields, and was made only to cash in on his radio popularity. While not technically a sequel, it was the last entry in an attempted series. There were "Big Broadcasts" released in 1935, '36, and '37—all were plotless musical-comedy revues featuring Paramount contract players. *The Big Broadcast of 1937*, for example, had starred Jack Benny, George Burns, and Gracie Allen, and was a hit for Paramount. *The Big Broadcast of 1938* was written with Benny, Burns, and Allen in mind, along with Martha Raye. Benny was replaced by Fields, Burns and Allen dropped out of the project during pre-production (Burns felt the script was too farcical), while Raye remained.

Fields performs a truncated variation on his golf game ("Stand clear and keep your eye on the ball!"), and has a few other scenes that are amusing, but the picture really belongs to Bob Hope. The thirty-four-year-old comedian is funny, affable, and truly stands out in a great musical number with Shirley Ross, "Thanks for the Memory," which would become his theme song. Until this time, Hope's screen career had consisted of a handful of lackluster short films. (About his first short, *Going Spanish*, he quipped, "When they catch Dillinger they're going to make him watch it twice.").[92] With his performance in *The Big Broadcast of 1938*, it was apparent that a career in feature films was just beginning.

Fields liked playing two different roles, but he realized there was little he could do with the material. He took his anger out on the director, Mitchell Leisen, who admitted that he did not find Fields at all funny. This tension resulted in clashes throughout the production until Fields was allowed his own unit, separate from the film's director. This did not bode well for the overall structure of the film. The stress on Leisen was so great that he suffered a heart attack shortly after production was completed.

Fields did get along well with Bob Hope, however, given the young comic's vaudeville training. Hope recalled that while he was sitting in Fields' dressing room, there was a knock at the door. Fields opened it to find a man asking for a charitable contribution. Fields stated that he only donated to the F. E. B. F., which stood for "Fuck Everybody but Fields."[93]

Critics generally complained that for a film heralding the return of

Fields (left), Shirley Ross and newcomer Bob Hope pose for a publicity still for the Paramount musical-comedy *The Big Broadcast of 1938*, the film that introduced Hope's theme song, "Thanks for the Memory."

W. C. Fields to the screen after a year's absence, it was unfortunate that he had so little to do. Bob Hope was often singled out as being the highlight, and nearly ever critic responded favorably to "Thanks for the Memory."

The Big Broadcast of 1938 turned out to be a box-office flop, and Fields was plagued by illness again shortly after its completion. Unfortunately, despite past successes, W. C. Fields came to be perceived as something of a liability. Also, many of the executives who had championed him were no longer at Paramount. Thus, he was let out of his contract.

Shortly after Paramount gave him the hook, Metro-Goldwyn-Mayer offered him the title role in *The Wizard of Oz*. He was pleased with the opportunity, having been a fan of the L. Frank Baum stories, and MGM planned a lavish production with color and music. An enthusiastic Fields began making notes as to how he would approach the character, and was planning to call a meeting with MGM representatives about the project. However, Fields also realized this would be a one-shot deal; there would be no longtime contract with MGM. He knew he needed to secure something steady in movies after shooting *The Wizard of Oz*. Reluctantly, Fields turned down the offer, and was replaced in the role by Frank Morgan.

Fields did not want to go "backwards" and perform onstage again. He was even looking toward the possibility of a career in television: the prospect of bringing visuals to his radio success intrigued him. But it would be more than a decade before TVs started to become a staple in American households.

Needing a studio to produce and distribute his myriad ideas, W. C. signed a contract with Universal studios. Once again proving the doctors wrong, The Great Man was about to appear in some of his best and most famous films.

You Can't Cheat an Honest Man

Production and Distribution: Universal
Producer: Lester Cowan
Director: George Marshall (Uncredited: Edward F. Cline, A. Edward Sedgwick)
Screenplay: Charles Bogle, Everett Freeman, Richard Mack, George Marion, Jr.
Camera: Milton R. Krasner
Editor: Otto Ludwig
Release date: February 17, 1939; rereleased: 1949 (Realart)
Running time: 79 minutes
Cast: W. C. Fields (Larson E. Whipsnade), Edgar Bergen (The Great Edgar),
    Constance Moore (Victoria Whipsnade), John Arledge (Phineas Whips-

nade), James Bush (Roger Bel-Goodie III), Eddie Anderson (Rochester), Thurston Hall (Mr. Bel-Goodie), Mary Forbes (Mrs. Bel-Goodie), Edward Brophy (Corbett), Arthur Hohl (Burr), Ivan Lebedeff (Ronnie), Jan Duggan (Mrs. Sludge), Grady Sutton (Chester), James C. Morton (judge), Walter Tetley (kid with candy cane), Evelyn Del Rio (crying girl with dog), Delmar Watson (boy with slingshot), Bill Wolfe (ticket buyer; World's Smallest Giant), Bill Worth (World's Largest Midget), Ernie Adams (Eddie), Irving Bacon (jailer), Charles Coleman (butler), Eddie Dunn (cop), Si Jenks (hillbilly), Byron Munson (ping pong player), George Offerman, Jr. (Western Union delivery man), Ralph Sanford (truck driver), Minerva Urecal (screaming lady), Ethelreda Leopold (girl at party), Blacaman, Princess Baba (themselves).

Universal was looking for more stars. The studio had scored during the early 1930s by launching a spate of classic horror films, featuring Dracula, the Frankenstein monster, the Mummy, and the Invisible Man. However, as the 1930s concluded, these series, though still popular, had been relegated to the B-movie level. By 1939, the studio's biggest moneymaker was young musical actress Deanna Durbin, whom they realized would eventually grow out of her roles as an effervescent teenager, and it could never be predicted if a younger star could effectively transition to adult roles.

When Fields signed his contract with Universal in August of 1938 he became the biggest star on the lot. He already had a story ready, and arrangements were made to use Edgar Bergen and Charlie McCarthy as co-stars in his first film for the studio. Production was set to start in October of 1938.

You Can't Cheat an Honest Man was a difficult shoot for all involved, mostly because Fields clashed at every turn with director George Marshall. Marshall was already a veteran director, having helmed Laurel and Hardy's feature *Pack Up Your Troubles* (1932), among many others. Stan Laurel, like Fields, had a specific way of working, and essentially directed himself. However, while Marshall was able to connect with Laurel, he did not respond as well to Fields. Part of the problem was that Fields was not interested in playing the Everyman whose comedy was based upon sympathy and reaction. He instead wanted to exploit his popular radio persona and use more joke-ridden dialogue. Marshall disagreed with this approach. It got to be such a problem that director Eddie Cline, a friend of Fields who had helmed *Million Dollar Legs*, was brought in to direct the scenes with Fields, while Marshall directed the sequences featuring the rest of the cast. Somehow, the movie still held together and remains among Fields' funniest.

Fields plays Larson E. Whipsnade, head of a traveling circus that always manages to stay one jump ahead of the sheriff. Whipsnade is presented as comically unscrupulous from the outset, whether he's throwing a lit match at a union rep who requests a light for his cigar, or shortchanging ticket buyers. The dialogue is delightfully sarcastic. When a patron complains "I'm short," Whipsnade retorts, "No need to feel bad about it, I'm only five-feet-eight myself!" When a woman passes the ticket window and complains to her date, "I won't walk another step," Whipsnade yells from the window, "Make him drag you lady, he got you drunk."

The quick-tempered and impulsive circus owner angrily throws a roll of tickets at a worker who calls him "Rib steak" instead of Whipsnade. The crowd starts diving for the tickets, while Whipsnade does a double-take, then hops onto the back of one of the men in the crowd to retrieve some of what he had tossed. His conning manner is exhibited early when he presents, at a side show, two regular-sized men, introducing them to the gullible circus-goers as "the World's Tallest Midget and the World's Shortest Giant." Adding to his own hype, he shouts, "They baffle science!"

Bergen and McCarthy represent one of the more popular acts of the circus, and because of their radio stardom, they get a lot of screen time with *and* without Fields. Bergen is not the most adept ventriloquist (his lips are constantly and obviously moving), although his timing in the changing of voices and maintaining different characters is still impressive. Another of his characters, a yokel by the name of Mortimer Snerd, makes occasional appearances in the film as well, and his voice is distinctly different from either Bergen's or McCarthy's.

The film is really a series of vignettes playing off the Fields character, the conflicts with McCarthy, and even some out-and-out slapstick scenes. What story there is involves Whipsnade's circus being deep in debt. Because of this, he is constantly having to outsmart process servers. When Whipsnade's attractive daughter, Vicki, learns that her father could go to jail, she agrees to enter into a loveless marriage to a rich society boy. In truth, the girl is in love with the more down-to-earth Edgar. The romantic scenes between the two are kept from being syrupy by Charlie's sardonic asides. The conflict occurs when Charlie wants to leave the circus, but Bergen wants to stay only because of Vicki (even to the point of duping Charlie by stating she has a little sister that he can date). They even make a joke about Bergen's limitations as a ventriloquist:

> VICKI: How do you talk without moving your lips?
> BERGEN: Well, now you're asking an awful lot.
> CHARLIE: And you're asking the wrong guy!

What is most entertaining about *You Can't Cheat an Honest Man* is that each scene creates a consistent thread based upon the characters. Sometimes there are opportunities to showcase actual performers (lion tamer Blacamon, for example, goes into the lions' cage when it is feared Charlie has been eaten by one of them). But, for the most part, the film is at its best when Fields is alone or trading barbs with McCarthy.

One memorable scene has Whipsnade showering by having an elephant spray him on command. Another has him in drag as Buffalo Bella, the female sharpshooter. At one point he is approached by a loudly crying girl who insists that an elephant stepped on her dog. To shut the girl up, he gives her money for another dog. A moment later, he sees the cunning child pick up her perfectly healthy dog from a hiding place. Caught trying to con the con man, she shrugs, "I guess he got better."

In an especially hilarious sequence, when Edgar feigns hiccups and claims he can't go on (he wants to secretly rendezvous with Vicki), Whipsnade takes his place by putting on a large fake mustache that covers his mouth and holding a large, grotesque puppet on his knee. He then does what can only be described as a pathetic ventriloquist act in which the dummy tells old jokes (including the one about the cat's tail being "fur to the end") and singing a tuneless old song. When Fields later discovers that his daughter has taken up with the not-so Great Edgar, he cuts the rope of a hot-air balloon, the basket of which is currently occupied by Bergen, McCarthy, and Snerd, causing them to float away, high in the sky.

The society party to announce the wedding of Vicki and the rich playboy is the climactic highlight. Of course, the society family does not realize she comes from common circus folk. This is disastrously revealed when Whipsnade, wearing an ostentatious cape with his name on it, arrives at the party and causes a series of disruptions. He is loud and crude. He plays an outrageous game of ping-pong with one of the party attendants. He tells a story about going big-game hunting while surrounded by snakes. Every time he mentions the word "snake," Vicki's mother screams and faints. Enraged at Whipsnade's presence, her stuffy fiancé asks his intended, "Why didn't you tell me your father was just—a—a—*person*?" In the end, Vicki ends up with Edgar.

Frank S. Nugent, of the *New York Times*, was underwhelmed by the movie:

> Charlie, possibly because the audience is on his side but more because Mr. Bergen makes him such a cute little tike, has all the best of the picture. At least, his material is as fresh as he is and appears to have survived editing and censoring with less damage. The Fields sequences, on the other hand, have a mutilated look. Several of

them are quite pointless; others, after a promising beginning, trail off into broad slapstick. It was all most disappointing.[94]

While *You Can't Cheat an Honest Man* is today considered among Fields' funniest, there is something to what reviewer Frank S. Nugent writes concerning the film's disjointedness. The aforementioned two directors had something to do with this, along with the fact that the movie is more loosely episodic and has less of a linear cohesion than the usual comedy feature. Originally, Fields had intended to have a scene where Whipsnade's wife, Madame Gorgeous, the star of the circus, passes away. He wanted to play a tender, dramatic scene, and have that event also be the catalyst to his company's lack of financial success. This scene was not used, and the film opens with Whipsnade already a widower. His refusal to pay his performers is now due, apparently, to his unscrupulous activity rather than the fact that he lost his wife and most popular performer. In other words, Whipsnade is not a sympathetic character.

Along with the radio-influenced conflict with Bergen and McCarthy, Fields draws from several standard themes associated with his films, such as the sympathetic daughter, the clashes among classes, the central character's sneakiness, and the troublesome characters who inconvenience him. Even these tried-and-true scenes were difficult to shoot. Fields would write scenes with his staff each day, based upon his original story, and then Edgar Bergen would come in with scenes he had written with his staff. Somehow, the two would blend their scenes and make them work. But while the conflict with Bergen and McCarthy was just an act, Fields' conflict with director George Marshall was quite real. Marshall did not find Fields at all funny, and balked at many scenes (including the wild ping-pong game during the engagement reception). Eddie Cline worked with Fields through his scenes, but also kept peace with Marshall so the film's scenes would not conflict. Marshall was still the supervisory director; Cline's unit was specifically brought in at Fields' demand.

Things became especially difficult regarding the story involving Whipsnade's wife. Fields wanted to play the bereaved husband whose wife is dying, and complained loudly when studio-hired screenwriters consistently left out that scene. When it became evident that it would never be shot, Fields walked off the picture. The Cline unit was dismissed, and Marshall finished the film by shooting around Fields and using a double. Producer Lester Cowan told studio head Cliff Work that, without this scene, Whipsnade comes off as a con man who lacks the impetus to give

Opposite: **One-sheet for** *You Can't Cheat an Honest Man* **(Universal, 1939).**

his grown children a better chance in life. One scene that ended on the cutting-room floor had Whipsnade pouring his heart out to the children in the end, explaining the reason behind his actions.

Fields became angry when he learned that the film was being completed without him, and requested a meeting with the producer, the studio head, and the director. The Universal executives were displeased that Fields had overstepped his authority, even beyond the level of creative control a movie star was allowed, causing the film to go over-budget.

You Can't Cheat an Honest Man, for all its problems, was a big hit for the studio. It broke the house record at the Rivoli Theatre in New York, and reports from theatre owners indicated that audiences "laughed themselves to tears."[95] As it stands today, *You Can't Cheat an Honest Man* is one of the defining W. C. Fields comedies, offering several noted elements of his character, a setting in which such a character can thrive, and aspects of his persona that later became legendary, including his feud with Charlie McCarthy.

Fields, of course, was not around to see how *You Can't Cheat an Honest Man* would survive the passage of time, but he was fully aware of its being a well-received moneymaker upon its initial release. Still, he was unhappy with the movie. He felt the film was essentially taken from him, and made without his vision or original concept.

A determined Fields told the top brass at Universal that he intended to write the screenplay for his next film, that it would be a vast improvement over its predecessor, and that it would make even more money. The executives wanted to please Fields, as he continued to be the most bankable star on the lot. Thus, he was allowed further provisions in his contract, including more creative control and the opportunity to choose his own directors. His friend Eddie Cline would helm his next three features.

My Little Chickadee

Production and Distribution: Universal
Producer: Lester Cowan (Uncredited: Jack J. Gross)
Director: Edward F. Cline
Screenplay: Mae West, W. C. Fields
Camera: Joseph A. Valentine
Editor: Edward Curtiss (Uncredited: Paul Landress)
Song: "Willie of the Valley," by Ben Oakland and Frank Skinner
Sung by Mae West
Release date: March 15, 1940; rereleased: 1948 (Realart)
Running time: 83 minutes
Editor: Edward Curtiss

Cast: Mae West (Flower Belle Lee), W. C. Fields (Cuthbert J. Twillie), Joseph Calleia (Jeff Badger), Dick Foran (Wayne Carter), Ruth Donnelly (Aunt Lou), Margaret Hamilton (Mrs. Gideon), Donald Meek (Amos Budge), Fuzzy Knight (Zeb), Willard Robertson (John), George Moran (Milton), Fay Adler (Mrs. Allen), Russell Hall (Candy), Otto Heimel (Coco), Anne Nagel (Ms. Foster), Otto Hoffman (Pete), Billy Benedict (Lem), Lane Chandler (porter), Bill Wolfe, Al Bridge, Bob Burns (bar patrons), Clyde Dembeck (boy on train), Jimmy Conlin ("Squawk" Mulligan), Addison Richards (judge), Delmar Watson, Jackie Searl (boys), Betty Roche (Salvation Army girl), Lloyd Ingraham, Walter McGrail, Joe Whitehead, Hank Bell, Robert McKenzie, Mark Anthony, Wade Boteler (townsmen) Lita Chevret (squaw), Bing Conley, Eddie Butler (henchmen).

On February 16, 1939, the Masquers Club held a testimonial dinner to commemorate W. C. Fields' fortieth year in show business. The sponsoring committee included Groucho Marx, Charlie Chaplin, Harold Lloyd, Jack Benny, Eddie Cantor, and Edgar Bergen. Each took a turn at the microphone roasting the comedian. Charlie McCarthy insisted, "I'm just here for the food."[96] Fields was delighted. One of the more significant occurrences at this event was the appearance of a witty anthropologist (and future scriptwriter and author) Dr. Leo Rosten, who said, "The only thing I can say about W. C. Fields, whom I have admired since the day he advanced upon Baby LeRoy with an icepick, is this "Anyone who hates babies and dogs can't be all bad."[97] This line, including a few variations, has often been attributed to Fields himself, when in fact it was said *about* him, but never said *by* him.

W. C. Fields was at the height of his career, an impressive accomplishment given all the setbacks and illness he had battled. Still dismayed by his previous movie, despite its box-office success, Fields was eager to begin production on a film in which he would co-star with Mae West. A longtime admirer of Mae West's work, Fields had written a screenplay he had titled "December and Mae." La West was, by 1939, no longer sought after in movies. Her pre–Code films had been hits for Paramount, but she had since been declared box-office poison. She considered going into independent production, but could not secure the requisite funds. It is because she had fallen upon somewhat desperate times that she agreed to co-star with W. C. Fields. But not until she made some changes to the script.

Those in charge at Universal were not terribly enthused with the screenplay, which they believed was a bit too genteel, but loved the idea of teaming West and Fields. West had not been in a film in two years and the studio knew they could acquire her services for less than they were

Fields and Mae West, the co-stars of *My Little Chickadee* (Universal, 1940).

paying Fields. They did feel, however, that her name was still strong enough to bring in her own contingent of fans.

Both Mae West and W. C. Fields were very much solo performers and not interested in teaming with anyone. And while Fields had often cited in the press that Mae West was his favorite actress, West was not one to give compliments to other performers. Be that as it may, she was grateful for the opportunity to be working in a movie again.

Fields' original screen treatment was turned over to screenwriter Grover Jones, but neither Fields nor West were interested in working from a prepared script by a studio screenwriter; both were accustomed to writing their own material. As it turned out, Mae West wrote most of the story directly involving her, while Fields wrote his solo scenes. They often ad-libbed during their relatively few scenes together, but that was the extent of their collaboration.

The completed film, titled *My Little Chickadee*, like its predecessor *You Can't Cheat an Honest Man*, is essentially a series of blackout routines, some involving West; others involving Fields. The story takes place in the American Old West of the 1880s. A masked bandit is not only terrorizing the town of Greasewood City, he is also romancing the town's visiting beauty, Flower Belle Lee (West, naturally), a singer from Chicago. West exudes the persona she had established onstage and in her early Paramount films. She remains completely unflappable, despite the occasional high level of danger. She does her nails while the train in which she is traveling is under attack by Indians, even as arrows whiz past her and stick into a nearby wall. As with most of her films, her character spends most of the time purring her dialogue and sashaying about in a flirtatious manner.

Cuthbert J. Twillie (Fields, naturally), a con man Flower Belle meets on the train which had brought her to this one-horse town, is caught off guard when Flower Belle agrees to marry him ("Can't we be lonesome together?" Twillie asks while wooing her). Having been driven out of a previous town due to her promiscuity, Flower Belle (who catches a glimpse of what she believes to be Twillie's satchel, stuffed with money) hopes their phony wedding (performed on the train by a gambler who looks like a minister), will give her some level of respectability in her temporary surroundings.

My Little Chickadee is as much a Mae West vehicle as it is a W. C. Fields film. One of Flower Belle's best scenes has her spending a day running the local school room. She effortlessly charms the ogling, overaged male students. When they whistle at her, she purrs, "There'll be no more of that," with a sly smirk that belies her objection. She looks over the sentences written on the blackboard, reading them aloud: "'I am a good boy,' 'I am a good man,' 'I am a good girl'—What is this, propaganda?"

Twillie is a delight as he dupes a gambler out of $100 in gold during a game of high card cut, and waxes nostalgic about his days as a bartender on the lower east side of New York. Jimmy Conlin, as fellow bartender "Squawk" Mulligan, is nearby. Twillie recalls one particularly rough encounter with a drunken female.

> TWILLIE: You remember the night I knocked Chicago Molly down?
> SQUAWK: *You* knocked her down? *I* was the one that knocked her down!
> TWILLIE: Yeah, but I was the one who started kicking her!
> [...]
> SQUAWK: She came back the next night and beat up the both of us.
> TWILLIE: Yeah, but she had another woman with her. An elderly woman with gray hair...

In another highlight, Twillie disguises himself (ineffectually) as the masked bandit and goes to Flower Belle's room, with sex on his mind. The screams from another woman as he attempts to make his escape result in his being arrested. Sentenced to be hanged, he is asked if he has any last requests, Twillie states, "Yes, I'd like to see Paris before I die." When it is obvious his request is outlandish, he concedes, "Philadelphia will do!"

Flower Belle clears Twillie's name and arranges for the real bandit to return his spoils to the town, not unlike Robin Hood. Learning the bandit's identity is that of the saloon owner, Flower Belle intends to leave town, also leaving behind an idealistic newspaper editor who has also fallen for her. Twillie leaves as well, off on another money-making venture of his own. He and Flower Belle part amicably, with Fields delivering West's classic line, "Come up and see me sometime." West replies, "Mmm, I will, my little chickadee," playfully mimicking her co-star's voice.

While Fields and West got along well enough during the creative process of preparing the script, the same cannot be said for Fields and producer Lester Cowan. Cowan, who had come to Fields' defense during the script changes for *You Can't Cheat an Honest Man*, insisted on using the script Grover Jones submitted. West liked that script as a basis, but planned to write her own material, which Fields encouraged. He and West agreed that she would get top billing as an actress and as a writer, while he would be allowed to choose their director. Fields wanted Eddie Sutherland, and West supported this because Sutherland had directed her most recent movie, *Every Day's a Holiday*. However, Sutherland was committed to another project. Fields then chose Eddie Cline, and West had no objection to working with him.

Fields did not like the script Jones submitted. He felt there were not enough opportunities for him or his co-star to use any of their routines. The dynamic between Fields and West, in which they each wrote their own scenes, was somewhat similar to the situation on *You Can't Cheat an Honest Man*, where Bergen and Fields had separate writing teams.

Unfortunately, once shooting began, the egos of the stars took hold and they didn't get along as well as they had during pre-production. Part of the problem was that Fields was now a major film star, and West no longer was. Once the highest paid actress on the Paramount lot, West was now making substantially less for *My Little Chickadee* than Fields. Thus, she began bolstering her contribution. While the movie was still in production, West told reporters that *she* wrote the script and all Fields did was make suggestions. She stated that despite his meager contribution, she generously allowed him to get screenwriting credit alongside her. Fields, justifiably offended, retaliated by describing West as "a plumber's version of Cleopatra."[98]

Despite their off-screen conflict, the two ex-vaudevillians demonstrated great chemistry onscreen. The problem with the movie overall is due to the fact that both of their characters are of dueling for screen time, so instead of having one hero to root for—like we would in a typical Fields film—we have two who are dividing the film's focus.

The film received mixed reviews upon its initial release, but the public enjoyed it. It was made for $625,000 and grossed over $2 million. The press favored Fields over West, indicating that her style of comedy was no longer relevant. As a result, Mae West came away from this project feeling with a feeling of contempt for both the film and her co-star. While he would speak well of her to the end of his days, West, who outlived Fields by over thirty years, was not so benevolent. She would continue to insist that *she* penned the actual script, would claim it was a project she had in the works, and that Fields was added later; she even said that the *only* scene he contributed was the sequence where he talks about Chicago Molly.

When W. C. Fields became an icon on college campuses during the late 1960s and early 1970s, West, still living at the time, would be asked about this movie more than any of her others, much to her chagrin. She would say that the movies W. C. Fields made were usually just B-movies, and it was her kindness that allowed him to appear in a top-flight project with her. Of course, this is patently false. Now, with both Fields and West long gone, if *My Little Chickadee* has retained any classic status in the 21st century, it is equally for her as it is for him. Both are somewhere near their best in this production.

At about the time that W. C. Fields completed work on *My Little Chickadee*, he engaged in an extracurricular project. He and writer Charles Rice collaborated on a book called *Fields for President*. It was not a big success, but Fields' ideas ("Instead of a New Deal, we will have a New Deck")[99] were amusing enough. It is now a collector's item.

While *My Little Chickadee* was enjoying great box-office success and *You Can't Cheat an Honest Man* continued to pull in moviegoers who were paying to see it for the second or third time, W. C. Fields began preparing what turned out to be one of the finest of his entire career. The *Bank Dick* would be among the films that would later serve to represent the screen work of W.C. Fields, and would also be his finest movie since *The Man on the Flying Trapeze*.

The Bank Dick

Production and Distribution: Universal
Executive Producer: Cliff Work

Associate Producer: Jack J. Gross
Director: Edward F. Cline
Collaborating Director: Ralph Cedar
Screenplay: Mahatma Kane Jeeves (Fields) (Uncredited: Richard Carroll)
Camera: Milton R. Krasner
Editor: Arthur Hilton
Release date: November 29, 1940; rereleased: 1949 (Realart)
Running time: 72 minutes
Cast: W. C. Fields (Egbert Sousé), Cora Witherspoon (Agatha Sousé), Una Merkel (Myrtle Sousé), Evelyn Del Rio (Elsie Mae Adele Brunch Sousé), Jessie Ralph (Mrs. Hermisillo Brunch), Grady Sutton (Og Oggilby), Franklin Pangborn (J. Pinkerton Snoopington), Shemp Howard (Joe), Dick Purcell (Mackley Q. Greene), Russell Hicks (J. Frothingham Waterbury), Pierre Watkin (Mr. Skinner), Al Hill (Filthy McNasty), George Moran (Cozy Cochran), Bill Wolfe (Otis), Jack Norton (A. Pismo Clam), Reed Hadley (Francois), Harlan Briggs (Doctor Stall), Bill Alston (Mr. Cheek), Nora Cecil (Lompoc Ladies Auxiliary member), Jan Duggan (mother in bank), Bobby Larson (boy in bank), Patsy Moran (lady with fruit hat), Margaret Seddon (old lady in car), Eddie Dunn (James), Billy Mitchell (black man withdrawing money), Fay Adler (secretary), Eddie Acuff (reporter).

Using the pseudonym Mahatma Kane Jeeves (a variation on the Broadway drawing-room play cliché "My hat, my cane, Jeeves!"),[100] Fields wrote the screenplay for his next feature, *The Bank Dick*. His recent box-office successes allowed him to ask for certain supporting actors whose work he admired. Since Fields wrote his scripts piecemeal, submitting only portions at a time, he felt he could effortlessly write in a role for any actor who joined the project, no matter how late he or she was signed.

One actor Fields reportedly wanted to cast as his son was Mickey Rooney, then the number-one box-office star in America. Although Fields had a good relationship with MGM, Louis B. Mayer wasn't about to lend Rooney to a rival studio, especially since Mayer had been grooming Rooney as the wholesome Andy Hardy, not as support for the nefarious character Fields would play. Fields assured Mayer that Rooney would be given the top billing befitting a star of his magnitude, and the teaming would really be no different than Rooney and Wallace Beery in MGM's own *Stablemates* (1938). Mayer still nixed the request.[101] Others Fields sought, including Ann Sothern and Gloria Jean, were also unavailable. However, he did manage to land Grady Sutton, Franklin Pangborn, Una Merkel, Evelyn Del Rio, and Shemp Howard.

In *The Bank Dick*, Fields is Egbert Sousé ("accent grave [sic] over the 'e'"), who barely tolerates his dysfunctional family and tries to get by on dreams and schemes. Unlike earlier Fields ensembles, the Sousé family (pronounced Su-say), of Lompoc, California, are not an average middle-class family with pretensions to a higher standard. Nor, for that matter, is Egbert an earnest, hard-working, sympathetic Everyman. He is, basically, a lazy guy who tries to get by with as little effort as possible. The family dynamic is familiar, albeit more cartoonish than in earlier films. There is a wife, a mother-in-law, and two daughters. Their hair is mussed, they wear drab flower-print dresses, and have a generally unkempt appearance.

In the opening scene, the family (minus the patriarch) sits, with sullen expressions, at a dining area table. Egbert's mother-in-law is in the process of slamming his character, describing him as someone who ekes out a meager living by entering slogan contests and has been robbing his youngest child's piggy bank, putting in IOUs. At this point, Sousé comes down the stairs, tries to hide the cigarette he is smoking, and forcefully takes his detective magazine from his youngest daughter, who kicks him. He hits her on the head with the rolled-up magazine. She bounces a ketchup bottle off his head. He goes out the door and comes back with a large potted plant that he fully intends to throw at the child.

This establishing scene effectively shows us the family dynamic. The long-suffering wife is sarcastic and disrespectful. The mother-in-law is cranky and judgmental. The youngest daughter is a brat. The oldest is aloof and self-involved; she is smitten with bank teller Og Oggilby ("Og Oggilby," her father muses. "Sounds like a bubble in a bathtub"). Grady Sutton plays Og, an amiable dumb ox who is eager to please those around him.

The early portion of *The Bank Dick* meanders a bit before it connects with a discernible narrative, but Fields apparently wants to further establish the Sousé character. An entire scene in Egbert's sanctuary—a bar called the Black Pussy Café, with the familiar face of Shemp Howard as bartender Joe—offers the following bit of dialogue:

> SOUSÉ: Was I in here last night and did I spend a twenty-dollar bill?
> JOE: Yeah!
> SOUSÉ: Oh, what a load off my mind! I thought I *lost* it.

Into the bar comes a harried studio rep who is supervising a production being filmed on a nearby location. The director is drunk, causing a delay in production. Egbert begins to brag that he once worked at the Mack Sennett studios, directing "Fatty Arbuckle, Charlie Chaplin, Buster Keaton, and the rest of 'em." A scene where Sousé attempts to take over direction of what is apparently a drawing-room drama is a study in absurdity. Sousé

Fields takes his job as security guard seriously, in *The Bank Dick* (Universal, 1940).

changes the narrative to "a circus picture," where the leading man "makes touchdown after touchdown."

The narrative finally begins when Sousé is relaxing on a park bench and reading a newspaper, just as Og is held up at the bank by two bandits. The crooks discover their car has been removed from a towing zone where they had hastily parked, and flee on foot. An argument between the two crooks ensues, one knocking out the other and throwing his gun away, hitting Sousé, who topples backward onto the other bandit. The cops arrive at the scene and Sousé is believed to have captured the crook after a tussle and recovered the bank's money. Considered a hero, he is given the position of security guard, or—"in the parlance of the underworld—a bank dick."

Within these narrative structures, Fields offers a series of hilarious sequences, each of which is organic to the story. For example, when Sousé returns home with the evening paper, featuring a front-page story on his supposed act of heroism, his wife, again at the dining table, summarily tosses the paper into the fireplace without looking at it. Then everyone takes a turn admonishing Sousé for helping the bank that holds the mortgage on their house. Sousé is given little respect outside of the home, and none within. So when he *does* get some positive attention for thwarting the robbery, he relishes it. Never revealing his actions as a mere set of accidental circumstances, he instead delights in signing autographs for neighborhood children, and entertains them with cigarette tricks (including sticking it in his ear and blowing out smoke through his mouth).

As the bank detective, Sousé takes his job quite seriously. He sees a little boy brandishing a toy pistol, and grabs him by the neck.

"Is that gun loaded?" he asks the boy's mother.

"No," she snaps. "But I think *you* are!"

When the child comments on Sousé's big nose, his mother replies, "I bet you'd like to have a nose like that full of nickels!"

As the mother and son take their leave, Egbert mutters under his breath, "I'll put him in the waste basket the next time he comes in here."

Another tangential plotline occurs when a Mr. Waterbury, representing something called the "beefsteak mines," talks Sousé into investing in some stocks. Consequently, Egbert convinces Og to "borrow" funds from the bank, to be returned when he gets paid in four days, which he would then give to Waterbury. In a case of bad timing, a prissy bank examiner, J. Pinkerton Snoopington (Franklin Pangborn) shows up to go over the books. The scenes with Snoopington are among the film's best moments. Sousé is determined to keep this fuddy-duddy from going over the books until Og can replace the money he took to pay for the beefsteak mines. He takes him to the Black Pussy after gently talking the teetotaler into having a drink. Sousé arranges with Joe to slip his guest a "Michael Finn," which results in Snoopington becoming "deathly ill." Sousé solicitously assists the inebriated bank examiner to the Lompoc Hotel, where a doctor friend of Sousé's admonishes the patient to remain in bed for four days (giving Og enough time to replace the money). Meanwhile, Sousé only exacerbates Snoopington's condition by offering to bring him everything from goulash and chili con carne to "a chocolate éclair with whipped cream." Each of these suggestions sends poor Snoopington running to the bathroom. However, the next day, Snoopington still shows up at the bank to work, stating, "I would travel to the tsetse-fly area of darkest Africa and brave sleeping sickness if there were books to be examined."

Fields' screenplay adds a great deal of comic tension to the proceedings, and has everything wrap up at about the same time. The beefsteak mines are declared a "bonanza" before Snoopington finishes examining the books, so the money is returned in time. The bandit who got away earlier in the movie returns to the bank to hold it up again, sticking a gun in Sousé's back and using him as a human shield. Sousé is also forced, at gunpoint, to drive a getaway car with the bandit in tow. Director Eddie Cline, recalling his silent comedy past, turns this sequence into a wild car chase. Sousé races down dirt paths, well off the main roads, driving over areas where workmen are digging, and forcing the following police cars and motorcycles to go over the same areas. Second unit director Ralph Ceder brilliantly choreographs the extras and doubles. Director Cline borrows some visuals from films he had done with Buster Keaton, especially the classic *Sherlock Jr.* (1924), when a motorcycle dips into a ditch and rides through as workmen come popping out. Sousé calmly offers asides to the bandit, pointing out interesting aspects of the area ("These are Catalpa trees") as if guiding a tour. When the frantic criminal demands the wheel, Sousé pulls it off and hands it to the bandit, saying, "It won't do you any good in that backseat." With a combination of fast-paced editing, dry dialogue, and frantic action, the chase is a perfect capper for *The Bank Dick*. By the time Sousé reaches a dead end where there is a body of water ("We'll have to swim from here"), the hapless criminal has passed out in the backseat. He is apprehended by police, the money is recovered, and just as they are about to leave the scene, the studio rep arrives and offers Sousé a contract to make movies. The studio heads, it seems, loved his ideas.

Sousé is now as a rich man, living in luxurious surroundings, with servants at his beck and call. The family members act as though they are aristocrats: they are sharply dressed, well-coiffed, and speak with affected accents. When the "Pater" leaves for work in the morning, they all kiss him goodbye. But just as Sousé gets out the door, he heads straight for the Black Pussy.

There are several elements that make *The Bank Dick* an exceptional film. It examines comic stereotypes with more depth than any of Fields' previous efforts. On full display are his prejudices against both the upper and lower classes. The bank president is a man of sober refinement, and when he goes to shake Sousé's hand, his "hearty handclasp" consists of his barely touching his fingers to Egbert's palm. The man selling the beefsteak mine is every bit the con man Sousé is, albeit even more successful in that he manages to con the con man. Small-town people are suspicious, business men and bankers are not trustworthy, families are critical and unsupportive. The people shooting a movie are inept and haughty. There is a

Lobby card for *The Bank Dick* (Universal, 1940), featuring Shemp Howard (left), Dick Purcell, Fields and Bill Wolfe.

persnickety women's club president, bumbling criminals, paranoid bank tellers, amiable fools. The only people with whom Sousé feels comfortable are his bartender and the patrons in the Black Pussy.

Speaking of that establishment's moniker, it was but one of many items in the script that came under fire from the censors, known as the Breen Office. Fields argued that his friend Leon Errol owned an establishment with that very name. The censors insisted it be changed to the Black Pussy *Cat* café. Fields complied to an extent. But whenever his character mentions the bar, he refers to it as the Black Pussy, not the Black Pussy Cat. Another line the censors nixed was, upon hearing Og Oggilby's name, Fields wanted Sousé to respond, "Sounds like bathtub flatulence." He changed it to "Sounds like a bubble in a bath tub," which is, arguably, funnier.

As with most of his productions, Fields didn't always stick to the script, even though the screenplay was his own. He continued to add things as he filmed, and members of the supporting cast commented that

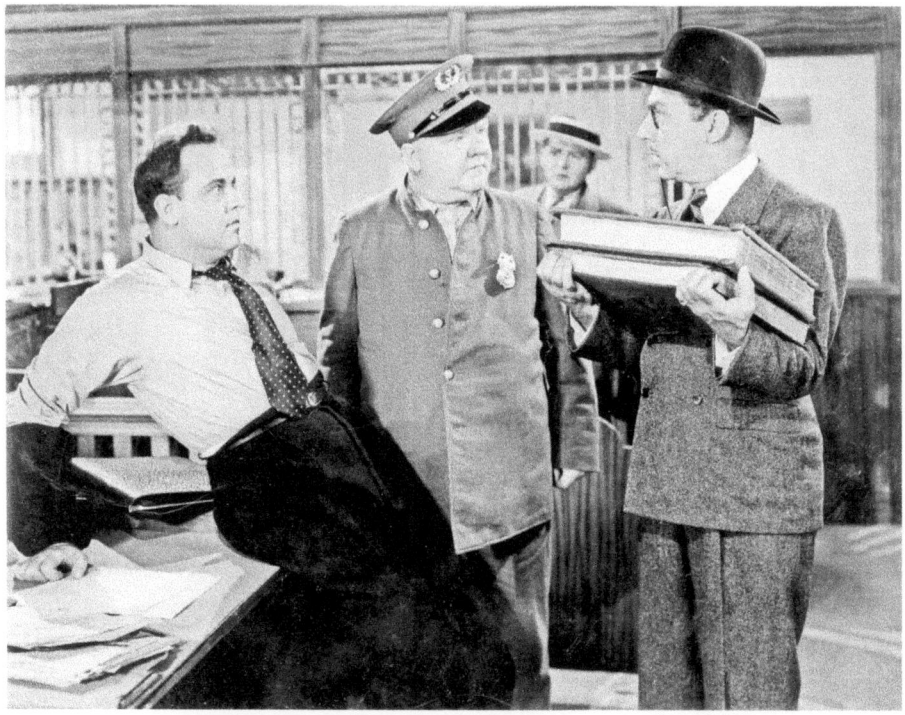

Grady Sutton (left), Fields and Franklin Pangborn in *The Bank Dick*.

they had trouble with their cues. Many of the actors, though—old pros like Franklin Pangborn and Shemp Howard—had comedy backgrounds and knew how to improvise. Some of Sousé's dry asides are quite funny. When Snoopington indicates he has an eighteen-year-old daughter, for instance, Sousé says amiably, "I'd like to meet her. I am very fond of children—girl children around eighteen to twenty."

Fields, now sixty, moved more slowly and worked shorter days, yet remained adept at physical comedy. When he believes a sickly Snoopington is safely tucked in bed at the hotel, he shows up at the bank, standing behind Sousé. When the bank president greets the bank examiner, Sousé screams, turns around, and bumps into Snoopington. Later, when a grateful Og discovers the beefsteak mines will net big money, he goes to hug Sousé, who jerks away comically, muttering, "Cut it out."

The Bank Dick owes at least some of its success to the stellar supporting cast. Fields knew when he had found someone with whom he felt comfortable working and insisted on their being involved in the production. Grady Sutton told Leonard Maltin in *Film Fan Monthly*:

I don't know who it was but the powers-that-be wanted this other guy [in the role of Og]. Fields said, "No, I want Grady. I like to work with him. I like the way he reacts to me." And they said, "No, we want so-in-so." He said, "All right then—get yourself another Fields." They had to hire me, but I didn't work out there again for three years or so, they were so mad at me.[102]

And Una Merkel, who played Egbert's daughter Myrtle, told Maltin, "Mr. Fields was just wonderful to me."[103]

The Bank Dick enjoyed good reviews from most of the leading critics. *Variety* offered the following:

> Story is credited to Mahatma Kane Jeeves, Fields' own humorous nom de plume. It's a deliberate rack on which to hang the varied Fieldsian comedic routines, many of them repeats from previous pictures but with enough new material inserted to overcome the antique gags. A wild auto ride down the mountainside for the climax is an old formula dating back to the Mack Sennett days, but director Edward Cline [and "collaborating director" Ralph Ceder] has refurbished the episode with new twists that make it a thrill-laugh dash of top proportions.[104]

Bosley Crowther, of the *New York Times*, loved it as well:

> With such a part to play around with, old Bill has the time of his life—growling, feinting, being official and forever preserving his flyblown dignity. No one who fancies madcap comedy can reasonably afford to miss the spectacle of Bill creeping up and pouncing upon a kid with a cap-pistol in the bank; or of Bill solicitously attending a bank examiner whom he has fed a "Michael Finn"; or of Bill at the wheel of the car in which a desperate bandit is attempting to escape. "The resale value of this car," says Bill from the corner of his mouth, "is going to be practically nil when we get through with this trip." In fact, for anyone who simply likes to laugh at the reckless manities of an inspired buffoon, we recommend *The Bank Dick*. It's great fun.[105]

Fields, however, was his own worst critic, and never seemed to believe that the finished product was as good as he had envisioned it. The more he saw the movie at various previews, the less enthusiastic he became. He tended to speak dismissively of the film, and this word-of-mouth spread. He pointed out how its comic competition included Chaplin's much-anticipated talkie debut *The Great Dictator*, and the Marx Brothers' latest, *Go West*.

Unfortunately, Fields did little to publicize *The Bank Dick*, which might have been a reason the film was not a box-office success. Reports indicate that it was popular the first few days, but moviegoer attendance fell off sharply after that. Universal executives believed that the public was simply growing tired of W. C. Fields films. The new influx of comedians like Bob Hope and Abbott and Costello were a generation younger and provided the sort of fast-paced rat-a-tat dialogue that probably made Fields' slow-moving methodical style seem dull by comparison. Even Laurel and Hardy, who left their longtime home at the Hal Roach studios to make movies at 20th Century-Fox in 1941, had to adapt their style to more contemporary sensibilities. But Laurel and Hardy were one old-guard act that continued to be very popular with moviegoers. Films like *Great Guns* (1941) and *The Big Noise* (1944) were big moneymakers for Fox and made the duo popular with new, younger audiences.[106]

Universal, however concerned they might have been, were not ready to release Fields from his contract just yet. Perhaps the box-office failure of *The Bank Dick* may have been just an aberration. Either way, he had just one more chance to prove himself.

Never Give a Sucker an Even Break

Production and Distribution: Universal
Director: Edward F. Cline
Associate Producer: Jack J. Gross
Screenplay: John T. Neville and Prescott Chaplin, from a story by Otis Criblecoblis (Fields)
Cinematographer: Charles Van Enger
Editor: Arthur Hilton
"Estrellita," (1912) Written by Manuel M. Ponce, Sung by Gloria Jean
"Hot Cha Cha," Written by Charles Previn, Sung by Gloria Jean
"Voices of Spring," (1882) Music by Johann Strauss, Sung by Gloria Jean
"Ochi Chyornye," Arranged from the Russian ballad by Harry Horlick, Gregory Stone
Sung by Gloria Jean
"Chickens Lay Eggs in Kansas," (unknown) Written and Sung by W. C. Fields
"Comin' Thru the Rye," Music (Traditional) Lyrics by Robert Burns
Sung by Susan Miller
Release date: October 10, 1941; rereleased: 1949 (Realart)
Running time: 71 minutes
Cast: W. C. Fields (himself), Gloria Jean (his niece), Leon Errol (his rival), Butch and Buddy / Billy Lenhart and Kenneth Brown (his hecklers), Margaret Dumont (Mrs. Hemoglobin), Susan Miller (Ouilotta Hemoglobin), Franklin Pangborn (Mr. Pangborn, the producer), Mona Barrie (Mrs. Pangborn), Charles Lang (engineer), Anne Nagel (Madame Gorgeous), Nell O' Day (salesgirl), Irving Bacon (soda jerk), Jody Gilbert (Tiny, a waitress), Minerva Urecal (cleaning woman), Dave Willock (Johnson), Jack "Tiny" Lipson (Huge Turk on plane), Claud Allister (Englishman on plane), Irene Coleman and Marcia Ralston (stewardesses), Kay Deslys (Mrs. Wilson, the woman on her way to the maternity hospital), Leon Belasco (studio pianist), Billy Wayne (studio foreman), Emil Van Horn (gorilla), Jack Roper (Joe), Bill Wolfe (man wanting a job in the movie).

W.C. Fields had offered several examples of the family dynamic in his films, examining various negative stereotypes with his central character as the put upon Everyman who wins in the end. Upon completing *The*

Bank Dick, Fields began writing a film that took issue with movie studio heads and his difficulty getting them to understand his offbeat comedy ideas. *Never Give a Sucker an Even Break* is perhaps his most offbeat idea of them all. Originally titled *The Great Man,* Fields casts himself, under his own name, in the title role as he brings a script to Esoteric Studios and attempts to sell the idea to a producer. He has a part earmarked for his niece, and has arranged for her to be rehearsing songs that she will sing in the production.

The film shows the producer reading Fields' script, and as he reads, we see what he is reading played before us. Every so often when things get too absurd, we cut back to the producer slamming the script on his desk and saying things to Fields like, "this is an insult to anyone's intelligence, even mine!" So the movie shows Fields, as himself, presenting his latest script to a producer, and the film that would be made from that script. It is all quite surreal in and of itself, but the details within make it even more outrageous. And, through it all, *Never Give a Sucker an Even Break* remains one of W.C. Fields' funniest and most remarkable screen achievements.

During the early part of the writing process, Fields' work on this project was interrupted by tragedy. While he was out doing some errands, the two year old son of his neighbor, actor Anthony Quinn, wandered into Fields' yard and was attracted by a toy sailboat Fields kept in a shallow pond on his property. He reportedly enjoyed relaxing in his back yard and watching the wind gently blow the toy boat across the pond. The child fell into the pond and drowned. This incident devastated Fields, who retreated into his home for several days and refused to communicate. He gradually returned to meeting with his writing staff and going back to working on the script, after the shock of the tragedy began to subside.

Once the script was completed, Universal responded to it in the same way as the fictional producer in the screenplay. They failed to understand its lack of a linear structure, its leisurely meandering from one scene to another, and its cutting back and forth between stories. Furthermore, the censors looked it over and took offense at one scene taking place in a bar, some of the double-entendres, et al. Fields tampered with the script a bit and eventually got approval. However, 1941 turned out to be an extremely busy year for Universal. There were several films being made at once, including popular horror movies, the new team of Abbott and Costello that had become a sensation, and other such activities. Director Eddie Cline told Fields that none of the studio executives were going to pay enough attention to their movie to make a difference, so they planned to shoot the script as Fields envisioned it.

Fields and Gloria Jean made a pleasant pair in *Never Give a Sucker an Even Break* (Universal, 1941).

Fields would be addressed by his own name onscreen. Actress Gloria Jean, whom he had wanted for *The Bank Dick*, was now available and would play his niece, also under her own name. The cast would be rounded out with such welcome veterans as Leon Errol, Margaret Dumont, Franklin Pangborn, and, on a far lesser level, a juvenile team known as Butch and Buddy (or "Buddy and Butch," as W. C. refers to them).

Gloria Jean represents Fields' idealized daughter figure, only in this case, she is cast as his niece. There is an even greater poignancy here than in earlier films. Gloria is younger than the usual girl playing his daughter, being only fifteen at the time of filming. And, at sixty-one, Fields is old and rather doddering, more along the lines of the girl's grandfather. His devastating illnesses over the past five years had truly taken their toll. His face and body are bloated, and his nose more bulbous than ever. The skin condition that he suffered from, rosacea with rhinophyma, had made his nose seem as big and red as it does when he is caricatured. In essence, he has become a living, breathing cartoon, albeit one with fast-diminishing energy. He began working fewer hours and shorter days as the shoot progressed.

The reason for Gloria being entrusted to the care of her uncle Bill is not made clear in the story. Gloria's mother, the performer Madame Gorgeous, appears in one brief scene early in the film. Once again, similar to what was planned for *You Can't Cheat an Honest Man*, the script had Madame Gorgeous die (with Fields playing the scene straight), and thereafter Gloria would be entrusted to Uncle Bill. Without that scene, the reasons behind this arrangement remain unknown. Regardless of this, Gloria looks up to Uncle Bill with warmth and affection, but she also tries to look after him, being aware of his penchant for imbibing.

Gloria Jean gets a lot of time to sing in this film, first being presented as rehearsing numbers, ostensibly for a film Fields has prepared as his next project. First rehearsing the fun, bouncy "Ha-Cha-Cha," because "that's the song Uncle Bill told me to sing," harried producer Franklin Pangborn instructs Gloria to instead rehearse a very long variation on the more serious "Voices of Spring." While these scenes had the potential for killing any comic momentum, director Eddie Cline creatively surrounds the sequence with workmen building a set, other acts rehearsing, and a host of distractions to enhance both the movement within the frame and adding a certain level of silliness. Dancers tap by and producer Pangborn, who starts to dance away with them, does a double-take, and then breaks free. Workers get in the way. A lift rises beneath Pangborn's feet and elevates him high above the set. It's all as crazy as it sounds.

Fields, on his way to the studio, stops to look at a large roadside ad for his latest movie, *The Bank Dick*. The obnoxious Butch and Buddy put down the movie, and Fields threatens them with a "kitten stocking" which he explains is a "a sock on the puss." A fruit vendor goes by hawking "raspberries," as his tire makes a flatulent noise. Fields reacts as if it is a comment on his movie.

This opening scene establishes that Fields is playing himself, and makes fun of how his films, specifically *The Bank Dick*, are perceived by members of the public. This provides a smooth transition in which he will be submitting another screenplay, and likely receiving the same negative reaction.

In preparation for his meeting, Fields stops for breakfast at a diner where, as he complains, "The flies get the best of everything." It is immediately evident that he is at odds with the waitress, Tiny, portrayed by heavyset comedienne Jody Gilbert, who specialized in playing wisecracking characters. Fields is continuously thwarted as he attempts to order. He asks about the steak, and Tiny crosses it off the menu with her pencil. He asks about pork chops, and Tiny crosses off several more items. Fields is left with little to choose from, but gamely orders:

Franklin Pangborn (left), Fields and Mona Barrie in *Never Give a Sucker an Even Break* (Universal, 1941), the Great Man's final starring film.

> FIELDS: Two four-minute eggs in a glass—
> TINY: Cup.
> FIELDS: Cup, yes. And some whole wheat—
> TINY : White.
> FIELDS : Yes, some white bread. And a cup of mocha java, with cream.
> TINY : Milk.
> FIELDS: Milk, yes, that's fine.

The banter continues as Fields eats. Tiny admonishes that he not be so free with his hands, indicating he once physically assaulted her. Fields responds, "Don't be so sensitive, honey. I was only trying to guess your weight!" She then responds, "There's something awfully big about you." Fields, sensing a compliment, starts to thank her, when she concludes, "Your *nose*." She then turns around, Fields looks at her backside and mutters, "There's something awfully big about you, too."

Fields depicts himself as basically friendly on the surface, but contemptuous of those around him. As he walks to get his hat upon finishing his meal, he passes a table where another diner makes a mild joke ("I was diagnosed with high blood pressure, but I lost my dough and had to give it up") that amuses the others at his table. "Very comical," Fields mutters sarcastically. (His comment is indicative of how Fields responds to what is accepted as humor by the general public, while his offbeat comic ideas are dismissed by that same element. The scene is brief, only seconds long, but makes its point effectively.) As he leaves the diner, he attempts to steal a new fedora off the hat rack, but is caught by Tiny. Forced to return the hat, he reluctantly settles for his familiar boater with the ripped lid.

This scene is followed by Fields' arrival at the studio and the meeting with Mr. Pangborn. As the producer reads the screenplay, the scenes are visualized. What we see is a surreal film-within-a-film, filled with wonderfully comic absurdities. The producer, who perceives the script to be merely illogical, periodically slams the script on his desk angrily protesting its unintelligible content.

One such sequence has Fields jumping from a plane in flight to retrieve a fallen bottle of liquor. Fields is seen falling through the air, catching the bottle as well as the cork, and recorking it while still plummeting to the ground. He miraculously lands on an outdoor cushioned couch on a mountaintop home. Borrowing from the slapstick visuals of his silent movie past, director Cline shows Fields bouncing several times as he lands, finally coming to a stop. He is met by a beautiful young woman who has never seen a man before. Fields asks the girl if she has ever played the game of squidgilum; she has not; the only game she ever played was beanbag. "Ah, beanbag, beanbag," he says knowingly. "I saw the championship played in Paris. Many people were killed." He then goes on to demonstrate squidgilum by asking the girl to close her eyes, raise her hands above her head, and pucker up. She does so, and Fields kisses her on the lips. She reacts to this unusual feeling, and prepares herself for Fields to do it again. At that moment, he offers a great double-take. Her beastly looking mother comes out, along with a Great Dane, sporting visible fangs (Fields dubs them Romulus and Remus). The woman, Mrs. Hemoglobin (Margaret Dumont), wants to join in the game. A horrified Fields escapes by jumping into a basket that plummets to the ground. This interesting visual shows movement on the right side of the screen where the mountain is, and a still background on the left side. This off-kilter visual only adds to the scene's surreal quality.

It is at this point that we cut back to Pangborn, slamming the script down and objecting to its absurdities:

> You drop from a plane ten thousand feet in the air and you land without a scratch. You play post-office with a beautiful blonde and then you throw yourself over a cliff in a basket. It is impossible, inconceivable, and incomprehensible. And besides that, it's no good!

While Pangborn plays it for comic effect ("Do you think I'm a dope?—*And don't you answer that!*"), the objection to Fields' offbeat vision is as interesting as the surrealism of the story he is presenting. The things Pangborn lists as "impossible" are, in fact, possible, since we have just witnessed them.

After his tirade, Pangborn then asks, "What's happened to Gloria Jean?" It just so happens that she is featured in the screenplay's next sequence. The girl is seen waiting at the airport when she gets a call on a nearby payphone from her uncle. Upon hearing his voice, she shouts, "Uncle Bill!" and starts looking up at the sky (a neat comic touch likely added by director Cline). Fields indicates he is in a Russian village and instructs her to go there. While in the village, Fields hears that Mrs. Hemoglobin had taken her infant daughter to live on the mountaintop when she was betrayed by her husband. She vowed that her daughter would never see or hear the word "man" as long as she lived. But he also discovers she is extremely wealthy, so he returns with Gloria Jean, Butch and Buddy, and a complete wedding outfit, in an attempt to marry the woman. He is followed by rival Leon Errol, who overhears the same information and gets there first. A younger man joins them, his designs being on the pretty daughter.

The level of absurdity here is delightful. The very concept of a woman existing on top of a mountain with only a basket to access food, clothing, etc., is completely outrageous. How are Butch and Buddy suddenly in this area and part of the wedding party Fields hastily assembles? If this woman hates men, why is she immediately attracted to Fields? And to Leon Errol as well? None of these questions truly matter because the film's lack of continuity and structure is precisely the point, and precisely why producer Pangborn is reacting as he does. However, by this time, it has gotten to be too much. He is so upset that he attempts to tear the script in half, but cannot. He then kicks Fields out of his office and says, "*Go!* Get a drink! Get a *dozen* drinks!" alluding to the comedian's penchant for imbibing on the job. The producer, who now has no intention of greenlighting the film, is past caring how drunk Fields might get.

Fields is next seen in an ice cream parlor, where he orders a "double chocolate soda." He looks straight into the camera, smiles, and says, "This scene was supposed to be in a saloon, but the censor cut it out." He wasn't kidding.

Learning that her uncle had been let go by the studio, Gloria Jean angrily walks off the lot. The two decide to leave town together. While she is in a store to buy some necessities, Fields waits in his car. Within earshot, a heavyset woman loudly states that she must deliver clothes to a maternity hospital and then catch a flight. Fields, overhearing this, assumes she is about to go into labor. He offers her a ride, she accepts, and he races down the street, through heavy traffic. The shocked woman faints, and Fields fears that time is running out, so he pushes the gas pedal all the way to the floor and darts through heavy traffic.

Fields had originally planned this scene to be used in *It's a Gift* but it disrupted the flow of the narrative so the idea was jettisoned. It is resurrected for *Never Give a Sucker an Even Break* where it doesn't fit in any better, but that works out more effectively for a movie the purposefully has no linear structure and is constructed in such a haphazard manner.

The chase—once again supervised by second-unit director Ralph Ceder—is outrageous and hilarious. Motorcycle cops spin out of control. A traffic cop gets caught on Fields' car door as he races down the street, and ends up hanging from his collar from a bus as the two vehicles pass each other. Motorists are endangered, and a fire-engine ladder connects to the roof of Fields' car, with the fireman in back stuck between the two vehicles as they race down the street. The shots, the stunts, and the editing are all tightly paced, making this conclusion the highlight of the entire feature. When Fields finally crashes into the hospital, his car totaled, he triumphantly leaves the auto as the woman is brought in on a stretcher. She wakes up in the hospital, and starts shoving her way out, confusing the attending nurses. Meanwhile, Gloria Jean catches up to Fields in a cab, looks directly at the camera, in close-up, and says, "My Uncle Bill. But I still love him."

Gloria Jean enjoyed her experience working on this film, and liked Fields, even though she admits he was quiet and distant on the set. She said Franklin Pangborn was very kind and friendly toward her, assuring her that Fields adored her and that anything negative she heard about him was untrue. As Gloria recalled for her biographers, Scott and Jan MacGillivray:

> My dialogue was cut and dried, but every day it changed. You never knew [what your new lines would be]. You memorized stuff, but they said, "Forget it, W. C. wants it this way." He was notorious for never sticking to the script. He did say to me, "Now listen, dear, you're going to have to go along with me in these scenes, because I may not say what you read in the script. But you go ahead and say what you have to say. I won't throw you." And he didn't throw me, because he'd look at me a certain way and I knew exactly how to come back. I kind of stuck to Pangborn because he clued me in on a lot of things and we'd laugh together.[107]

Gloria recalls Fields entertaining her by doing some juggling on the set between takes, and she was also invited to his home, which is something he rarely did with other actors. Fields was quite fond of Gloria's mother, who was on the set as a chaperone, because she was a former circus performer and shared Fields' dry sense of humor.

There were scenes that were shot and later discarded, such as a shooting gallery sequence in a carnival scene featuring Fields, Gloria Jean, and Leon Errol. Stills of that scene still exist, as do photos of the scene in which Madame Gorgeous dies.

Somehow the disparate elements of *Never Give a Sucker an Even Break* all come together with enough cohesion to make it a satisfying viewing experience. But Universal was displeased with the finished product, audiences were confused, and, despite some critical acclaim, the movie was a box-office flop. It was considered by the studio to be so unimportant that they put it out as the second feature on a double bill with the Alfred Hitchcock drama *Suspicion*.

With the dismal response to his last two films, and the comedian's declining health causing filming delays, Universal decided not to renew Fields' contract. His starring days were over forever.

The Final Years: 1942–1946

Despite being without a home studio, Fields did have an immediate job upon completing *Never Give a Sucker an Even Break*. Producer Boris Morros, perhaps best known for producing the Laurel and Hardy feature *The Flying Deuces* (1939), was a longtime fan and wanted Fields for an episodic all-star project he was preparing at 20th Century–Fox. The story would concern a tuxedo that is handed off from person to person; each segment of the film would be devoted to a different wearer. One would be Professor Diogenes Pothlewhistle (Fields), a temperance lecturer. W. C. indicated that he would have to complete his current project first, asked for $25,000 per week with a guarantee of one week's work, and also demanded creative control over the script pertaining to his episode. Morros agreed, and Fields began filming the nine-minute "Sequence E," directed by Malcolm St. Clair, for *Tales of Manhattan* in January of 1942. Phil Silvers, who appeared in the segment as a used clothing salesman, recalled:

> The scene was intended to be a piece of whimsy or irony, preferably both. We placed wallets, stuffed with paper, in a pocket of shabby coats; the customers, feeling a wallet, would quickly buy the coat just to get the wallet. The store had a trick mirror that transformed the tawdry tailcoat on Fields into a new costume. To film this illusion, the movement of Fields, savoring the new tails in the mirror, had to exactly match the movement of Fields seeing himself in the old coat, so that it could be superimposed. But Fields, who was in his dotage, never made the same gesture twice; he was always improving. This was a very difficult bit of business, even if you were cold sober. Fields' valet encouraged him every day with a thermos bottle of lemonade. And every day the producers appeared on the set to plead with Fields: "Please don't drink while we're shooting—we're way behind schedule. After this is over, we'll take you on the biggest binge of your life—you can drink all week!" Fields merely raised an eyebrow. "Gentlemen, that is only lemonade. For a little acid condition affecting me." He leaned on me. "Would you be kind enough to taste this, sir?" I

took a careful sip. Pure gin. I answered the producers a little scornfully, "It's lemonade!"[108]

Fields, wearing the storied tailcoat, proceeded to give a lecture on the benefits of coconut milk to a group of gullible society people (including Margaret Dumont). The milk has been spiked ahead of time.

In an episodic movie that contained interconnecting stories featuring such top stars as Edward G. Robinson, Veronica Lake, and Charles Laughton, a decision was made to cut the Fields sequence from the release. It was not seen until 1996, when the sequence was restored to the movie for its video release.

Fields was then back at Universal to do his pool table bit in another all-star movie, *Follow the Boys*, made for the war effort. Although he had performed it in earlier films, it is impressive that, even as his health continued to fail, he retained the dexterity necessary to perform what was already embraced as a classic routine.

Fields (left) and Bill Wolfe (right) in the all-star military revue, *Follow the Boys* (Universal, 1944).

The Final Years: 1942–1946

Fields next did a cameo in Charles Rogers's production *Song of the Open Road*, in which singing ingénue Jane Powell plays a pampered celebrity who runs away from her studio and joins a youth corps to enjoy some freedom. In the setting of a California orange grove, Fields has some rather watered-down exchanges with Edgar Bergen and Charlie McCarthy (and even Charlie McCarthy, Jr.). Later, seated alone, W. C. painfully attempts an over-the-shoulder juggling move with an orange. "This used to be my business," he mutters to no one in particular. "But it isn't anymore."

W. C. Fields' final appearance before a movie camera was in *Sensations of 1945* for Andrew Stone Productions, in which he was to revive his "Caledonian Express" routine from vaudeville. However, once Fields arrived on the set, it was clear he wasn't up to doing such a scene. He spoiled several takes, making it a frustrating experience for the cast and the director. Finally, the scene had to be scrapped. Fields indicated he would do whatever was necessary to remain in the movie, so the producers instead hired the acrobatic comedy team of Fritz and Jean Hubert and had Fields appear in the background, muttering asides.

Fields remained active on the radio, which was physically less taxing, and the three movies he did all came out around the same time. His image was continually caricatured in cartoons, and his likeness was also utilized in advertising. When there was no work in 1945, Fields considered writing his memoirs. Some of the notes and materials he collected were later gathered by his grandson and released in book form as *W. C. Fields by Himself* in 1973.

In the summer of 1946, Fields was hired to put a couple of his monologues on record: "The Day I Drank a Glass of Water" and "The Temperance Lecture." Fields reported to the garage studio of legendary electric guitarist Les Paul, who recalled to James Curtis:

> I was making my first multiple recording. I was expecting Fields, but I was busy recording in my garage. All of a sudden from behind me he says, "That sounds great, Les." I said, "Bill, you're not supposed to hear this." And he said, "You sound like an octopus." So when I invented the multitrack tape recorded, I called it The Octopus. [Fields] sat out on the swing [in the backyard] and we talked about it. I said, "We're making something new, and you're the first person to hear it. It's a multitrack recording." So he says to me, "It reminds me of when I was in vaudeville. I used to play the banjo." I never knew he played the banjo.[109]

Fields recorded both routines, with Paul providing background musical accompaniment. The session took a total of around three hours, and everyone was satisfied. James Curtis writes in his biography of Fields:

When Fields exited the garage studio that day, after witnessing the birth of multi-track recording, a career spanning forty-eight years in most every facet of show business was over. He had given his final performance.[110]

Although Fields' health had been steadily on the decline since *Never Give a Sucker an Even Break*, he had kept fairly active and continued to accept offers. He agreed to appear with Bing Crosby on a radio show that was set for December 22, 1946. Fields was ill, but was determined to do the show, and for weeks Crosby touted the appearance. However, Fields' health worsened and by the date of the show he was bedridden. Mickey Rooney agreed to take Fields' place. The public was told that Fields' appearance was merely postponed. But three days later, on Christmas Day 1946, William Claude Fields died at the age of sixty-six.

There is a story, perhaps apocryphal, that, throughout his career, Fields had always spoken negatively about Charlie Chaplin, because Chaplin was always hailed as the number-one comedian in movies; Fields would never match Chaplin's level of fame during his lifetime. When word got out among Hollywood insiders that Fields was in serious condition, he received telegrams from virtually every luminary in show business. One of the telegrams he received was from Charlie Chaplin. It read: "You were always number one to me, Bill."[111]

The W. C. Fields Legacy

After Fields' death, his estate was fought over by his mistress, Carlotta Monti, as well as Fields' widow (they never divorced), his son, other family members, etc. It was quite a mess and remained in the courts for years.

In the late 1960s—a quarter of a century after the comedian's passing—a renaissance occurred. By 1969, W. C. Fields films were a standard fixture on college campuses, his image was used in cartoon form to sell Fritos corn chips, and he was once again a part of popular culture. His name and image were known by a new generation.

Before the advent of home video, however, it was quite difficult to access Fields' films. Although some of his more popular films were rereleased to theatres, and his Paramount sound films were later shown on television (usually late, late at night, and interrupted by countless local car commercials), it was difficult to see the Great Man when you wanted to. Fortunately, this was about to change—but it would be a slow process.

In 1946, Universal studios president Nate Blumberg created a new division of the company called United World Films, which dealt with producing and distributing entertainment, educational, and religious subjects for the nontheatrical market on 8mm and 16mm film. They bought a controlling interest in the home-movie distributor Castle Films and began releasing some of their Walter Lantz cartoons. The cartoons would be offered in complete nine-minute versions, black and white or color, in sound or silent, depending on what type of projector the buyer owned. Abridged four-minute 8mm silent versions were also available.

In 1948, Castle Films began to offer highlights from Abbott and Costello comedies, which were retitled and issued as one-reel short subjects. For instance, a chase scene from their feature *Ride 'em Cowboy* (1941), was issued as *No Indians, Please!* Neither Bud Abbott nor Lou Costello was aware of this practice at first. But, when Lou Costello discovered that his and Abbott's films were being issued in truncated form, under different titles, without their permission or any form of compensation, the duo sued Universal and won a $2 million settlement, as well as a percentage of any Castle Films short in which they appeared. The popularity of these home-movie edits was so profitable that the studio paid Abbott and Costello off and struck a deal rather than halting production of the short subjects.

Due to the popularity of these comedies, Castle Films began issuing scenes from the W. C. Fields films in the one-reel format. In the fall of 1949, the chase scene from *The Bank Dick* was released as *The Great Chase*. A year later, the chase scene from *Never Give a Sucker an Even Break* came out as *Hurry, Hurry!* Some isolated scenes from *You Can't Cheat an Honest Man* were issued as *Circus Slicker*.[112]

In the era of streaming complete movies in high definition, it is perhaps difficult to understand how exciting the early days of home movies were for the collector. It was a thrill to have a star like W. C. Fields projected on a screen in your living room. Films like *The Great Chase* or *Hurry, Hurry!* were essentially visual, so the less expensive silent versions played just as well. It was affordable to have a home theatre during a time when something like home video was far into the future.

By the 1960s, Castle Films expanded to offer the new Super 8mm format, and also acquired the right to use clips from the Fields Paramount films. So, the juggling scene from *The Old Fashioned Way* became the one-reel abridgement *The Great McGonigle*. *It's a Gift* actually resulted in two single-reel excerpts: the grocery store scenes became known as *The Big Thumb*; the Bissonette family's trek out west was *California Bound*. As late as the 1970s, Castle Films was coming out with new Fields entries. His "road hog" segment in *If I Had a Million* came out in 1971, under that original title. The golfing scene from *You're Telling Me* was issued in 1976 as *Much Ado About Golf*.

In 1977, Castle Films became Universal 8, and the company expanded, as did the home movie market. Now they released longer, twenty-minute digest versions of their films, under their original titles, and did away with the retitled one-reel shorts. Rather than create a new twenty-minute edit, Universal simply took the two *It's a Gift* highlights—*The Big Thumb* and *California Bound*—spliced them together and issued them under the film's original title. However, when Universal 8 issued a digest print of *Never Give a Sucker an Even Break*, it abruptly ended with Fields in the ice cream parlor. It contains none of the car chase footage that Castle Films had issued as *Hurry, Hurry!*

Trade ad for the first Castle Films release featuring W. C. Fields, *The Great Chase*, which included the climactic chase scene from *The Bank Dick* (Universal, 1940).

By 1980, a rise in the cost of silver (used for black-and-white film processing) made home movie releases too expensive to produce. Also, by the end of the 1970s, VHS and Beta tapes containing entire full-length features started were being marketed. At the end of the 1980s, videotape had only grown in popularity, driving the prices down, and soon a full-length feature could be had for less than a Super 8mm digest print once cost.

The W. C. Fields features began coming out on VHS tapes in the 1980s and '90s. Due to their public domain status, poor transfers of *The Golf Specialist, The Dentist, The Pharmacist, The Barber Shop*, and *The Fatal Glass of Beer* were available throughout the 1980s. However, by the end of the decade, a handful of the features were readily available on tape, including a few of the silents, *Sally of the Sawdust, It's the Old Army Game,* and *Running Wild*.

VHS was eventually eclipsed by the DVD. In 2004, the *W. C. Comedy Collection Volume One* came out in an attractively packaged, affordable box set, containing *International House, It's a Gift, You Can't Cheat an Honest Man, My Little Chickadee,* and *The Bank Dick*. In 2007, a second volume came along, including *The Old Fashioned Way, Poppy, You're Telling Me, Man on the Flying Trapeze,* and *Never Give a Sucker an Even Break*. By the mid–2010s, *If I Had a Million, Tillie and Gus,* and *Mississippi* came out as video-on-demand releases, as did the once obscure *Her Majesty, Love*. On the 2000 Criterion DVD release *6 Short Films with W. C. Fields*, one can find beautifully restored, high-definition transfers of the four Sennett shorts, *The Golf Specialist*, and even *Pool Sharks*.

In June of 2015, W. C. Fields' grandchildren Harriet and Ronald hosted a centennial event at the New Amsterdam in Los Angeles to commemorate the 100th anniversary of Fields' film career. In September of that year, Harriet co-hosted a marathon of W. C. Fields films on the Turner Classic Movies channel. Although these films no longer enjoy the trendy popularity they once had among college students, and younger people may not be aware of who he is, Fields remains a cinematic icon to his fans.

In the 21st century, the Fields films are more accessible than ever before. Many of these films are as fresh and hilarious as they were when they were first released. After a century in the public eye, W. C. Fields remains among the most creative, challenging, and talented comedians of all time.

Notes

1. Roger Ebert, "Great Movies," rogerebert.com, December 10, 2000.
2. David Pierce, *The Survival of American Silent Feature Films: 1912-1929* (Washington, D.C.: Library of Congress, 2013).
3. "Big Stars for Mutual Program," *Reel Life* (September 1915).
4. "His Lordship's Dilemma," *Moving Picture World* (October 3, 1915).
5. "Janice Meredith," *Film Daily* (August 7, 1924).
6. "Sally of the Sawdust" review, *Photoplay* (September 1925).
7. "Sally of the Sawdust" review, *Picture Play Magazine* (September 1925).
8. "W. C. Fields Interview," *Motion Picture Magazine* (August 1926).
9. "That Royle Girl," *Photoplay* (March 1926).
10. "That Royle Girl," *Motion Picture Magazine* (April 1926).
11. "W. C. Fields Signs with Paramount," *Motion Picture News* (December 19, 1925).
12. W. C. Fields Interview, *Motion Picture News*, January 1926.
13. In many studies, Louise Brooks's character is referred to as Mildred Marshall. However, in the print screened for this study, a title card introduces her as Marilyn Sheridan.
14. "Studio Life by Mickey Bennett," *Motion Picture* (July 1926).
15. Louise Brooks, *Lulu in Hollywood* (New York: Knopf, 1982).
16. "It's the Old Army Game," *Film Daily* (July 12, 1926).
17. "It's the Old Army Game," *Motion Picture Classic* (July 1926).
18. "It's the Old Army Game," *Moving Picture World* (July 1926).
19. "So's Your Old Man," *Motion Picture News* (March 1926).
20. "So's Your Old Man," *Film Daily* (November 9, 1926).
21. "So's Your Old Man," *Exhibitors World* (January 21, 1928).
22. "The Potters," *New York Times*, January 18, 1927.
23. "The Potters," *Motion Picture News* (February 4, 1927).
24. "W. C. Fields Signs with Paramount," *Motion Picture News* (March 1927).
25. "Running Wild," *Motion Picture News* (June 24, 1927).
26. "Running Wild" *Picture Play* (September 1927).
27. "Two Flaming Youths," *Exhibitors Herald* (January 1928).
28. Ibid.
29. James Curtis, *W. C. Fields: A Biography* (New York: Random House, 2003), p. 204.
30. "Limit on Footage Set for 'Tillie' remake," *Film Daily* (January 4, 1928).

31. "Tillie's Punctured Romance," Paramount publicity release, January 1928.
32. "Tillie's Punctured Romance," *Exhibitors Herald* (October 1928).
33. "Tillie's Punctured Romance" review, *Motion Picture News* (September 29, 1928).
34. "Fools for Luck," *New York Times*, June 12, 1928.
35. "Fools for Luck," *Exhibitors Herald* (October 1928).
36. "Topekans Off Fields and 'Fools' Hits Bottom," *Variety* (June 27, 1928).
37. "The Golf Specialist," *Motion Picture News* (July 5, 1930).
38. "The Golf Specalist," *Variety* (August 6, 1930).
39. "Her Majesty, Love," *Motion Picture Herald* (November 14, 1931).
40. "Million Dollar Legs," *Hollywood Filmograph* (June 25, 1932).
41. "Million Dollar Legs" review, *New York Times*, July 9, 1932.
42. Michael Wilmington, "Million Dollar Legs' rates critic Kael's high opinion," *Chicago Tribune*, February 10, 2006.
43. Paramount Publix Corporation was the company's actual name from 1930–1933. This was due to the importance to the studio of the Publix Theatre exchange in New York City. Paramount Publix officially went bankrupt in 1935, due to overexpansion by the studio's president, Adolph Zukor. In 1936, in his new capacity as chairman of the board, Zukor reorganized the company as Paramount Pictures.
44. www.davemanuel.com (accessed September 20, 2016).
45. Lou Jacobs, "If I Had a Million" review, *Hollywood Filmograph*, December 10, 1933.
46. Brent Walker, *Mack Sennett's Fun Factory* (Jefferson, NC: McFarland, 2010), p. 215.
47. "The Dentist," *Hollywood Filmograph* (December 3, 1932).
48. "The Dentist," *Motion Picture Herald* (December 3, 1932).
49. The re-release included background music to some scenes.
50. "The Dentist," *Motion Picture Herald*, December 16, 1933.
51. Donald Deschner, *The Films of W. C. Fields* (New York: Citadel Press, 1966).
52. Ibid.
53. *Motion Picture Herald*, July 8 1933.
54. "Fatal Glass of Beer" review, *Variety*, June 20, 1933.
55. Walker, *Mack Sennett's Fun Factory*, p. 216.
56. "The Pharmacist" review, *Film Daily*, April 24, 1933.
57. Curtis, *W. C. Fields: A Biography*, p. 267.
58. *Variety*, 8/15/33.
59. "The Barber Shop" review, *Variety*, 8/15/33.
60. "International House," *Motion Picture Herald*, November 7, 1933.
61. "International House," *New York Times*, May 27, 1933.
62. Simon Louvish, *Man on the Flying Trapeze: The Life and Times of W. C. Fields* (New York: W. W. Norton, 1999).
63. Mordaunt Hall "Tillie and Gus" review, *New York Times*, November 13, 1933.
64. "Tillie and Gus," *Motion Picture Herald* (February 17, 1934).
65. Curtis, *W. C. Fields: A Biography*, p. 278.
66. "The Laugh Team Speaks Up!" *Screenland*, August 1934.
67. Ibid.
68. Author's interview with Buster Crabbe, 1980.
69. "You're Telling Me," *Motion Picture Herald*, October 13, 1934.

70. "Just a Loveable Old So-and-So," *Film Weekly* (December 7, 1934).
71. Ibid.
72. "The Old Fashioned Way," *Screenland* (August 1934).
73. William Drew, *At the Center of the Frame: Leading Ladies of the Twenties and Thirties* (New York: Vestal Press, 2000).
74. Curtis, *W. C. Fields: A Biography*, p. 296.
75. Ibid.
76. "Mrs. Wiggs of the Cabbage Patch," *New York Times*, October 29, 1934.
77. "Mrs. Wiggs of the Cabbage Patch," *Motion Picture Herald* (March 16, 1935).
78. W. C. Fields papers, Los Angeles, CA.
79. Curtis, *W. C. Fields, A Biography*, p. 307.
80. "It's a Gift," *Motion Picture Herald* (June 16, 1935).
81. "It's a Gift," *New York Times*, January 5, 1935.
82. "David Copperfield," *Variety* (January 22, 1935).
83. "David Copperfield," *The New Yorker*, January 26, 1935.
84. "Missisippi" review, *New York Times*, April 18, 1935.
85. "Mississippi" review, *Motion Picture Herald* (March 30, 1935).
86. "Mississipi" review, *Variety* (March 27, 1933).
87. "Man on the Flying Trapeze," *New York Times*, August 3, 1935.
88. Ted Okuda and Edward Watz, *The Columbia Comedy Shorts* (Jefferson, NC: McFarland, 1998) p. 204.
89. "W. C. Fields Laughs at Death," *Hollywood* (August 1936).
90. Ibid.
91. "Poppy" review, *New York Times*, June 18, 1936.
92. James L. Neibaur, *The Bob Hope Films* (Jefferson, NC: McFarland, 2005), p. 10.
93. Ibid., p. 14.
94. Frank S. Nugent, "You Can't Cheat an Honest Man" review, *New York Times*, February 20, 1939.
95. "What The Picture Did For Me" column.
96. Curtis, *W. C. Fields: A Biography*, 393.
97. *Time* magazine, February 27, 1939; Curtis, *W. C. Fields: A Biography*, 392.
98. Original source unknown, but this line is ubiquitous in books of quotations.
99. W. C. Fields, *Fields for President* (New York: Dodd, Mean & Co., 1940).
100. Curtis, *W. C. Fields: A Biography*, 393.
101. Author interview with Mickey Rooney.
102. Leonard Maltin interview with Grady Sutton, *Film Fan Monthly* (October 1969).
103. Leonard Maltin interview with Una Merkel, *Film Fan Monthly* (January 1971).
104. "The Bank Dick" review, *Variety* (November 30, 1940).
105. Bosley Crowther, "The Bank Dick" review, *New York Times*, December 13, 1940.
106. Scott MacGillivray, *Laurel and Hardy: From the Forties Forward* (New York: Vestal Press, 1998).
107. Scott and Jan MacGillivray, *Gloria Jean: A Little Bit of Heaven* (Lincoln, NE: iUniverse, 2005), p. 64.

108. Phil Silvers, *This Laugh Is on Me* (New York: Prentice-Hall, 1973), p. 116.
109. Curtis, *W. C. Fields: A Biography*, p. 476.
110. Ibid., p. 477.
111. This is one of those stories that's been going around for years. No source is known.
112. Scott MacGillivary, *Castle Films: A Hobbyist's Guide* (Lincoln, NE: 2004).

Bibliography

Books

Agee, James. *Agree on Film.* Boston: Beacon Press, 1958.
Allen, Steve. *The Funny Men.* New York: Simon & Schuster, 1956.
Bergman, Andrew. *We're in the Money: Depression America and Its Films.* New York: New York University Press, 1971.
Brooks, Louise. *Lulu in Hollywood.* New York: Knopf, 1982.
Curtis, James. *W. C. Fields: A Biography.* New York: Random House, 2003.
Deschner, Donald. *The Films of W. C. Fields.* New York: Citadel Press, 1966.
Drew, William. At the Center of the Frame: Leding Ladies of the Twenties and Thirties. New York: Vestal Press, 2000.
Durgnat, Raymond. *The Crazy Mirror.* London: Faber & Faber, 1970.
Eames, John Douglas. *The Paramount Story.* New York: Crown, 1985.
Everson, William K. *The Art of W. C. Fields.* New York: Bobbs-Merrill, 1967.
Fields, Ronald J. *W. C. Fields: A Life on Film.* New York: St. Martin's Press, 1984.
Fields, W. C. *W. C. Fields by Himself: His Intended Autobiography.* Englewood Cliffs, NJ: Prentice-Hall, 1973.
_____. *Fields for President.* New York: Dodd, Mead & Co., 1940.
Gehring, Wes. *W. C. Fields: A Bio-Bibliography.* Westport, CT: Greenwood Press, 1984.
Hirschorn, Clive. *The Universal Story.* New York: Crown, 1983.
Knight, Arthur. *The Liveliest Art.* New York: Macmillan, 1957.
Louvish, Simon. *Man on the Flying Trapeze: The Life and Times of W. C. Fields.* New York: W. W. Norton, 1999.
Maltin, Leonard. *The Great Movie Comedians.* New York: Crown, 1978.
_____. *The Great Movie Shorts.* New York: Crown, 1972.
Massa, Steve. *Lame Brains and Lunatics.* Atlanta, GA: BearManor Media, 2013.
Mast, Gerald. *The Comic Mind.* Indianapolis, IN: Bobbs-Merrill, 1973.
McCaffrey, Donald. *The Golden Age of Sound Comedy.* New Jersey: A. S. Barnes, 1973.
MacGillivray, Scott. *Castle Films: A Hobbyist's Guide.* Lincoln, NE: iUniverse, 2004.
MacGillivray, Scott, and Jan MacGillivray. *Gloria Jean: A Little Bit of Heaven.* Lincoln, NE: iUniverse, 2005.
Monti, Carlotta, with Cy Rice. *W. C. Fields and Me.* NJ: Prentice-Hall, 1971.
Neibaur, James L. *The Bob Hope Films.* Jefferson, NC: McFarland, 2004.
Rocks, David T. *W. C. Fields: An Annotated Guide: Chronology, Bibliographies,*

Discography, Filmographies, Press Books, Cigarette Cards, Film Clips and Impersonators. Jefferson, NC: McFarland, 1993.
Sennett, Mack, with Cameron Shipp. *King of Comedy.* New York: Doubleday, 1954.
Shipman, David. *The Great Movie Stars: The Golden Years.* New York: Bonanza, 1970.
Silvers, Phil. *This Laugh is On Me.* New York: Prentice-Hall, 1973.
Stumpf, Charles. *ZaSu Pitts: The Life and Career.* Jefferson, NC: McFarland, 2010.
Taylor, Robert Louis. *W. C. Fields: His Follies and Fortunes.* Garden City, NY: Doubleday, 1949.
Walker, Brent. *Mack Sennett's Fun Factory: A History and Filmography of His Studio and His Keystone and Mack Sennett Comedies, with Biographies of Players and Personnel.* Jefferson, NC: McFarland, 2010.

Articles

"Big Stars for Mutual Program." *Reel Life,* September 1915.
"Just a Loveable Old So-and-So." *Film Weekly,* December 7, 1934.
"The Laugh Team Speaks Up!" *Screenland,* August 1934.
"Limit on Footage set for 'Tillie' remake." *Film Daily,* January 4, 1928.
"Studio Life by Mickey Bennett." *Motion Picture,* July 1926.
"Topeka Off Fields and 'Fools' Hits Bottom." *Variety,* June 27, 1928.
"W. C. Fields Interview." *Motion Picture Magazine,* August 1926.
"W. C. Fields Laughed at Death." *Hollywood,* August 1936.
"W. C. Fields Signs with Paramount." *Motion Picture News,* March 1927.

Reviews

"The Bank Dick." *Variety,* November 30, 1940.
"The Dentist." *Hollywood Filmograph,* December 3, 1932.
"The Dentist." *Motion Picture Herald,* December 3, 1932.
"Fools for Luck." *New York Times,* June 12, 1928.
"Fools for Luck." *Exhibitors Herald,* October 1928.
"The Golf Specialist." *Motion Picture News,* July 5, 1930.
"The Golf Specialist." *Variety,* August 6, 1930.
"His Lordship's Dilemma." *Moving Picture World,* October 3, 1915.
"If I Had a Million." *Hollywood Filmograph,* January 1933.
"International House." *New York Times,* May 27, 1933.
"It's a Gift." *New York Times,* January 5, 1935.
"It's the Old Army Game." *Film Daily,* July 12, 1926.
"It's the Old Army Game." *Motion Picture Classic,* July 1926.
"It's the Old Army Game." *Moving Picture World,* July 1926.
"Janice Meredith." *Film Daily,* August 7, 1924.
"Man on the Flying Trapeze." *New York Times,* August 3, 1935.
"Million Dollar Legs." *Hollywood Filmograph,* June 25, 1932.
"Mrs. Wiggs of the Cabbage Patch." *New York Times,* October 29, 1934.
"The Old Fashioned Way." *Screenland,* August 1934.
"The Potters." *Motion Picture News,* February 4, 1927.
"The Potters." *New York Times,* January 18, 1927.
"Running Wild." *Motion Picture News,* June 24, 1927.
"Running Wild." *Picture Play,* September 1927.

Bibliography

"Sally of the Sawdust." *Photoplay*, September 1925.
"Sally of the Sawdust." *Picture Play Magazine*, September 1925.
"So's Your Old Man." *Film Daily*, November 9, 1926.
"So's Your Old Man." *Exhibitors World*, January 21, 1928.
"That Royle Girl." *Photoplay*, March 1926.
"That Royle Girl." *Motion Picture Magazine*, April 1926.
"Tillie's Punctured Romance." *Motion Picture News*, September 29, 1928.
"Tillie's Punctured Romance." *Exhibitors Herald*, October 1928.
"You Can't Cheat an Honest Man." *New York Times*, February 20, 1939.

Exhibitor Comments

From the *Exhibitors Herald* and later *Motion Picture Herald* in their regular feature "What the Picture Did for Me," where theater owners commented on how films fared in their theaters.
"The Dentist." December 3, 1932.
"The Dentist." July 8, 1933.
"Her Majesty, Love." November 14, 1931.
"It's a Gift." June 16, 1935.
"Mrs. Wiggs of the Cabbage Patch." March 16, 1935.
"Tillie's Punctured Romance." October 25, 1928.
"Two Flaming Youths." January 21, 1928.
"You're Telling Me." June 1, 1934.

Online Articles and Sources

The Internet Movie Database
www.rogerebert.com
Turner Classic Movies
Wikipedia

Interview

Buster Crabbe, by the author, 1980.

Index

Abbott and Costello 163, 165, 177, 178
Allen, Gracie 83, 95, 95, 142
Allen, Judith 106
Apfel, Oscar 57, 133
Arbuckle, Roscoe (Fatty) 9, 157

Baby LeRoy 88, 89, 105, 151
Ballyhoo 54
Bartholomew, Freddie 119, 120
Beaudine, William 105, 106
Beery, Wallace 89, 156
Bennett, Mickey 27
Bergen, Edgar 140, 145, 146, 147, 149, 151, 154, 175
The Big Parade 21
Blanche, William (Shorty) 31, 51, 53, 95
Blane, Sally 48
Blue, Ben 49
Boland, Mary 95, 97
Bow, Clara 24
Brennan, Lillian 28
Brian, Mary 37, 127, 128, 133
Brock, Lou 50
Brooks, Louise 27
Bruckman, Clyde 73, 133, 134
Burns, George 83, 84, 85, 95, 96, 142
Burton, Tim 91

Calloway, Cab 81
Cantor, Eddie 134, 1151
Carroll, Lewis 90
Cavanna, Elise 68, 75, 101
Chaplin, Charlie 9, 21, 28, 43, 61, 151, 157, 163, 176
Chase, Charley 10
Christie, Al 42, 43, 45
Cline, Eddie 60, 145, 149, 150, 154, 160, 163, 165, 167, 169, 170
Clyde, Andy 60, 62, 133
The Comic Supplement 24

Conklin, Chester 40, 41, 42, 43, 45, 47, 48, 49, 55, 56, 65
Conklin, Heinie 60
Cooper, Gary 64, 107
Corrado, Gino 57
Cowan, Lester 145
Crabbe, Buster 101
Crosby, Bing 67, 107, 108, 119, 122, 123, 124, 176
Curtis, James 43, 78, 95, 110, 175

Dames 107
Davies, Marion 14, 15, 16
DeHavilland, Olivia 112
Del Rio, Evelyn 156
Dempster, Carol 19, 20, 21, 135
Dent, Vernon 60
Dickens, Charles 118, 119, 120
Dieterle, William 56, 57
Diplomaniacs 58
Dressler, Marie 43, 89
Duck Soup 58
Duggan, Jan 106
Dumont, Margaret 169

Earl Carroll's Vanities 49, 67, 83
Ebert, Roger 2
Eburne, Maude 57
Errol, Leon 55, 57, 161 164, 165, 170, 172
Erwin, Stuart 83, 85

The Family Ford 51
Fazenda, Louise 43
Fellows, Edith 110
Fields, Hattie 6, 8
Fields, William Claude, Jr. 8
Fields, William Rexford 8
Fleming, Susan 61
The Flying Deuces 173
Follow the Boys 174
For Heaven's Sake 32

190 Index

Gable, Clark 120, 124
Gibson, Wynne 64
Gilbert, Billy 58
Go West 163
Going Spanish 142
The Gold Rush 21
Grant, Cary 107
The Great Dictator 163
Grey, Shirley 53
Griffith, D.W. 16, 19, 19, 20, 21, 28, 135, 137

Hall, Mordaunt 34
Hammerstein, Arthur 54
Hardy, Sam 134
Hearst, William Randolph 15, 16
Henry, Charlotte 91
Herbert, Hugh 60
Hitchcock, Alfred 172
Hope, Bob 124, 141, 144, 163
Howard, Kathleen 101, 118, 127, 129, 130, 133
Howard, Shemp 157, 161, 162
Hubert, Fritz 175
Hubert, Jean 175
Hughes, Harriet *see* Fields, Hattie

Jean, Gloria 156, 164, 166, 167, 170, 171, 172
Johnson, Carmencita 110
Jones, Newt 93
Joyce, Peggy Hopkins 83, 85

Kael, Pauline 62
Kane, Eddie 57
Kapp, Jack 121
Karns, Roscoe 64
Kelly, Patsy 61

La Cava, Gregory 32, 35
Lake, Veronica 174
Lantz, Walter 177
Laughton, Charles 64, 119, 120, 174
Laurel, Stan 96
Laurel and Hardy 40, 41, 145, 164, 173
Le Baron, William 35, 50, 98
Lewis, Vera 127, 133
Littlefield, Lucien 133
Lloyd, Harold 32, 33, 35, 45, 47, 134, 151
Luden, Jack 48
Lugosi, Bela 81
Lusk, Norman 38
Lyon, Ben 55

Maltin, Leonard 162, 163
Marie, Rose 81

Marsh, Joan 101
Marshall, George 145, 149
Marx, Groucho 62, 151
Marx, Harpo 61
Marx Brothers 58, 70, 163
Mayer, Louis B. 119, 156
McCarey, Leo 40, 96
McEvoy, J.P. 24, 27, 33, 34, 35, 97, 102, 111, 114
McLeod, Norman Z. 91
Menzies, William Cameron 91, 92
Merkel, Una 156, 163, 183
A Midsummer Night's Dream 112
Miller, Marilyn 54, 55, 56
Monti, Carlotta 132, 177
Moran and Mack 49
Morrison, Joe 106
Morros, Boris 173
Mutiny on the Bounty 120

No Indians Please 177
Normand, Mabel 10, 43
Nugent, Frank S. 147, 149

Oakie, Jack 60, 61, 62, 63, 66

Pangborn, Franklin 80, 83 159, 162, 166, 167, 168, 169, 170, 171
The Patsy 16
Paul, Les 175
Pierce, David 9
Pitts, ZaSu 109, 110
Poole, Bessie 7–8
Powell, Jane 175

Raft, George 64
Raye, Martha 142
Raymond, Gene 64
Reid, Laurence 39
Reinhardt, Max 112
Ride 'Em Cowboy 177
Roach, Hal 40, 49, 61, 163
Roberti, Lyda 60, 61, 62
Roberts, Florence 57
Robinson, Edward G. 174
Robson, May 64
Rogers, Charles 175
Rogers, Will 134
Rooney, Mickey 156, 176
Ross, Lanny 121, 123
Ross, Shirley 142
Rosten, Leo 151
Rouverol, Jean 112
Ruggles, Charlie 64, 95, 97

St. Clair, Malcolm 173

Index

St. John, Al 10
Saturday Night Live 1
Sellon, Charles 113, 115, 118
Selznick, David O. 119
Sennett, Mack 9, 43, 46, 58, 60, 62, 66, 67, 68, 70, 73, 75, 79, 80, 100, 101, 108, 113, 163
Sennwald, Andre 85, 110, 118
Sensations of 1945 175
Shakespeare, William 12
Show Boat 54
Show People 16
Silvers, Phil 173
Sinclair, John 41, 42, 135
Skipworth, Alison 64, 65, 66, 86, 87, 89, 93, 94, 95, 96
The Skyrocket 83
Snow White and the Seven Dwarfs 92
Sothern, Ann 156
Stablemates 156
Sterling, Ford 55, 57
Suspicion 172
Sutherland, Edward 27, 28, 32, 43, 45, 83, 94, 121, 135, 154
Sutton, Grady 76, 127, 133, 157, 162
Swain, Mack 43

Tales of Manhattan 173
Taxi Boys 49

Tillie's Nightmare 43
Tiomkin, Dimitri 93
Todd, Thelma 61
Treasure Island 107
Tully, Jim 110
Turpin, Ben 58

Vallee, Rudy 81
Venable, Evelyn 110
Vidor, King 16, 21

Walker, Brent 67, 73
Wayne, John 124
West, Mae 70, 83, 98, 107, 150–155
Westmore, Wally 93
Wilmington, Michael 62
Wilson, Clarence 57
Work, Cliff 149

Young, Loretta 48
Young, Tammany 95, 100, 101, 106, 110, 114, 118, 138

Ziegfeld Follies 5, 6, 14, 19, 24, 25, 28, 31, 35, 39, 54, 55, 56, 66, 83, 95, 106, 111, 138